Uncle John's
BATHROOM READER.

ATTACK OF THE
FACTOIDS

By the
Bathroom Readers'
Institute

Ashland, Oregon,
and San Diego, California

UNCLE JOHN'S BATHROOM READER®
ATTACK OF THE FACTOIDS

"Bathroom Reader," "Portable Press," and
"Bathroom Readers' Institute" are registered trademarks
of Baker & Taylor. All rights reserved.

For information, write:
The Bathroom Readers' Institute,
P.O. Box 1117, Ashland, OR 97520
www.bathroomreader.com
e-mail: mail@bathroomreader.com

Series cover design by Michael Brunsfeld
Book cover design by Sara Gillingham Studios

ISBN-13: 978-1-62686-040-7 / ISBN-10: 1-62686-040-8

Library of Congress Cataloging-in-Publication Data
Uncle John's bathroom reader attack of the factoids.
    pages cm
  ISBN 978-1-62686-040-7 (pbk.)
1. American wit and humor. 2. Curiosities and wonders.
I. Bathroom Readers' Institute (Ashland, Or.) II. Title: Bathroom
reader attack of the factoids.
  PN6165.U522 2013
  081--dc23
                                        2013028128

Printed in the United States of America
First Printing
1 2 3 4 5   18 17 16 15 14

Our "Regular" Readers Rave!

"I love these books! I read them on my commute bus in the morning, and during my lunch hour. They are definitely not just for the bathroom."

—**Alison G.**

"Uncle John's Bathroom Readers are the entire reason I started collecting rubber ducks. I have over seventy."

—**Sara C.**

"I LOVE your books, my whole family are avid BRI readers. Thanks!"

—**Shannon D.**

"My friend in school was reading Bathroom Readers, so then I bought a couple, and now my mom says I'm just threatening her with my intelligence."

—**Chase O.**

"If I walk out of 'the John' still reading 'the John,' does that make me weird or is that normal???"

—**Lisandro G.**

"I have learned so much from you guys. Thank you for being amazing!"

—**Reece T.**

"I just happened to see one of these sitting on the back of a friend's toilet one time eight years ago. Instead of reading the shampoo bottle, I picked this up. I have been hooked ever since."

—**Angela D.**

"Long live Uncle John!"

—**Denis S.**

iii

Thank You!

The Bathroom Readers' Institute sincerely thanks the people whose advice and assistance made this book possible.

Gordon Javna	Sydney Stanley
JoAnn Padgett	Peter Norton
Melinda Allman	Lilian Nordland
Jack Mingo	Brian Boone
Lidija Tomas	Kim Griswell
Madaline Woodard	Ginger Winters
Karin Arrigoni	Jennifer Magee
Angela Kern	Mana Monzavi
John Dollison	Monica Maestas
Derek Fairbridge	Rusty von Dyl
Blake Mitchum	Publishers Group West
Aaron Guzman	Raincoast Books
Trina Janssen	Sophie and JJ
Jay Newman	Thomas Crapper

* * *

Uncle John's Bathroom Reader Attack of the Factoids is a compilation of new material and running feet and articles selected from various books in the Bathroom Reader series.

Contents

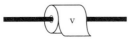

Greetings, Fellow Fact-hounds!

Welcome one and all to our third big book of short facts. If I do say so myself, it's our best collection yet.

When it comes to bite-sized bits of information, we at the BRI hold ourselves to a very high standard. A fact can't just be factual—it has to be so interesting and surprising that you feel compelled to share it with others. (Or if you're me, attack them with it.) For example:

- Female fruit flies lay eggs in rotting fruit...as many as 500 eggs a day for up to 10 days.
- The number of grains of sand on all of the world's beaches is about 7.5 quintillion.
- The first person to add sugar to gum was a dentist: William Finley Semple, in 1869.

See what I mean? You'll find thousands of fascinating facts like that about all kinds of things, from fitness and fatness to fish, flags, First Ladies, and food phobias—even subjects that don't start with F. We've got you covered from aardvarks to zombies...and everything in between.

But before you attack these pages, I'd like to throw a huge shout-out to the freaky folks who made this masterpiece possible: Jack, Lidija, Sara, Madaline, and Karin. Each and every one of you rocks! And that's a fact. So without further ado...charge!

And as always…

Go with the flow!

—Uncle John and the BRI Staff

The Fastest...

...street-legal, mass-produced car: The 2011 Bugatti Veyron, made by Volkswagen, can go 267 mph. (It's also the most expensive, selling for $1.7 million.)

..."furniture": In 2007 a motorized sofa drove at 92 mph, setting a world record.

...known insect: The Australian dragonfly, which (depending on what expert you believe) can reach a top speed of 35–60 mph.

...bird: Eider ducks can fly at 47 mph.

...land animal: Cheetahs, 71 mph.

...reptile: Sea turtles can swim as fast as 35 mph.

...checkmate: The "Fool's Mate" in chess takes just two moves. It gets its name from the fact that the first player must play very badly (or foolishly) on his first two moves for the second player to achieve the checkmate.

...winds ever measured: 318 mph during a 1999 Oklahoma tornado.

...elevator: It was installed in China's 2,000-foot-tall Shanghai Tower in 2014. It climbs at about 59 feet per second, or 40 mph.

...roller coaster: Formula Rossa at Ferrari World in Abu Dhabi (149 mph).

Hot Dog!

Between Memorial Day and Labor Day, Americans consume seven billion hot dogs.

The most popular condiment is mustard. Then come onions, chili, ketchup, relish, and sauerkraut.

Nathan Handwerker opened Nathan's Famous Hot Dogs (which remains a Coney Island institution) in 1916. To counteract the stories of unhealthy ingredients in hot dogs, Handwerker hired men to wear surgeons' smocks and eat lunch in his restaurants.

The largest seller of hot dogs is 7-Eleven, with 100 million served annually.

If you ask for a "hot dog" in New Zealand, you'll get it battered on a stick like a corn dog. To get one on a bun, you have to ask for an "American hot dog."

A "Chicago-style" hot dog never includes ketchup.

Hot dogs cause about 17 percent of all food asphyxiation deaths in children under 10.

According to Guinness, the most expensive hot dogs ever were ¾-pound, 18-inch dogs sold for charity in 2012 at a Sacramento, California, restaurant. Topped with an impressive array of fancy condiments—moose milk cheese, maple-syrup bacon, organic baby greens, whole-grain mustard, and cranberries—the dogs cost $145.49 each, with proceeds donated to a children's hospital.

The most hot dogs (with buns) consumed by one person in 10 minutes: 68. Joey Chestnut holds the record—he established it at an annual contest in Coney Island in 2009 and tied it in 2012.

The world's longest hot dog stretched 196.85 feet and was prepared by Japan's Shizuoka Meat Producers in 2006.

In the 1880s or '90s, frankfurters (from Germany) and wieners (from Austria) became known as "hot dogs"—possibly because of the sausages' similarities to dachshunds or maybe because of rumors about where the meat came from. (Germans regularly ate dog meat back then.)

There's a Word for It

If you're not *quite* an atheist, you may be a **minimifidianist**, defined as "someone who has *almost* no faith or belief."

If you say it out loud, you can almost guess the definition of **abecedarian**: "Somebody who is learning the fundamentals of something, like the alphabet."

Do some politicians suffer from **empleomania**? It means "an unnaturally high enthusiasm for holding public office."

Mamihlapinatapai is "a look between two people who both want something to happen, but with neither wanting to make the first move."

What's a **scroggling**? A small, runty apple left on the tree after a harvest.

A dictionary of Old English defines a **spatherdab** as "a scandal-monger who goes from house to house dispensing news."

Another from Old English: A **pilgarlick** is a "poor, ill-dressed person; an object of pity or contempt."

And one more: A **snoker** is "one who smells at objects like a dog."

Left-Handers

About 10 percent of the world's population is left-handed.

16 percent of American presidents have been, including five of the last seven (Ford, Reagan, George H. W. Bush, Clinton, and Obama).

The 2008 election was the first in which both candidates were left-handed.

Kermit the Frog is also left-handed.

The word "sinister" began as a slur on left-handers—it's from the Latin *sinestre*, which meant both "left-handed" and "wicked." So was *gauche*, French for both "left" and "social awkwardness"—it's from an old word, *gauchir*, that means "to become warped."

Premature infants are more likely to be left-handed than full-term babies.

22 percent of all twins are left-handed.

On average, left-handed women enter menopause sooner than right-handed women.

Left-handed people tend to scratch with their right hand.

More male cats are left-pawed than female cats.

Pennsylvania's Juniata College offers a scholarship for left-handed students.

Three sports officially forbid players from playing left-handed: jai alai, field hockey, and polo.

In hand-to-hand combat, left-handers are more likely to prevail because most fighters haven't had much practice handling punches, thrusts, and jabs from the left.

Ultrasounds during pregnancy increase the chances of having a left-handed baby.

When Neil Armstrong walked on the moon, he took his first step with his left foot.

Loose Change

The first known coins, minted in about 2000 BC, were bronze pieces shaped like cattle.

In 1124 England's King Henry I ordered 94 workers castrated for producing bad coins.

In 1783 Thomas Jefferson, Benjamin Franklin, Alexander Hamilton, and David Rittenhouse proposed the currency system that we use today. One difference from now: when their proposal passed Congress, the 10-cent coin was spelled *disme*, a French term that meant "1/10th."

The words "In God We Trust" first appeared on pennies, half-pennies, and nickels during the Civil War, to drive home the idea that God was on the Union's side. It disappeared from the nickel in 1883 and didn't reappear until 1938.

Then, "In God We Trust" was added to U.S. paper currency during the Cold War in 1957 as a way of differentiating the (largely Christian) United States from the (officially atheistic) Soviet Union.

Only 25 percent of a nickel is actually made of nickel. The rest is cupro—an alloy of 75 percent copper, 25 percent nickel, and a pinch of manganese. A penny is only 2.5 percent copper and 97.5 percent zinc. Dimes, quarters, and half-dollars are all 8.33 percent nickel and the rest cupro.

Can't find the second Abe Lincoln on a pre-2009 penny? Look very carefully at the back of one with the memorial on it.

In 1737 Samuel Higley of Connecticut minted America's first copper coins. Value: 3 pence.

When George Washington was shown a half-dollar design with his image on it, he denounced it as a trapping of monarchy that was inappropriate for a democracy. Instead, he suggested Lady Liberty. She graced American coins until 1909, when Abraham Lincoln's image replaced her on the penny. This started a trend of using former presidents, and in 1932—despite his wishes—Washington's image was put on the quarter.

1600 Pennsylvania Avenue

John and Abigail Adams were the first First Couple to live in the White House. When they moved there in 1800, Washington, D.C., was largely covered in swamps. President Adams once got lost in the woods while trying to find his way back to the White House.

Presidents William Henry Harrison and Zachary Taylor both died in the White House. (Harrison caught pneumonia and died after just a month in office; Taylor died of a stomach ailment, possibly cholera.)

Andrew Jackson's first official act as president: ordering spittoons for the White House.

Abraham Lincoln was a fan of actor (and assassin) John Wilkes Booth and once even invited him to the White House. Booth declined.

First Lady Louisa Adams (wife of John Quincy) bred silkworms in the White House. She even made silk cloth from them.

There are 132 rooms in the White House...35 of them are bathrooms.

President James Monroe once chased his Secretary of the Treasury from the White House with fire tongs.

Jimmy Carter watched the most movies in office. He had 480 films projected during his four-year term. The first was *All the President's Men*, about the downfall of Richard Nixon.

Thomas Jefferson's daughter, Martha "Patsy" Jefferson Randolph, was the first woman to give birth in the White House. Frances Cleveland, wife of Grover, was the only First Lady to do so.

In 1860, when the Prince of Wales visited the White House, President James Buchanan gave up his bedroom and slept on a sofa in the hallway.

The first White House phone number was simply...1.

Before They Were Famous

Mary Tyler Moore's first acting job was in 1955. At the age of 17, she played a pixie named Happy Hotpoint in early TV dishwasher commercials.

Mike Wallace's (60 *Minutes*) first TV job was as a product pitchman on the 1949 kids' show *Super Circus*.

Charles Dickens grew up poor and, at the age of 12, was forced to take a job pasting labels on bottles at a shoe-polish factory.

Writer Virginia Woolf briefly worked as a teacher, but she quit.

Before cartoonist Gary Larson started drawing *The Far Side*, he had jobs as a jazz guitarist and animal cruelty investigator for the Seattle Humane Society.

Poet Walt Whitman worked as a low-level Washington bureaucrat during the Civil War.

Evel Knievel was once fired from a mining job for making a dirt-moving machine do a wheelie.

What do O. Henry, Henrik Ibsen, and Dante Alighieri have in common? They were all once pharmacists.

When Wyatt Earp's pal Doc Holliday wasn't drilling people with his gun, he was drilling them in other ways. In his day job, he was a dentist.

Another dentist, Dr. Pearl Grey, eventually changed his first name to Zane and became a very successful writer of Old West fiction.

*   *   *

HAIR THIS!
Natural blonds have more individual hairs on their heads (about 140,000) than brunettes, who have about 105,000. Redheads? Only around 90,000.

Rhino Facts

Rhinos got their name because, in Greek, *rhinos* meant "nose" and *keras* meant "horn."

Rhino horns are made of keratin, the same stuff that's in hair and fingernails.

What do you call more than one rhinoceros? Some linguists in the late 1800s suggested "rhinocerotes," but were universally ignored. So even though it sounds awkward and is hard to say, it looks like we're stuck with "rhinoceroses." (Or, of course, "rhinos.")

A group of rhinos is called a "crash."

The two main types of rhinos—black rhinos and white rhinos—are different colors, but are closely related and were the same species five million years ago. The main difference in their appearance is the shape of their mouths, which evolved to suit local vegetation. White rhinos eat mostly grass and have wide, flat lips for grazing; black rhinos eat leaves and have longer, more pointed lips for grazing.

Besides the black and white rhinos, there are also the Sumatran and Javan, both considered "critically endangered," and the Indian, considered "vulnerable." Reports indicate that there may be just 275 Sumatran rhinos in the wild, and only 35 Javan.

The extinct *Elasmotherium* was an Ice Age rhinoceros that could be about 26 feet long.

Lightning Strike

The U.S. city with the most lightning displays is Tampa, Florida—it has about 100 "thunderstorm days" each year.

Oak trees grow to great heights, have deep roots, and retain more water than most. But because water and height are good conductors of electricity, oak trees are also more likely to be struck by lightning than shorter trees.

1 in 8 of all lightning fatalities in America take place on a golf course.

There's enough electricity in a single lightning bolt to power 10,000 electric chairs.

In 2001 singed duck carcasses rained on Hot Springs, Arkansas, after a flock flying by was struck by lightning.

Only about one in five lightning bolts strikes the earth. The rest just jump from one cloud to another.

A lightning bolt can be more than 10 miles long, but most are only about an inch in diameter. They look thicker because they light up the foggy air around them.

Every year, about 24,000 people are killed by lightning strikes worldwide, and 240,000 are injured.

A Trip to the Islands

Thousand island salad dressing got its name from its birthplace—the Thousand Islands of the St. Lawrence River along the border of the U.S. and Canada.

The world's shortest regularly scheduled airline flight takes place between the Scottish islands of Westray and Papa Westray, a distance of 1.5 miles. The flight takes 2 minutes, including taxiing.

In the early 1900s, immigrants at Ellis Island were welcomed to America with a serving of Jell-O.

Victoria Island in Canada's far north is the world's eighth-largest island. On Victoria is Tahiryuak Lake. In that lake, there's an unnamed mile-long island. On that island there's an unnamed lake, about 200 by 300 yards. And in *that* lake, there's yet another island that measures 20 by 30 yards. Whew.

According to host Jeff Probst, *Survivor*'s worst location was the Marquesas Islands. The reason? Biting sandflies.

The first American cattle ranch opened on Long Island in 1747.

Today, Coney Island is a peninsula, but it was an island before it was connected to the mainland with landfill. Before the Europeans, the native Lenape tribe called it Narrioch ("land without shadows"). The Dutch called it Conyne Eylandt and the British translated that into Coney Island; both meant "rabbit island."

Another island that isn't: Rhode Island. In 1524 explorer Giovanni da Verrazzano thought that a small island off of the New England coast looked like the island of Rhodes in Greece. The name "Rhode Island" stuck and people began referring to the mainland region that way as well.

Tiny canned herrings are called "sardines" because there were so many in the waters off the Italian island of Sardinia.

The 1902 eruption of Mount Pelée killed 29,000 people on the Caribbean island of Martinique. Only two people survived.

HAM, I Am

DOTS & DASHES

- HAM Radio was a network of amateur shortwave broadcast-ers who, from 1912 to the present day, have numbered in the millions. Before Facebook or Twitter, it was a social network that connected people all over the world.

- Why were they called "HAMs"? Before there was radio there were telegraphs. In the 19th century, the term "ham" meant "unskilled," and telegraph operators applied the ham label to any of their peers whose Morse code skills were slow, sloppy, or inaccurate—all reasons that caused frustration for the operators on the other end who were trying to decode the messages. Early radio operators adopted the insult for their peers and then for any amateur who broadcast his own signal. The amateurs, however, took the insult on as a badge of honor.

- To get a license to broadcast on the amateur radio bands, partici-pants had to pass a rigorous test covering electronics, radio theory, and, ironically, Morse code speed and accuracy. Until 1991, when things loosened up, a HAM radio operator needed to be able to transmit five words per minute to get the lowest, Morse-only HAM radio license. To work up to a general amateur license, which allowed someone to talk into a microphone, he needed to transmit 13 words per minute.

- The dots and dashes of Morse code were a slow way of communi-cating, though, so HAM also used shorthand like we do today in texts and e-mails. There were no smiley faces or ROFL back then, but close: The equivalent to the modern "LOL" in Morse code was "HI HI," because the sound (di-di-di-dit / di-dit / di-di-di-dit / di-dit) sounded like someone chuckling.

MORE HAM SLANG:

- **CQ:** "Attention!" or "Looking for..." A pun on "seek you."
- **YL:** "Young lady," used to address or refer to any female HAM broadcaster of any age.

- **73:** "Best wishes" or some comparable expression of goodwill, used as a signoff.
- **88:** "Love and Kisses."
- **Elmer:** A HAM teacher or guru, named after Elmer "Bud" Frohardt, who was a mentor to many beginning HAM users in the Chicago area in the 1960s.
- **Handle:** Name or alias. This is one that leaked into the CB radio culture of the 1970s. It was originally cowboy slang.
- **Mayday:** "Help me!" A corruption of the French word *m'aidez*. A similar saying is "Pan Pan," from the French word *panne* (meaning "equipment breakdown").
- **33:** In 1939 the relatively few women HAMs organized into a club called the Young Ladies Radio League. They decided that 73 as a sign-off was too formal, and 88 was too romantic. So they coined their own sign-off: Technically, 33 means "love sealed with friendship between one YL and another YL."

*   *   *

FAMOUS DROPOUTS

- **Grade school dropouts:** Mark Twain, Henry Ford, William Faulkner, President Zachary Taylor, Charlie Chaplin, Isadora Duncan, Charles Dickens, Frank Sinatra, Dean Martin, Jack London, Al Pacino, Richard Branson, and Cher.

- **College dropouts:** Edgar Allan Poe, Bill Gates, Mark Zuckerberg, Steve Jobs, Larry Ellison, Marc Rich, Sheldon Adelson, David Geffen, Ted Turner, and Ralph Lauren.

- And much to his family's displeasure, Harry Lillis Crosby dropped out of law school to play drums and sing in a jazz band. In the end, though, Harry, who also went by "Bing," did OK.

Hodgepodge

More than 60 percent of the world's lawyers live in the United States.

68 percent of Americans over 65 consider TV a "necessity."

A "pregnant" crash-test dummy is called a Maternal Anthropometry Measurement Apparatus Version 2B—or a "MAMA2B."

In the 1890s, the University of Nebraska football team changed its name from the Bugeaters to the Cornhuskers.

In May 1996, a tornado hit an Ontario, Canada, drive-in theater. The movie scheduled to be shown that night: *Twister*.

Bear cubs are born toothless, blind, and bald.

A car traveling at 100 mph would take 29 million years to reach theclosest star outside the solar system. Traveling to our own star, the sun, would require 106 years.

One of the most frequently recycled items before the 20th century was bones.

Hitler owed the equivalent of about $8 million (in today's money) in back income taxes when he seized power in 1933. He never paid up.

The U.S. spends about $203 million dollars per year on barbed wire.

Earth's human population inhales more than 6 billion tons of oxygen annually.

Alooooha!

Hawaii consists of eight main islands: Oahu, Maui, Kauai, Molokai, Niihau, Lanai, Kahoolawe, and the Big Island (aka, Hawaii).

Niihau, one of the smallest, is inhabited by only 130 people and a few low-profile military personnel. It was the only Hawaiian island that voted against U.S. statehood in 1959.

Hawaii produces about a third of the world's pineapples.

Hawaii has its own time zone.

The summit of Mauna Kea on the Big Island rises 13,796 feet above sea level and stretches another 18,000 feet below sea level to the ocean floor. Combined, that makes it the tallest mountain in the world.

The first people to settle Hawaii were Polynesians who traveled by canoe.

The only royal residence in the United States is Iolani Palace in Honolulu, the former home of the Hawaiian royals.

There are only 12 letters in the Hawaiian alphabet: A, E, H, I, K, L, M, N, O, P, U, and W.

There is no single ethnic majority in Hawaii. There are also no billboards, seagulls, squirrels, rabies, or poison ivy.

The Wit and Wisdom of Ben Franklin

"Wise men don't need advice. Fools don't take it."

"Waste not life; in the grave will be sleeping enough."

"Wish not to live long as to live well."

"If you would keep your secret from an enemy, tell it not to a friend."

"Read much, but not too many books."

"He that falls in love with himself will have no rivals."

"Nothing brings more pain than too much pleasure; nothing more bondage than too much liberty."

"If you want to lose a troublesome visitor, lend him money."

"Be civil to all; sociable to many; familiar with few; friend to one; enemy to none."

"Beware of little expenses. A small leak will sink a great ship."

"Search others for their virtues, thyself for thy vices."

"It is hard for an empty bag to stand upright."

"Make haste slowly."

"The used key is always bright."

"Industry pays debts, while despair increases them."

"He that lives upon hopes will die fasting. There are no gains without pains."

"If your head is wax, don't walk in the sun."

"When you have bought one fine thing, you must buy ten more, that your appearance may be all of a piece. It is easier to suppress the first desire than to satisfy all that follow it."

"Many men die at 25 and aren't buried until they are 75."

"One today is worth two tomorrows."

"Lost time is never found again."

This Little Piggy...

The technical name for your big toe is the "hallux," and the little toe is called the "minimus." The other toes, however, officially go by "second toe," "third toe," and "fourth toe."

Artist John G. Chapman's *The Baptism of Pocahontas* hangs in the U.S. Capitol's Rotunda, but Chapman made a slight mistake—one of the Native Americans in the painting has six toes on one foot.

Horses run on their toes. (Hooves are considered toes.)

A pig stands on two of its toes, but actually has four on each foot. The two higher ones don't touch the ground when a pig walks.

Actor Dan Aykroyd has webbed toes.

A cat with six toes is considered a "polydactyl."

Cats usually have five toes on each of their front feet, but only four on their hind legs.

In 2000 Al Capone's toenail clippings were sold at an auction for $9,500.

Some marathon runners have their toenails removed to make running easier.

During Robert Peary's trek through Greenland in 1898–99, he lost eight toes to frostbite.

The Downtown Hotel bar in Dawson City, Yukon, features a unique drink: the Sourtoe Cocktail. It's a beer stein of champagne with a severed toe in it. (Swallowing the toe has happened a few times, but is not recommended.)

In the original version of *Cinderella*, one of the wicked stepsisters cuts off her big toes to fit into Cinderella's shoe.

*   *   *

Q. Where do people drink the most beer?
A. In the Czech Republic, which averages 41.4 gallons per person per year.

Battle of the Sexes

Women's bodies reject heart transplants more often than men's do.

One study found that a majority of men thought white was the best color for a bedroom. Women preferred blue.

Men are more likely than women to change lanes without signaling and to run red lights.

Men are more likely to part their hair on the left.

Women are almost twice as likely to file for divorce.

Researchers found that two-thirds of men reported having fallen in love with an older woman, but only half of women reported having fallen in love with a younger man.

Women typically have higher core body temperatures than men. They are also more likely to have cold hands and feet.

Researchers say that underweight men tend to worry more about their weight than overweight men. For women, it's the reverse.

Elderly women are more likely to die in the week after their birthday. Men, in the week before.

Let's Talk Turkey

Ben Franklin despised eagles and lobbied hard to name the turkey our national bird. (He lost.)

There are about 4.5 million wild turkeys living free in the United States. They can fly 55 mph and run 25 mph. Domesticated turkeys, however, have been bred to be so overweight and front-heavy that they can't build up any significant speed, loft, or distance.

For more than 100 years Massachusetts had no wild turkeys. But thanks to a reintroduction program in nearby New York in the 1970s, more than 20,000 now roam the state.

Most American ice-cream trucks play a song called "Turkey in the Straw." (British trucks play "Greensleeves.")

Big Bird's costume includes about 6,000 turkey feathers dyed yellow.

The first in-flight meal: turkey and vegetables, served aboard the luxury 16-passenger Russian Ilia Mouriametz biplanes in 1914. The meals stopped later that year when the large airplanes were converted into heavy bombers for World War I.

First Swanson's TV Dinner, released in 1954: turkey, cornbread dressing, frozen peas, and sweet potatoes.

Turkeys originated in Mexico.

Introduced to Spain in the 1500s, Turkish merchants sold the birds all over Europe (one theory as to how they got their name). The turkeys we eat today are descendants of those European birds.

The Pilgrims were familiar with turkeys before reaching the New World—they brought them in 1620.

*   *   *

THE BIG CHEESE

The 1964 World's Fair in New York exhibited the world's largest piece of cheese—it was as big as a van and weighed 17.5 tons. It was made with 183 tons of milk, one day's production for 16,000 cows.

Balloonatic

On June 4, 1783, French papermakers Jacques-Etienne and Joseph-Michel Montgolfier launched a hot-air balloon they'd designed. That first successful, untethered balloon launch lasted just 10 minutes.

Average weight of an inflated Macy's Thanksgiving Day Parade balloon: -330 pounds, meaning it takes 330 pounds to keep it from floating away.

Albert Lamorisse, the French filmmaker who directed the classic short *The Red Balloon* (1956), also invented the board game Risk.

On August 27, 1783, J. A .C. Charles and his colleagues launched the first unmanned hydrogen balloon. It floated 15 miles to the village of Gonesse, France, where panicked inhabitants attacked it with pitchforks. (The men made the first manned balloon flight later that year.)

How hot-air balloons work: Earth's atmosphere is heavier than hot air, so it slides under a balloon and pushes it up.

First Internet character balloon in the Macy's Thanksgiving Day Parade: Jeeves the Butler (from Askjeeves.com) in 1999.

During World War II, the Japanese navy launched about 9,000 balloon incendiary bombs into the United States. Most landed harmlessly, but one in Oregon drew curious folks on their way to a church picnic. The bomb then detonated, killing five children and one adult.

Record for most balloon animals made in one hour: 747 (one animal about every five seconds).

In October 1874, two performers in P.T. Barnum's circus held the first wedding aboard a hot-air balloon.

Average weight of a Macy's Thanksgiving Day Parade balloon, uninflated: 300 pounds.

In 1982 Californian Larry Walters tied 45 weather balloons to his lawn chair, hoping to fly 300 miles to the Mojave Desert. Instead, he rose to 16,000 feet… and used a pellet gun to pop the balloons on the way down.

Relatively Speaking

Francis Scott Key wrote "The Star Spangled Banner," but his son Philip Barton Key also made a name for himself—he was shot and killed in 1859 by New York congressman Daniel Sickles for having an affair with Sickles's wife, Teresa.

Francis Scott Key was also a very distant cousin and namesake of author F. Scott Fitzgerald. (Fitzgerald's "F" stands for Francis.)

Presidents Theodore Roosevelt and Franklin D. Roosevelt were fifth cousins. Franklin and Eleanor Roosevelt were fifth cousins, once removed.

Elvis Presley was related to both Abraham Lincoln and Jimmy Carter.

Glenn Close and Brooke Shields are second cousins.

Madonna and Céline Dion are both distant cousins of Prince Charles's second wife, Camilla.

Al Capone's brother Vince was a policeman in Homer, Nebraska.

Phone Home

It was Thomas Edison who popularized the tradition of saying "hello" to answer the phone. In 1877 he wrote a letter to a forerunner of AT&T suggesting it. Now, using "hello" has spread worldwide, with most phone users saying it or a close approximation like *allo, hallo, halo,* or *hola.*

But telephone inventor Alexander Graham Bell's preferred greeting for answering a ringing phone was "Ahoy!" or "Hoy! Hoy!"

Taiwan and Luxembourg both have more cell phones than people.

February 2012 was the first month that nearly half of all Americans owned smartphones.

The telephone was originally called a "harmonic telegraph."

The average lifespan of a cell phone is 18 months. Americans throw out 350,000 of them every day.

One in three iPhone owners has ended a relationship via text message.

More than 100 million telephone calls connect through New York City every day.

New York City's first phone directory, published in 1878, contained listings for just 256 numbers.

Americans use about 6 billion minutes of cell phone talk time every day.

*   *   *

Q. What inspired Herman Melville to write *Moby-Dick?*

A. On November 20, 1820, an 80-ton sperm whale sunk the *Essex,* a whaling ship from Nantucket, Massachusetts. The 20 crew members escaped in small whale boats and began to row more than 3,000 miles back to civilization. The boats were rescued after four months, and just five men survived (some killed and eaten by fellow sailors), giving Melville the idea for his most famous work.

Class Notes

As early as 1647, Massachusetts passed a law mandating that all towns with more than 50 families set up a school or face a fine.

Milton Hershey made chocolate in order to fund the Milton Hershey School for Orphaned Boys. The school trust still owns 56% of the company's stock.

First person to go over Niagara Falls in a barrel: a Michigan schoolteacher named Annie Taylor (1901).

Textbook titles used to be a lot longer. Here's one from the 19th century: *Osgood's Progressive Fifth Reader: Embracing a System of Instruction in the Principles of Elocution, and Selections for Reading and Speaking from the Best English and American Authors: Designed for the Use of Academies and the Highest Classes in Public and Private Schools.*

In their first year of school or preschool, kids average 6 to 10 colds.

In 1969, 90 percent of kids who lived within a mile of their school walked or biked. In 2001 that number was 31 percent.

Schoolhouses in the 1800s were painted red for the same reason that barns were: Red paint was cheap and it contained a chemical called ferrous oxide (iron rust), which killed the mold that grew in and weakened the wood.

The average high school student has a vocabulary of about 60,000 words.

Benito Mussolini was a substitute teacher before he became the fascist dictator of Italy. (Many schoolkids will tell you this makes perfect sense.)

*   *   *

GOING EXTINCT

In the mid-1990s there were 2.7 million pay phones in the United States; in 2004 the number was down to 1.8 million. And by 2013, there were fewer than 500,000 left in the country.

Food Fears

Turophobia:
Fear of cheese.

Lachanophobia:
Fear of vegetables.

Alliumphobia:
Fear of garlic.

Mycophobia:
Fear of mushrooms.

Arachibutyrophobia:
Fear of peanut butter sticking
to the roof of your mouth.

Carnophobia:
Fear of meat.

Ichthyophobia:
Fear of fish.

Oenophobia:
Fear of wine.

Cibophobia:
Fear of eating.

Fashion Sense

France's King Louis XIV wore some of the first high heels—he stood only 5'4" and had height added to his boots.

First TV-inspired fashion fad: All-black clothes, inspired by 1950s TV cowboy Hopalong Cassidy.

The 1980s soap opera *Dynasty* once had its own fashion line based on costumes from the show.

The *Mona Lisa*'s lack of eyebrows was not a mistake by Leonardo da Vinci. It was the style of the day in Florence, Italy; women plucked their eyebrows off.

In 2006 a London fashion show called "Naked Fragrance" featured nude models wearing different brands of perfume and walking in front of a blindfolded audience.

Average measurements of a fashion model: 5'11" and 117 pounds. Average American woman: 5'4" and 140 pounds.

For centuries, hatmakers needed beaver skins, nearly driving the animals to extinction. Luckily, in 1850, England's Prince Albert began wearing silk hats. Fashion followed, and the beaver was saved.

Gerald Ford once worked as a fashion model.

Mick Jagger and Ian Anderson (of the band Jethro Tull) both tried to revive the codpiece as fashion. They failed.

Leave It to Beaver

In winter, you can tell a beaver is at home if you see steam rising from the vent at the top of its lodge. Like all mammals, beavers generate heat, and the moist air from their wet fur and breath creates a plume of steam when it rises.

Beaver teeth keep growing throughout their lives—the animals wear their teeth down by chewing wood.

Beavers never stop growing. During a full 24-year lifespan, they can grow to be about 55 pounds. But unlike most mammals, female beavers generally grow larger than males.

Beavers don't hibernate or hunt much for food during the winter. Instead, they store a huge supply of branches inside their lodges and eat the bark.

On a single breath of air, a beaver can swim for a half-mile...or hide quietly for 15 minutes without emerging from the water.

Beavers don't move out of their parents' lodges until they're three years old.

When I Get Older

By age 75, most people will have spent 25 years of their lives sleeping.

Every day, about 7,900 Americans turn 60 years old.

On your 75th birthday, you'll have lived for 27,760 days...or 2,398,000,000 seconds.

Studies show that most people feel about 13 years younger than they actually are.

The average life span after retirement in 1900: 1.2 years. In 2000: 19.2 years.

Worldwide, there are now about 340,000 people who are at least 100 years old. The country with the highest percentage of people over 100 is Japan, with 34.85 centenarians per 100,000 people. That's twice as high as the United States (17.3 per 100,000).

Supreme Court justice Oliver Wendell Holmes was 90 when he retired in 1932, making him the oldest justice so far.

Of all the states, Florida has the highest percentage of senior citizens. Alaska has the lowest.

About 50 percent of elderly women live alone.

Directors' Cuts

In 1968 Steven Spielberg and George Lucas took a directing class taught by Jerry Lewis.

During the famous "chest bursting" scene in *Alien* (1979), director Ridley Scott got the reaction he wanted by unexpectedly showering the actors with real blood.

Youngest movie director: Kishan Shrikanth of India directed a full-length film at age 9.

13 of the 100 top-grossing films of all time were made by Steven Spielberg or George Lucas.

Only one person has won Emmys for acting, writing, and directing: Alan Alda (for M*A*S*H).

Supposedly, Wes Craven named his horrifying character, Freddy Krueger, after a kid who used to bully him in school.

Leonard "Mr. Spock" Nimoy costarred in the 1985 Bangles video "Going Down to Liverpool."

Of the more than 250 episodes of *Alfred Hitchcock Presents*, Alfred Hitchcock directed only 18.

The sketch that Jack drew of Rose in *Titanic* was actually drawn by director James Cameron. (Cameron has many talents: he was also once a school bus driver.)

David Lynch turned down the chance to direct *Return of the Jedi*.

Woody Allen disliked his film *Manhattan* so much that he offered to direct another movie for United Artists for free if they shelved it. (They refused.)

Italian director Frederico Fellini was nominated for 12 Oscars for writing or directing. Number of wins: 0.

Francis Ford Coppola is an honorary ambassador to Belize.

First movie Steven Spielberg ever saw: *The Greatest Show on Earth*, at age 4.

Earthquaaaake!

There are about 70 earthquakes in California...every day, Luckily, only a few are actually felt by anybody.

Before a large earthquake, ponds and canals may give off a strange smell, perhaps from earlier small shakes that disturbed sediment or released gas.

A 1775 earthquake in Portugal caused waves on Loch Ness in Scotland...1,240 miles away.

The tsunamis that sometimes follow an earthquake can be disastrous to land, but they don't usually damage ships at sea. People on a cruise ship just feel a slow rise and fall as the wave slides deep beneath them.

A 2007 earthquake lifted up the entire island of Ranongga, in the Solomon Islands, by 10 feet.

Even the UK gets earthquakes—about 300 a year. Most are pretty small, and only 11 people in history are known to have died in British quakes.

"The earthquakes" anagrams to "that queer shake."

About 2 million people died in earthquakes during the 20th century.

The deadliest earthquake in recorded history took place in 1556 in Shansi, China, killing nearly 830,000 people.

Charles Richter, who developed the Richter scale (for measuring earthquakes), was a nudist.

Thomas Jefferson's sister, Elizabeth, died from exposure after fleeing her home following a massive, rare earthquake that struck Virginia on February 21, 1774. (She thought she'd be safer outside...in the freezing cold.)

An earthquake that measures 4.0 on the Richter scale is 100 times stronger than one measuring 2.0. Each whole number on the scale is ten times stronger than the previous one. So a 5.0 would be 1,000 times stronger than a 2.0.

Within three years of the 1906 earthquake, 20,000 new buildings went up in San Francisco.

Driving Passions

Ferrari will sometimes custom mold a car's driver's seat to the buyer's body.

The average time it takes to go through a McDonald's drive-thru is 184 seconds.

In the 1950s, there were about 5,000 drive-in theaters in the United States. Today: about 368.

Nearly 800,000 senior citizens voluntarily give up their driving privileges each year.

Until 1923, drivers in Italy drove on the right in rural areas and on the left in cities. (Now they all drive on the right side.)

The first states to require driver's licenses were Massachusetts and Missouri, in 1903.

Henry Ford never had a driver's license.

There's no evidence that drivers of red cars get speeding tickets any more often, but Mercedes SL drivers get four times as many tickets than average.

On average, Americans lock themselves out of their cars nine times in a lifetime.

Collectively, New York City cab drivers log more than a million miles a day.

The first woman to drive coast-to-coast across the U.S. was Alice Ramsey in 1909. That was an especially impressive accomplishment at a time when cars weren't that reliable and there were only 152 miles of paved road along the 3,800-mile route. She was accompanied on her trip by two sisters-in-law and a friend, none of whom could drive.

76 percent of American commuters drive to work alone.

In the UK, nearly 500,000 car accidents a year are caused by women applying makeup while driving.

According to a survey, over a lifetime, the average driver spends 2 hours, 14 minutes kissing in the car.

Where's the Rest of Me?

ST. NICHOLAS'S BONES: The real Saint Nick (who lived in ancient Greece and had a penchant for secretly giving gifts) was buried in the town of Myra, now a part of Turkey. In 1087, authorities in Bari, a rival town in Italy, hired pirates to steal the saint's bones. The pirates managed to make off with about half of them, which are still stored in Bari. The rest of the bones were stolen by Venetian sailors ten years later during the First Crusade and deposited in a church there. In 2009 Turkey demanded the bones back from Italy; it's still waiting.

NAPOLEON'S PENIS: Allegedly removed during the French leader's autopsy in 1821 and given to a priest, the dried organ, which looked a lot like a one-inch piece of beef jerky, ended up in the hands of a urologist in New Jersey, who paid $3,000 for it in 1977. The man stored it under his bed for 30 years, and his daughter inherited it after his death.

MUSSOLINI'S BRAIN: Well, half of it anyway. After the fascist leader was executed and Italy was occupied at the end of World War II, the American government took away part of Mussolini's brain, allegedly to study it, but mostly as a victory trophy. The Americans returned the brain to Mussolini's widow in 1966.

THOMAS PAINE'S CORPSE: In 1819, ten years after the *Common Sense* author died a penniless, friendless drunkard in Manhattan, an admirer named William Cobbett dug up the writer's bones and carried them to England for a fitting memorial. Unfortunately, Cobbett's attempts at raising money for Paine's burial stalled, and the remains remained in a trunk in Corbett's attic…or so everybody thought. However, after Cobbett died in 1835, a thorough accounting of his belongings revealed that Paine's bones were gone. They still haven't turned up.

Sticking Their Necks Out

Giraffes don't make a lot of noise, but they are able to make sounds like grunts, hisses, snorts, and even moos.

Baby giraffes grow about an inch every day during their first week of life. But only about one giraffe baby in four makes it to adulthood. Big cats and jackals hunt them, and their mothers aren't great at defense

Giraffe males can be as tall as 18 feet; females, 14 feet.

Like cows, giraffes are ruminants, which means they have four compartments in their stomachs and they regurgitate and chew their cud.

A giraffe tongue measures about 2 feet long and is blue-black in color. Scientists think that might be so their tongues don't get sunburned.

A giraffe's legs are taller than the average human adult.

Giraffes have seven vertebrae in their necks—the same as every mammal.

A giraffe newborn falls from a height of about 6½ feet. Luckily, it's already about 6 feet tall at birth, so the fall isn't really that bad.

Male giraffes are often at more risk from predators than females, even though they're larger, because they spend a lot of time alone and are easy to sneak up on.

The giraffe has only one known relative: the okapi, a mammal native to rain forests in central Africa. Okapis somewhat resemble giraffes, but have black and white striped legs and short necks.

*　　*　　*

Apples float in water, but pears don't.

Up & Autumn!

Autumn (aka, fall) is the only season that has two names.

The autumnal equinox (September 22 or 23, depending on the year) is one of the two days each year that the entire world gets a day split into exactly half sun and half dark. It even happens at the North and South Poles...sort of. At the poles, the sun skims the horizon, beginning six months of uninterrupted daylight or darkness.

In 1908 Archibald Joyce wrote his popular waltz "Songe d'Autome" ("Dream of Autumn") in a slightly melancholic minor key. Maybe it was that calming, nostalgic sadness that inspired the *Titanic*'s eight-member band to play it as the ship floundered.

Certain autumn things like football and the Thanksgiving harvest festival make sense. But why do new cars come out then? That was President Franklin Roosevelt's idea during the Great Depression. He asked carmakers to shift the new car season from January so that auto workers would be working instead of laid off during the holiday season.

* * *

TWO FIRSTS IN SPACE

First toys: Eleven simple toys, like a top, a yo-yo, a flipping bear, and a jump rope, went up on April 12, 1985.

First human: Russian cosmonaut Yuri Gagarin, who orbited the Earth on April 12, 1961.

The Average Canadian...

... receives 200 e-mails a week.

...spends about $2.50 per week on condiments.

...spends about one week each year waiting in line—nearly half an hour a day.

...trusts firefighters more than pharmacists, doctors, or EMTs.

...would stay on the job, even if he or she got a windfall of money.

...checks food labels for fiber, vitamins, calories, and fat.

...man is 5'9" and weighs 182 pounds.

...works 36.6 hours per week and makes about $38,700 a year.

...household spends $2,200 a year on cell phone and Internet services.

...household has $40,000 more in net worth than the average U.S. household.

Neither Cocoa, Nor A Nut

Coconut milk can be used in place of blood plasma in emergencies.

The average mature coconut weighs about 2.5 pounds.

Nearly 150 people die every year from being hit on the head by falling coconuts.

A well-fertilized coconut palm can produce up to 75 fruits a year, but 30 is average.

Technically, coconut isn't just a fruit; it's a "fibrous drupe." Drupes are fruits that contain pits, like peaches, mangoes, apricots, nectarines, and plums.

To produce fruit, coconut palms need a lot of sun, a lot of rain and humidity, and heat—no colder than 54°F, but ideally 68–90°F. Even one night below freezing can kill a tree.

The brown fiber on the outside of coconuts is called "coir." It's strong and resistant to salt water. So it's used for ropes, fishing nets, upholstery and mattress filler, doormats, sacks, carpets, floor tiles, and brushes.

Tooth or Consequences

About 40 percent of American men do not brush their teeth every day.

If you're typical, you'll use about 68,000 gallons of water and spend five to seven weeks of your life brushing your teeth.

A person's teeth are home to nearly 11,000 million bacteria per quarter inch.

Dentists say that grazing is worse for your teeth than eating regular meals. Eating of any kind—whether a meal or a snack—activates the cavity-causing bacteria in your mouth for 20 minutes or more. So the fewer times you eat, the better off your teeth will be.

Archaeologists have found ancient mummies with metal braces on their teeth.

Odontophobia is the fear of dental treatment.

Every year, hundreds of people swallow their false teeth.

At one time, denture makers added uranium to false teeth to give them a "healthy" glow.

One in 10 men grind their teeth while sleeping.

The Catholic patron saint of dentists is Saint Apollonia—an angry mob knocked out all of her teeth when she wouldn't renounce her faith.

Russian czar Peter the Great loved playing dentist, especially extracting teeth.

Actor James Dean had two false front teeth. For fun, he liked to drop them into his glass while drinking.

One of Isaac Newton's teeth was auctioned in 1816 for $3,633 ($35,700 today).

*　　*　　*

The Catholic Saint Brigid of Ireland was sainted in part because she performed the miracle of turning water into beer.

Our Daily Bread

The Chillicothe Baking Company (Missouri) was the first to sell bread packaged and sliced (1928).

During the Middle Ages, people often used stale bread as plates.

The yeasts that make bread rise are similar to the yeasts that grow between your toes.

Yeast grows fast. Under ideal conditions, 200 grams will grow into 150 tons in just five days, enough to make a million loaves of bread.

Some San Francisco bakers still make sourdough bread from dough started in 1849. But despite San Francisco's association with sourdough bread, Oakland, just across the San Francisco Bay, produces more sourdough bread than any other city in the world.

New Yorkers eat more Wonder Bread per capita than do residents of any other U.S. city.

The word *pumpernickel* means "devil's fart" in German. It got its name in the 15th century when the bread was especially coarse, foul-smelling, hard to eat, and typically produced a lot of flatulence in the people who ate it.

Farmers in Kansas harvest enough wheat each year to make 36 billion loaves of bread.

Gallup poll results: 49 percent of Americans don't know that white bread is made from wheat.

Bread changes color and flavor when toasted due to a complex chemical reaction called the "Maillard reaction," after Louis-Camille Maillard, who first analyzed the effect in 1912.

*   *   *

GOT A DOLLAR?

Dollar bills typically wear out after about 18 months of circulation. Other denominations don't get as much day-to-day use, so they tend to last longer.

Hating Shakespeare

"With the single exception of Homer, there is no eminent writer, not even Sir Walter Scott, whom I can despise so entirely as I despise Shakespeare when I measure my mind against his. The intensity of my impatience with him occasionally reaches such a pitch, that it would positively be a relief to me to dig him up and throw stones at him."

—George Bernard Shaw

"Shakespeare never has six lines together without a fault. Perhaps you may find seven, but this does not refute my general assertion."

—Samuel Johnson

"I have tried lately to read Shakespeare, and found it so intolerably dull that it nauseated me."

—Charles Darwin

"Shakespeare's name, you may depend on it, stands absurdly too high and will go down. He has no invention as to stories, none whatever. He took all his plots from old novels, and threw their stories into a dramatic shape, at as little expense of thought as you or I could turn his plays back again into prose tales."

—Lord Byron

"What a crude, immoral, vulgar, and senseless work *Hamlet* is."

—Leo Tolstoy

"Enormous dunghill."

—Voltaire

Put a Sock in It

A company called Aetrex makes GPS-enabled shoes for tracking Alzheimer's patients. The shoes send a signal when the wearer roams out of a preset range.

According to a Chinese wedding custom, tossing one of the bride's red shoes from the roof ensures happiness.

For much of 2008, actress Natalie Portman had her own line of eco-friendly "vegan" shoes (not made of leather or animal glues). The economic downturn that year, however, drove the company that made them out of business.

George Washington's shoes were size 13.

In the shoe world, a clog is any shoe with a wooden sole. A klompen is a shoe that's carved entirely of wood.

The first zippers were put on shoes.

Foot-binding in China deliberately deformed women's feet from childhood, bending the toes under the soles, so they'd fit into tiny slippers.

In a pinch, you can shine your shoes with banana peels or vegetable shortening.

Until 1884, a shoe could be worn on either foot. The first store to sell boots matched into a left and right pair was Phil Gilbert's Shoe Parlor in Vicksburg, Mississippi.

GR8 PL8s

As early as 1884, license plates were used on horse-drawn carriages.

The mayor of Boston's official car had the same license plate number from 1914 to 1993: 576.

Early license plates were made of porcelain, leather, or cardboard.

In 1893, France became the first country to require license plates on cars.

New York was the first state to require license plates, in 1901.

19 states don't require front license plates, just back ones.

New Hampshire's license plate slogan is "Live Free or Die"...and they're stamped out by inmates at the state prison.

Virginia has the highest percentage of vanity plates at 16.1 percent, followed by New Hampshire (14 percent), Illinois (13.4 percent) and Nevada (8.2 percent). Texas has the fewest (just 5 percent).

*　　*　　*

UM...YUM?

The most popular pie dish in ancient Rome was placenta. But it's not as gross as it sounds—the human organ was actually named because it resembled this dessert, a sort of cheesecake pie.

Outbreak!

Influenza means "influence" in Italian. The illness was so named because doctors in 1743 believed its spread was under the influence of certain "evil" stars and constellations.

Almost all flu viruses first infect chickens, then pigs, and then spread to humans, mutating along the way. But the "chicken flu" of 1997 made medical news because it jumped directly from birds to humans, bypassing pigs.

People typically begin spreading the flu a day before they show any symptoms.

In 2003 a British fan claimed that Paul McCartney had given him the flu and tried to sell his germs on eBay. The bidding reached just $1.83 before eBay took down the offer.

Despite what you've heard, people with the flu often *do* sneeze and have runny noses. In many cases, even doctors have difficulty distinguishing the flu from a cold.

The "Spanish" flu didn't come from Spain. It began in Kansas in 1918, and America's soldiers spread it worldwide during World War I. But the disease got its name because Spain, as a neutral country during the war, had a fairly unrestricted press that was free to report about the pandemic, which gave the world the impression that the disease was more deadly in Spain.

Flu viruses can live up to 48 hours on hard metal or plastic surfaces. They can live 8 to 12 hours on dry porous surfaces like paper money, and only about 15 minutes on skin.

The "stomach flu" or "24-hour flu" is not at all related to influenza.

In general, older people were more protected against the 2009 swine flu outbreak than younger people, because many who had a flu illness before 1957 were infected with a similar virus and thus had some immunity.

Better Off Dead

Zombies originated from followers of the Vodou (Anglicized to "Voodoo") religion, which was born in Haiti and came to the U.S. with immigrants. The term "zombie" may come from the Caribbean word *jumbie* or the West African Kimbundu word *nzambi*, both of which mean "ghost."

The tradition of walking dead people appears in many cultures, though, including Chinese, Persian, Arabian, Native American, and European. In fact, in the Middle Ages, the French believed that the dead would awaken as emaciated corpses to avenge any crimes against them.

Vodou tradition says that you can get a zombie to return to the graveyard by feeding it salt.

A 1929 fictional book, *The Magic Island* by William Seabrook, brought zombies to mainstream America. In 1932 the first zombie movie appeared, a horror film starring Bela Lugosi, *White Zombie*.

Biologist Wade Davis investigated reports of zombie slaves in Haiti and discovered they may be true. A cocktail of poisons from puffer fish and cane toads can put a victim in a zombielike state.

In September,2012, FEMA offered a free webinar about being prepared for a zombie apocalypse.

According to mathematicians at the University of Ottawa, humanity would be unlikely to survive a full-scale zombie attack. In 2009 the researchers wrote: "While aggressive quarantine may contain the epidemic, or a cure may lead to coexistence of humans and zombies, the most effective way to contain the rise of the undead is to hit hard and hit often. As seen in the movies, it is imperative that zombies are dealt with quickly, or else we are all in a great deal of trouble."

Super Bowl Sunday

Each year, bets placed on the Super Bowl total about $10 billion.

In the 48 hours after the Super Bowl, 6 million people view (or review) the commercials on YouTube.

Most rewatched Super Bowl moment: Janet Jackson's 2004 "wardrobe malfunction."

Max McGee of the Green Bay Packers scored the first Super Bowl touchdown in 1967. He made a one-handed catch on a pass from quarterback Bart Starr and ran 37 yards to the end zone. The 34-year-old veteran went on to a total of seven catches, gaining 138 yards and two touchdowns, leading to a 35–10 victory over the Kansas City Chiefs.

Most Super Bowl wins as of 2013: Pittsburgh Steelers (6).

The only team to play in four consecutive Super Bowls is the Buffalo Bills (1991–94). They are also the only team to lose four consecutive Super Bowls.

Four teams have never gone to the Super Bowl: the Detroit Lions, Cleveland Browns, Jacksonville Jaguars, and Houston Texans.

In 2005, of the 93 million people who watched the Super Bowl, only 2 percent lived outside North America.

Number of footballs made exclusively for use in the Super Bowl every year: 144. Of those, 72 are to be used during the game, and 72 more are back-ups.

Cost of a 30-second Super Bowl commercial in 2012: $3.5 million.

Super Bowl I was broadcast live by both CBS and NBC, using the exact same video but with their own announcers.

Hall of Fame quarterback Roger Staubach holds the record for the most career Super Bowl fumbles: 5.

Collectively, Americans consume the most food on Thanksgiving, but Super Bowl Sunday is #2.

The Original Web Designers

Of the 35,000 known species of spiders, only about 500 can bite humans. And of those, only 20 to 30 are significantly poisonous.

Despite their name, black widow spiders don't really eat their mates any more often than other spiders, and they aren't *that* poisonous: 99 percent of people who are bitten survive.

Spiders can get caught in their own webs, so they walk on special dry strands that aren't sticky. If a spider gets stuck by mistake, it secretes an oily solvent to free itself.

Some spider babies eat their moms.

The weight of insects eaten by spiders every year is greater than the weight of all the humans on earth.

Not all spiders spin webs. Some just wait and leap out to catch bugs. Others chase bugs down. And the spitting spider spits out gobs of sticky, venomous fluid to capture its prey.

A butterfly's wings will not stick to spider silk.

A house spider can build a traditional web in about an hour.

A Hairy Tale

Jimmy Carter began his presidency with his hair parted on the right, but left office with his hair parted on the left.

To transform actor Lon Chaney Jr. into the Wolf Man (1941), Hollywood make-up artists spent five hours a day applying yak hair to his face and body.

Ringo Starr thought the Beatles would be a short-lived fad: he was just hoping to make enough money to open a hair salon.

Regular washings in saffron kept Alexander the Great's hair a bright orange.

On Easter in 1105, Bishop Serlo of Seiz chastised England's King Henry I and his court for "wearing their hair like women." After the service, the king begrudgingly allowed the bishop to cut his waist-length hair.

Walt Disney first started drawing cartoons in exchange for free haircuts.

Everyone's favorite redhead, Lucille Ball, actually had brown hair.

It was called "the most expensive haircut of all time" when Justin Bieber abruptly changed his look in 2010. Not expensive to *him*, but to all the manufacturers who had licensed his image to plaster on products like clothes, school supplies, and bags. One company that made Bieber dolls spent about $100,000 to trim their locks in time for the Christmas season.

John Reznikoff is the world's foremost collector of celebrity hair. He has bits from people like Michael Jackson (singed from his Pepsi ad accident) and Abraham Lincoln (cut by the surgeon after his assassination).

Bart Simpson has nine spikes of hair on his head.

The premise of the TV show *24* was that each season's 24 episodes took place in 24 hours of a single day. To keep the illusion, cast members had to get haircuts every five days.

Before people collected autographs, they collected locks of celebrity hair.

Dream Time

A 2008 study found that people who smell roses while they're sleeping are more likely to have pleasant dreams.

Typically, humans spend about 3 months of their lives dreaming.

On average, humans experience smells and tastes in 15 percent of their dreams.

Sign-language users have been known to sign in their sleep while dreaming.

A British study found that eating different cheeses before bed influenced dreams. The most bizarre dreams came after eating blue cheese.

The number of people who say they dream in color has risen by 53% since the 1940s.

People who are born blind do not see in their dreams; they employ the other four senses. That's also true of most people who lost their sight before age seven. However, those who lost their sight after age seven do often see in their dreams.

"He dreams." That's the literal translation of the Algonquin Indian word *powwaw*, which was a hallucinogen-enhanced religious gathering. (It's also where we got the word "powwow.")

Children's dreams are shorter than adults' dreams. Good thing, too, because about 40% of childhood dreams are nightmares.

Fiction readers have more surreal dreams that most, but the types of dreams differ by genre: Fantasy fans have are often aware that they're dreaming. Romance novel readers' dreams are the most emotionally intense. And children who read scary books are more likely to have nightmares.

Men dream more frequently about roads; women dream more frequently of water.

Studies show that only 8% of dreams are about sex.

Scientists say that the higher your IQ, the more complex your dreams.

Mooning the World

In the 1960s, astronauts trained for Moon voyages by walking on Hawaiian lava fields.

In many Western cultures, people see a man's face in the Moon's rock formations. But the Japanese see two rabbits making rice cakes. And the Chinese see one rabbit, pounding medicinal herbs for the moon goddess.

First manmade object to reach the Moon: the Soviet space probe *Luna 2* (1959).

There are still two golf balls on the Moon. Both were hit by astronaut Alan Shepard.

Astronauts have never visited the "dark side of the Moon," the side facing away from the Sun. Temperatures there drop to –280°F, and space suits can't handle such extreme cold. (Heat they can handle, though—the sunny side reaches 260°F.)

Astronauts have seen the Moon's dark side, though. On December 25, 1968, American astronauts Frank Borman, James Lovell, and William Anders became the first humans to see it from their *Apollo* 8 spacecraft.

If you weigh 150 pounds on Earth, you'd be only 25.5 pounds on the Moon.

The surface of the Moon has more than 30 trillion craters that are at least a foot wide… and 500,000 that are at least a mile wide.

The Moon is only 1.25 light-seconds away from Earth, meaning it takes that long for its reflected light to reach us.

The Moon turns slowly in relation to the Sun, so one lunar day averages 27.3 Earth days.

*   *   *

QUOTE ME
"Everyone is a moon, and has a dark side which he never shows to anybody." —**Mark Twain**

Putting Around

If a monkey steals your ball while you're golfing in the kingdom of Tonga, there's no penalty for replacing it.

Rule #10 on the first list of golf rules, compiled in Edinburgh, Scotland, in 1744: "If a ball be stopp'd by any person, horse, or dog, or anything else, the ball so stopp'd must be played where it lyes."

On September 14, 1963, Floyd Satterlee Rood teed up a golf ball at the edge of the Pacific Ocean and drove it due east. An incredible 385 days, 114,737 strokes, and 3,511 lost balls later, he'd covered 3,397.7 miles before driving a final ball into the Atlantic Ocean.

At the Jinja Golf Course in Uganda, you can drop a ball at the nearest safe spot if your shot lands dangerously close to a crocodile.

There are typically between 360 and 523 dimples on a golf ball. Each measures about 0.01 inch deep.

In the game of ice golf, the cold temperatures reduce a ball's flight by about 30%. To give players a fighting chance, the tees in this icy game are relocated a third of the way up the fairway.

The floor of the Oval Office once bore scars from President Dwight Eisenhower's golf spikes.

Canada has more recreational golfers per capita than any other country, yet it took years for one of them to win the Masters tournament. Mike Weir in 2003 was the first.

Odds of making a hole in one: 1 in 12,500.

Why do Japanese insurance policies offer hole-in-one insurance? Because getting an ace can be financially disastrous in Japan. It's such a big deal that you're expected to give parties and expensive gifts to friends to mark your good fortune, sometimes costing tens of thousands of dollars.

Poorly Executed

After a series of tests with corpses and sheep, French officials finally tried out their new guillotine on a live prisoner, highwayman Nicolas Jacques Pelletier, on April 25, 1792. (It worked.)

Remember: prisoners are "hanged," not "hung."

James Rodgers, a Utah murderer who faced a firing squad in 1960, was asked if he had a final request. His response: "Why, yes—a bulletproof vest."

In 1890 murderer William Kemmler of Buffalo, New York, became the first person ever executed by electric chair.

Only Confederate soldier (and only person in the U.S.) executed for war crimes: Henry Wirz. He ran the brutal Andersonville military prison, where nearly a third of the Union prisoners died of malnutrition and disease.

In 1888 the British Home Office issued a guide called the *Official Table of Drops*, prescribing the length of rope to be used for every body weight up to 200 pounds. The guide was popular with hangmen... until they discovered it was wrong because the rope lengths were too long. The Home Office issued a revised version in 1913, cutting the rope lengths two or three feet. For example, a 154-pound prisoner got 9 feet of rope in 1888, but 6½ feet in 1913.

It's traditional in a firing squad to load a blank cartridge in one random gun, allowing shooters to believe they didn't shoot the fatal bullet.

Being an axeman could be even worse than being a hangman. Take the anonymous beheader of Mary, Queen of Scots in 1587. Rather than one good clean head chopping, his first blow glanced off her lower skull and didn't kill her. A second blow killed her, but her head was hanging on by gristle, so he had to rock the axe blade back and forth to cut it. Her head finally detached and he triumphantly lifted it by the hair for the assembled company of nobles...but her hair was a wig, and her head slipped out and fell to the floor.

Rock the Vote

Ugly election campaigns aren't anything new: In 1800, during an especially bitter election, a pro–John Adams newspaper in Connecticut warned that electing Thomas Jefferson would mean "murder, robbery, rape, adultery, and incest will all be openly taught and practiced."

You can be jailed in Fiji, Chile, and Egypt for not voting.

Empleomania is "an unnaturally high enthusiasm for holding public office."

George Washington and James Monroe are the only U.S. presidents to win every state in an election. (Of course, this was when there were only 15 states, and they had no opposition.)

In ancient Athens, lawmakers were chosen by a lottery. They each served a one-year term and then were replaced.

Members of England's royal family do not vote because they are expected to remain politically neutral.

In 1893 New Zealand became the first country to allow women to vote in national elections—90,000 women showed up that year.

Wyoming was the first state to grant women the right to vote, in 1889. Nationwide, American women had to wait until 1920.

In 1997 Mike Soleto ran unopposed for the school board in Westmoreland, Kansas… and still lost. No one (including Soleto) voted for him.

In some states, if you vote by absentee ballot but die before Election Day, your vote still counts.

Congress chose early November for Election Day because it fell between the end of the fall harvest and winter's heavy snows. It's also always "the Tuesday after the first Monday" to avoid All Saints' Day on November 1.

The candidate who spends the most money usually wins the election.

Nine Facts About Eight Planets

Because it is so close to the Sun but has no atmosphere to hold heat or cold, Mercury has the largest temperature fluctuation of any planet in our solar system—from -280°F at night and 800°F during the day.

Venus turns so slowly that one Venus day (243 days on Earth) is longer than one Venus year (225 days on Earth).

Depending on their orbits at a given time, the distance between Mars and Earth can range from 3 light-minutes to 21. (A light-minute is the distance light can travel in a minute, just under 11,176,944 miles.)

Mars's sky has a pinkish tint because red dust from the planet's soil gets suspended in the atmosphere.

It would take 318 Earths to make one Jupiter.

Unlike most planets, Venus rotates clockwise, so the sun appears to rise in the west.

Jupiter is home to 66 of the 171 moons discovered so far in our solar system.

The tallest volcano on Mars is 17 miles high.

Besides Pluto, other dwarf planets include Ceres, Haumea, Makemake, and Eris. Ceres, Haumea, and Makemake are smaller than Pluto, but Eris is larger.

Pretty Fly for a Wright Guy

There are 15,095 airports or airfields in United States—more than in the next nine countries combined.

Every wonder how much loose change is left in those plastic bins at U.S. airport security checkpoints? Including foreign coins, the take for 2012 was $531,392, up from $487,869.50 in 2011.

Because more than 80 percent of Alaska's communities aren't connected by road to anyplace else, the state has 545 airports and airfields. Some of the state's airport codes include EEK (the town is actually named Eek), WOW (Willow), and GNU (Goodnews Bay).

London's Heathrow Airport got its name from a hamlet of that name that the airport displaced.

One of America's first airport hotels was Michigan's Dearborn Inn, commissioned by Henry Ford for his Ford Airport and finished in 1931. The hotel's still there, but the airport closed in 1933.

Oldest airfield: College Park Airport in Maryland, founded by Wilbur Wright in 1909 and still in use today.

Denver International Airport covers 53 square miles, making it larger than the city of Boston. However, Riyadh Airport in Saudi Arabia, which sprawls across 87 square miles of desert, is the world's largest.

The Pan Am Clippers of the 1930s didn't have wheels, and their runways didn't have pavement. The famous pioneering trans-Pacific planes were actually "flying boats" that took off and landed on water. Its mainland "runway"—an artificial harbor in San Francisco Bay—is still in Alameda, California.

Why does Chicago's O'Hare Airport have the code of ORD? It used to be called Orchard Place/Douglas Field.

The world's busiest airport is Atlanta International, serving 95 million travelers a year.

Base(ball) Instincts

A pitched baseball slows by about 8 mph by the time it reaches home plate.

Until 1845, it was legal to "plug" runners (i.e., hit them with a thrown ball to get them out).

The Cobb salad's namesake, Robert H. Cobb, was a first cousin of baseball legend Ty Cobb.

Baseball wasn't invented by one person, and various baseball-like games were around in England before the sport became popular in the United States. "Rounders" and "one old cat—two old cats—three old cats" were all popular variations in the early 1800s.

In 1910 Howard Taft began the presidential tradition of throwing out a ball to begin the baseball season.

Before he played baseball, Babe Ruth trained to be a tailor.

Average MLB player's salary: $3.4 million.

Baseball trading cards were once the "prize" that came with bubble gum, cigarettes, and Cracker Jacks. In the early 1960s, the cards were also printed on the backs of Post cereal boxes, requiring a steady hand with scissors to get them the exact right size and shape.

"Shoeless Joe" Jackson isn't in the Baseball Hall of Fame…but his shoes are.

Since 1997, David Lander (Squiggy on the 1970s TV show *Laverne & Shirley*) has been a pro baseball talent scout for the Los Angeles Angels and Seattle Mariners.

*　　*　　*

"There are two theories on hitting the knuckleball.
Unfortunately, neither works."
—**Charlie Lau, hitting coach**

Beetlemania

There's a species of beetle named *Agra vation*. It got its name from its habit of eating the lead covering from underground cables.

The "Hitler beetle," or *Anophthalmus hitleri*—a blind beetle found only in a few caves in Slovenia—was named in 1933 for Adolf Hitler. A furor of collecting has endangered it.

George W. Bush, Dick Cheney, and Donald Rumsfeld each have a slime-mold beetle named after them.

Other slime-mold beetles have been named for Pocahontas, the Aztecs, Hernán Cortés, and Darth Vader. (His beetle has a helmetlike head.)

The whirligig beetle, a water dweller, got its name because it swims in circles when frightened.

The deathwatch beetle got its name because its adults use a mating call that sounds like a ticking watch.

The museum beetle is so named because its larva feed on dried animal products, making them the scourge of natural history museums.

Mixing Apples...

Some apple varieties are as small as cherries. Others are as large as grapefruits.

Maria Ann Sherwood Smith found the first Granny Smith apple growing in her Australian orchard in 1868 from the remains of some French crabapples.

Canadian John McIntosh is to be given credit for the McIntosh apple. He found a seedling growing wild, probably from a discarded apple core, and cultivated it in 1811.

Most apple harvests are still picked by hand.

Apple cider can be frozen for up to a year. Just don't use a full or glass jug—it expands as it freezes.

The Gravenstein apple came to California sometime around 1820 with Russian immigrants, but it's been around for a while: In the 1600s, it first grew around Germany's Castle Graefenstein.

If you had eaten an apple a day from age 5 until you were 35, you would have eaten 10,957 apples.

The only apple native to North America is the crabapple.

It takes the energy from 50 leaves on an apple tree to produce one ripe fruit.

McDonald's buys 34 million pounds of fresh apples in a year, mostly from Michigan.

McDonald's keeps its Happy Meal apple slices from browning by dipping them in calcium ascorbate (a mix of calcium and vitamin C). They have a shelf life of two weeks.

The Red Delicious apple was cultivated by chance on a farm in Peru, Iowa. In 1872 it was first dubbed "Hiatt's Hawkeye" after the man who owned the farm.

Apple Currant was one of the first Pop Tart varieties.

...and Oranges

Oranges that grow higher on the tree have more vitamin C than the lower fruit.

A glass of orange juice contains about 22 grams of sugar. (Two squares of dark chocolate: 12 grams.)

The first oranges were cultivated in China as far back as 2500 BC. In a number of languages, including Dutch and German, the word for an orange translates to "China's apple."

Orange trees, unlike apple trees, don't lose all their leaves during winter (or ever).

Oranges won't ripen off the tree.

If you want your oranges pure, grow them separately from grapefruits, lemons, and limes. Oranges crossbreed easily with any of them.

The popular navel orange is a freak of nature: Every navel orange tree is a clone of a single tree that mutated 200 years ago. The trees are sterile and can be grown only by being grafted onto the roots of another tree.

It is possible to grow other types of orange trees from seeds.

Orange peels consist of two parts: the exocarp (the orange, exterior peel) and the mesocarp (the white, inner peel).

In 1894 Charles Chapman, a descendant of Johnny Appleseed, introduced Valencia oranges to America from his orange grove in California.

Oranges have less vitamin C than strawberries.

How many sections in an orange? 9 to 12.

* * *

A million dollars' worth of pennies weighs 288 tons.

Deaths on the Throne

WHO: Roman emperor, Elagabalus
WHEN: 222
CAUSE OF DEATH: Murder
Elagabalus became emperor as a teenager and was entirely
unprepared for the job. Initially, his erratic behavior was
entertaining, but eventually it became an embarrassment to the
Roman power structures. Three wives, several rumored homosexual
liaisons, and a few sacrilegious acts later, he was murdered in his
bathroom.

WHO: King Edmund II of England
WHEN: 1016
CAUSE OF DEATH: Natural causes…or murder
When Edmund became king of England, he battled the Viking
king Canute the Great for control of England. Edmund lost and
eventually struck a deal dividing the disputed territories, agreeing
that whoever died first would cede his territory to the other. Months
later, Edmund was found dead in his bathroom…and Canute took
over England. Officially recorded as death from natural causes,
some historians now believe the timing of Edmund's death was too
coincidental to be anything but murder.

WHO: Danish astronomer Tycho Brahe
WHEN: 1601
CAUSE OF DEATH: Burst bladder
The famed Danish astronomer, who invented an indoor pressure-
flow toilet, died in a terrible twist of fate: During dinner one night,
having consumed a large amount of alcohol, he politely refused to
leave the table to empty his bladder. By the time Brahe made it to
the loo, his overfull bladder had burst and killed him.

WHO: King George II of England
WHEN: 1760
CAUSE OF DEATH: Aortic dissection
George II ruled for more than 30 years…and then died from a

tear in the lining of the aorta while straining on the toilet. He made medical history as the first person to have "aortic dissection" recorded as the cause of death.

WHO: Empress Catherine the Great of Russia
WHEN: 1796
CAUSE OF DEATH: Unknown, but probably natural causes
Catherine the Great, Czaress of Russia, was making her way to the bathroom when something caused her to collapse on the threshold. That's where her attendant found her partially conscious. She died soon after.

WHO: Elvis Presley
WHEN: 1977
CAUSE OF DEATH: Drug overdose
The king of rock and roll died as the result of taking too many prescription drugs, including codeine from a dental visit. (He was known to have previously had an allergic reaction to codeine.) While in the bathroom, Presley apparently got sick, fell unconscious, and crashed to the floor. His autopsy stated he died from "cardiac arrhythmia" from ingesting too many drugs.

*   *   *

ACTUAL BOOK TITLES

- *How to Be Happy Though Married*, by E. J. Hardy (1885)

- *Life and Laughter 'midst the Cannibals*, by C. W. Collison (1926)

- *Sex Life of the Foot and Shoe*, by William Rossi (1977)

- *Children Are Wet Cement*, by Ann Ortlund (2002)

- *Be Bold with Bananas*, a cookbook by the Australian Banana Growers Council (1970s)

Our Biggest Star

The Sun travels through space at 230 miles per second—fast enough to go from New York to Los Angeles in 11 seconds.

The Sun may look bigger at sunrise and sunset, but it's actually about 8,000 miles closer to you at high noon.

Those "angelic" sunbeams pouring through clouds are technically called "crepuscular rays."

The pressure at the Sun's center is about 700 million tons per square inch—enough to smash atoms (which it does).

During our winter, Earth is 3 million miles *closer* to the Sun than in summer because of the way Earth tilts on its axis.

What is a *spectroheliokinematograph*? A special camera used to film the Sun.

The Sun contains 99.8 percent of the mass in the solar system. Jupiter has most of the rest.

The Sun shrinks by five feet every hour.

*   *   *

YOU WANT A PIECE OF ME?

Nineteenth-century poet and literary sex symbol Lord Byron got lots of requests for bits of his hair. He sent clippings from Boatswain, his Newfoundland dog.

Physical Fatness

As far as your body is concerned, fat is a fuel tank, storing energy to burn when you need it.

The human body contains about 30 billion fat cells.

Sumo wrestlers have to be at least 5'6" tall and weigh 165 pounds. Most champions are much heavier than that.

The body mass index measures how much fat you have on your body: Below 18.5 is "underweight." 18.5 to 24.9 "normal." 25 to 29.9, "overweight." 30 to 39.9, "obese." And over 40, "morbidly obese."

63 percent of Americans are overweight, obese, or severely obese.

For most of human history, obesity was a status symbol, signifying health, wealth, and fertility.

Not getting enough sleep can be one cause of obesity.

Minnesota and Utah have the lowest rates of childhood obesity (23.1 percent). Mississippi has the highest (44.4 percent).

Dads are less likely than moms to recognize that their child is overweight.

Let yourself go: 70.6 percent of married American men are overweight or obese. Married women: 48.6 percent

Studies show that most lottery winners gain weight after they win.

Thinking for one hour burns about 0.07 grams of fat.

For the average person, walking an extra 20 minutes every day burns 7 pounds of body fat per year. (It's more if you're overweight or obese.)

*   *   *

Turkeys can have stress-induced heart attacks.

It's a Living

A *qwylwryghte* is an ancient name for an old job: wagon-wheel mechanic.

A *muggler* takes care of pigs.

A *frobbisher* polishes metal for a living.

In the U.S. Army, "laundry and shower specialist" is an official job title, but it isn't much fun. Duties include spraying germicide on laundry.

"Wanted: Young, skinny, wiry fellows. Not over 18. Must be expert riders. Willing to risk death daily. Orphans preferred." Despite that ominous ad, 183 boys and men, age 11 to 40, became Pony Express riders. (Luckily, only one rider was killed in the 19 months the Pony Express existed.)

New Hampshire has an official state seagull harasser whose job it is to drive gulls away from nesting terns.

A *belly builder* is someone who puts together the parts inside a piano.

Gong farmer is an old British name for a person who cleans out privies and cesspools.

Coffee Break

A single coffee tree yields only about 2 to 4 pounds of roasted coffee annually.

It takes 18 coffee trees to feed the habit of a two-cup-a-day coffee drinker for one year.

Only about a penny of that latte you buy for four bucks goes back to the farmer who grew the coffee.

The coffee "bean" is not really a bean. It's the pit of the coffee "cherry," which is really a berry. Drying the discarded fruit makes a pleasant, fruity, and very caffeinated tea.

Math students, remember this request: "May I have a large container of coffee? Thank you." If you count the letters of each word, you'll get pi to ten digits: 3.141592653.

Americans consume coffee at the rate of 4,848 cups a second.

Rhode Island's official state drink is "coffee milk," a delicacy that's one part coffee to one part milk, and heavy on the sugar.

Hawaii is the only state that grows coffee.

The caffeine that's removed from decaf coffee is mostly used in soft drinks, aspirin, and over-the-counter stimulants.

Ten grams of caffeine can kill the average person. That's the equivalent of about 100 cups of coffee drunk in four hours.

Clownin' Around

How dangerous are circus jobs? Not that dangerous. In fact, spectators driving to and from the circus grounds suffer more injuries and death than performers do in their acts.

In circus jargon, a *doniker* is a toilet.

Calliopes—those whistling musical instruments housed in a wagon or train car—traditionally appeared only at the end of circus parades. That was partly to give a bang-up finish to the parade, but mostly because sometimes their steam boilers exploded.

Circus clowns have a hierarchy: The highest is called the *clown blanc* ("whiteface" in French), whose face is completely painted like Bozo or Ronald McDonald. The second tier is the Auguste, a fall-guy clown in flesh tones. At the bottom is the Character— tramps, cops, and clown-car fillers to act as foils and extras.

How many animals come in a box of classic Nabisco's Animal Crackers? Typically 22 cookies, in a random mix of 19 possible animal shapes.

Traveling shows with clowns and performers weren't called "circuses" until the 1790s.

There's no evidence that famous circus-master P. T. Barnum ever said, "There's a sucker born every minute."

There were seven Ringling brothers: Al, Gus, Otto, Alf, Charles, John, and Henry. They also had a sister named Ida.

A "flea circus" was a show that really *did* star performing fleas. Although flea circuses began in England during the 1500s, the tiny performances didn't become a big thing until the 1800s. The shows were short—usually 3 to 8 minutes—and could be attended by only a few people at a time. (After all, it's not like fleas can do that many tricks, and they were hard to see from a distance.)

China had the first school for circus arts, opened between the 7th and 10th centuries. The curriculum included sword dancing, rope walking, and pole tricks.

Gridiron Trivia

All NFL game balls are made by hand in Ada, Ohio.

Instant replay, invented by Tony Verna, was first used during a 1963 Army vs. Navy football game.

The worst shutout in football history took place in 1916, when Georgia Tech clobbered Cumberland University 222–0.

Most dangerous sport: Football. (#2: Basketball.)

U.S. sport with the most viewers: NFL football. (#2: NASCAR.)

Elvis Presley always wore a helmet when watching football on TV.

After years of adjusting the specific game rules and regulations, what's now considered the very first intercollegiate football game took place between Princeton and Rutgers in 1869.

Wearing a football helmets was optional in the NFL until 1943.

In 1873 Cornell's football team asked permission to travel to Cleveland for a game against the University of Michigan. "Absolutely not," roared the university's president, Andrew White. "I will not permit thirty men to travel 400 miles merely to agitate a bag of wind [to play football]."

Feats of Clay

A *pugger* is a person who mixes clay for ceramics.

Slings have been used as weapons since ancient times. In a pinch, throwers used rocks as ammo, but if they wanted accuracy, they used hardened clay balls instead.

Kaolin is a white clay best known for being used to make fine china. But it's also used to make paper glossy, keep pills together, protect crops from pests, and in diarrhea medicines (like Kaopectate) to make stools solid.

Clay was once baked into electrical fixtures for insulation.

Long before the first books, early Egyptian libraries lent out literature that had been pressed onto clay tablets.

Clay is part of most houses too, whether as brick, stucco, tiles, or "wattle and daub" (a building technique that trowels clay onto a wooden frame).

The oldest surviving love poem was etched onto a clay tablet in about 3500 BC.

Armadillos eat a lot of dirt with their diet of insects and snails, so their excrement comes out looking like round clay marbles.

In 1948 Edward Lowe of Cassopolis, Michigan, discovered that little bits of dried clay were perfect for cat boxes. He used that knowledge to found Tidy Cat.

The Mayans used cacao beans as currency, and painted clay counterfeit beans were common.

Doctors once prescribed eating a little clay for upset stomachs, and even today, you can still buy certain "medicinal" clays from alternative-medicine Web sites. Many users swear it works.

There's clay in the sidewalk. It's mixed with limestone and gypsum to make concrete.

Games People Play

It takes 17 hits to sink all of an opponent's ships in a game of Battleship.

When Fidel Castro took control of Cuba, he ordered all Monopoly game boards destroyed.

Nintendo's Mario character has appeared in more than 200 video games since 1981.

Video-game creators pay the NFL about $300 million to use real players in their games.

The board game Risk has released themed editions for Star Wars, Lord of the Rings, Godstorm, Narnia, Halo Wars, Metal Gear Solid, Transformers, and Napoleon.

"Flap-dragon" or "snapdragon" was a 16th-century game that included trying to pluck hot raisins from a shallow plate of burning brandy and flip them into your mouth, still burning. (Closing your mouth and biting down hard was usually enough to extinguish them.)

There are 1,326 possible hands you can be dealt in a game of Texas Hold 'Em.

At the game's peak in 2009, Farmville "farmers" outnumbered real farmers in the United States by 60 to 1.

* * *

"It may be that all games are silly—but then, so are humans."

—Robert Lynd

Christmas Presence

According to a central European folk tale, a child born on Christmas will become either a lawyer or a thief.

In his will, Robert Louis Stevenson left his November birthday to a friend who'd been born on Christmas…and wasn't happy about it.

A week before Christmas in 1958, a tape recorder inside a satellite played a "peace on earth, good will toward men" message from President Dwight Eisenhower. It was the first voice broadcast from space.

The first text message was sent December 3, 1992. The message: "Merry Christmas."

Each year during the Christmas season, more than half a million packages and letters come through the Santa Claus, Indiana, post office.

Despite having plenty of spruce and pine, Alaska imports most of its Christmas trees from Minnesota, Washington, and Oregon.

Technically, Christmas trees are edible…but they taste terrible.

For Christianity's first 200 years, its leaders believed it was sinful to celebrate Jesus's birthday because, in the Bible, the only birthday celebrations were for to Roman kings: Herod, during whose reign John the Baptist was beheaded, and the pharaoh who imprisoned Joseph (who wore the coat of many colors).

In 1643 the Puritans had the same thought. They declared Christmas carols, holly, plum pudding, and even holiday church services illegal.

Although the Puritan laws were officially repealed in 1681, New England leaders continued their war against Christmas for nearly two centuries, arresting merrymakers and discouraging public displays, decorations, and taking the day off from work. Until Christmas was made a federal holiday in 1870, Boston public schools remained open on December 25 and punished kids who didn't show up.

Four Facts About Bagpipes

1. SCOTLAND DIDN'T INVENT THEM.

Long before bagpipes reached Scotland, much of Europe, southwestern Asia, and northern Africa were already playing early versions of the instrument. In fact, many historians believe that it was a form of the bagpipe that the Roman emperor Nero famously played, not a fiddle as is commonly reported.

Bagpipes probably arrived on the English Isles sometime after AD 43 during Rome's 400-year occupation. But it wasn't until the late 13th century that they began to appear regularly in British art. Finally in the 14th century, *The Canturbury Tales* cemented the bagpipe's place in literature, describing a virtuoso this way: "A baggepype wel coude he blowe and sowne, / And ther-with-al he broghte us out of towne."

It was the Scots who made bagpipes famous worldwide, however. And in the late 20th century, electronic versions of the instrument appeared, shaped and played like the regular kind but with synthesized tones, no air, and no reeds.

2. BAGPIPES DON'T PLAY WELL WITH OTHERS.

There are a few reasons that bagpipers don't typically appear in jazz, country, or rock groups. First, bagpipes are made for outdoor use, so they're loud and not easily modulated to quieter tones. Second, they are hard to tune. But probably the biggest problem is that bagpipes are tuned to different tones than the notes of pianos, violins, guitars, horns, woodwinds...well, everything, actually. For example, an A on any other instrument is 440 hz (vibrations per second). But what is called an A on a bagpipe is anything between 476 to 480 hz, a tone between B-flat and B on any other instrument. As a result, when traditionally tuned bagpipes play with other instruments, the result sounds like horns in a traffic jam, only not quite so musical.

It's possible to modify a bagpipe to something close to the modern scale, but not with great accuracy, meaning that any accompanying instrument has to try to tune to the bagpipe. That's reasonably doable with brass and woodwinds, harder with stringed instruments, prohibitively time-consuming with pianos and electronic keyboards, and impossible with pipe organs, xylophones, and vibes. Also, any arrangements must avoid the bagpipe's high G: it won't be tuned right, no matter what you do.

3. A BAGPIPE DOESN'T PLAY THAT WELL BY ITSELF, EITHER.

If you're reasonably skilled on a modern Western musical instrument, you can play almost any song. That's because they all offer the 13 notes on the modern Western scale, tuned to the white and black keys on a piano: C, C sharp, D, D sharp, E, F, F sharp, G, G sharp, A, A sharp, B, and C. But that's not true of a bagpipe. It will play only two of the black-key notes (C sharp and F sharp) and won't play two of the white-key notes (C and F). Traditional bagpipes also have a note that doesn't appear on any other Western instrument: a high G that is halfway between G and G sharp.

4. ORIGINAL BAGPIPES AREN'T VEGETARIAN.

What's the bagpipe's bag made of? Today, it's usually something like Gore-Tex, but traditionally, players used the skin of whatever goat, sheep, pig, cow, or dog happened to be available.

*   *   *

THE GREAT CHEESE RACE

In a tradition that is about 500 years old, an annual "race the cheese" event takes place in Gloucestershire in the United Kingdom. Competitors in the Cooper's Hill Cheese-Rolling and Wake race a seven- to nine-pound wheel of Double Gloucester cheese (which is given a one-second head start) down a steep hill. The cheese usually wins, reaching speeds of up to 70 mph, so the first human to cross the finish line wins the race.

Byway or the Highway

The busiest stretch of highway in the United States is Interstate 405 from Los Angeles to Santa Ana, California.

Despite having no contiguous neighbors, Hawaii has more miles of "interstate highways" than Alaska, which has none.

Indiana has more miles of interstate highway per square mile than any other state.

Broadway doesn't just stop at the edge of New York City. It continues 150 miles to Albany. (Its official name is Highway 9.)

97 percent of the world's redwoods grow along the "Redwood Highway"—Highway 101 from Mendocino County in California to the Oregon border.

Despite higher speed limits, fatality rates on German autobahns are lower than on U.S. interstates.

Those yellow plastic impact barrels filled with sand or water that appear along highways are called Fitch barriers, named after race car driver John Fitch, who invented them.

Among highway engineers, raised reflective plastic disks and squares that mark off highway lanes are called "Botts' dots" to honor Elbert Botts, the California Department of Transportation chemist who created them.

Built in 1922, Oregon's Columbia River Highway was America's first designed for sightseeing along the way.

The font used on interstate signs is officially called FHWA Series Font, but known informally as Highway Gothic.

In 1938 Route 66 became the first American highway to be fully paved.

*　　*　　*

In traditional Hawaiian burials, bodies are wrapped in banana leaves.

Facebook Follies

For most people, Facebook is a fun way to keep in touch with family and friends or track down people they wish they hadn't lost touch with. For others, it brings disaster.

- In 2009 Lynn France of Ohio searched Facebook for the name of a woman she thought was having an affair with her husband. To her surprise, she found 200 recent wedding photos of her husband (dressed as Prince Charming) getting married to the woman (dressed as Sleeping Beauty) on the grounds of Walt Disney World.

- Arizona podcaster Israel Hyman admitted in 2009 that he shouldn't have tweeted the details of his vacation in the Midwest to his Twitter followers. While he was gone, he lost thousands of dollars worth of video equipment after burglars crawled in through a dog door at his home.

- In 2009 a 19-year-old broke into a house in Pennsylvania, but was caught after the victim discovered that he'd used her computer to log into Facebook and hadn't signed out. (The same year, a 27-year-old man in South Carolina robbed a bank of $3,924, but couldn't help bragging about it on MySpace: "On tha run for robbin a bank Love all of yall." He was arrested nine days later.)

- In 2010 Keri McMullen posted her plans for a night out on Facebook. Minutes after she left the house, two men broke into her home in New Albany, Indiana, and took $10,000 worth of computers and other valuables. But they left behind the hidden video cameras that recorded the whole thing. McMullen posted the video on Facebook and quickly ID'ed the culprits: One of her 500 "Facebook friends" recognized one of the men as another of McMullen's "friends," an old acquaintance better forgotten.

Creepy Suicide Stats

Most likely day for suicides: Wednesday. Least likely day: Thursday.

Since the Golden Gate Bridge opened in 1937, more than 1,600 people have jumped off it.

Approximate odds of surviving a plunge from the Golden Gate Bridge: 1 in 500.

American men are four times more likely to kill themselves than American women, but women have the most suicide attempts.

Each year, about 30 people attempt to commit suicide with BB guns. They usually fail since the odds of dying from a BB gun wound are very low.

According to a 20-year study of suicides in Memphis, Tennessee, 29 percent of people who commit suicide have alcohol in their systems.

Writers are 2.6 times more likely to kill themselves than nonwriters.

Only about 1 in 5 people who commit suicide leave a note.

The ten states with the lowest suicide rates have coastlines on an ocean or Great Lake.

China is the only country where female suicides outnumber those of men.

Suttee is the 1,600-year-old tradition in India of widows being expected to throw themselves onto the burning funeral pyres of their husbands. Although outlawed in 1829, the practice still occasionally surfaces in rural areas, in which social coercion—and sometimes forceable action—continues the practice.

Suicides by gun outnumber all other methods combined.

* * *

A 1911 Canadian silver dollar is worth more than $1 million today.

Just One Word, Son...Plastics!

It costs one cent to make a plastic grocery bag.

Worldwide, people use more than 500 billion plastic shopping bags each year.

Every year, manufacturers make enough plastic wrap to cover the entire state of Texas.

The first 100 percent synthetic material ever created was Bakelite, a plastic invented in 1907. Still used for some electronics, Bakelite ended up in a variety of early 20th-century objects: toys, pipe stems, sax mouthpieces, radios, cameras, clocks, billiard balls, chess pieces, and mah-jongg tiles.

Henry Ford funded research into making plastic car parts from plants. His experimental gardens included rows of soybeans and marijuana, from which he made a few prototype plastic car bodies before World War II shut down his research. By the war's end, it became clear that petroleum-based plastics were easier and cheaper to make than plant-based ones. However, the cost of oil has recently spurred manufacturers to start working with plant-based plastics again.

Australia started using plastic currency in 1988 and completely switched over in 1996. Printed on hard-to-tear material like that used for FedEx envelopes, it resembles paper, but is difficult to counterfeit and lasts four times longer. Since then, Thailand, Indonesia, Singapore, Bermuda, Romania, Vietnam, and many others have gone plastic as well.

Eye See You

The human eye can see about 10 million shades of color, including 100 different shades of gray.

Scientists believe that every blue-eyed person is descended from a single common ancestor.

Humans' eyes reach full size before puberty, and humans' retinas are fully grown by the age of four or five.

Some people can hear their eyeballs moving.

The photographic effect called "red eye" is most visible in people with blue eyes because of a melanin deficiency: The tissue behind the backs of their eyes is lighter colored and therefore reflects more light.

Arctic hares have black eyelashes that protect their eyes from the sun, like sunglasses.

Light a match in the dark. If it's a clear night without city lights or a moon, another person could see it from 50 miles away.

Beavers have a set of transparent eyelids to protect their eyes underwater.

Not every animal has two eyes— honeybees have five, and the box jellyfish has 24.

The tokay gecko uses its tongue to clean its eyes.

Frogs close their eyes when they swallow because their eyelids push their big round eyes backward, forcing struggling bugs into their throat.

Yellow stands out to the human eye more than any other color on the spectrum.

According to *Guinness World Records*, in 2006 Dong Changsheng of China pulled a 3,300-pound car 33 feet...using his lower eyelids.

As some people age, their eye color gets lighter.

Human eyes produce about a teaspoon of tears every hour.

Coffee Talk

35 percent of coffee drinkers drink it black.

GI slang for coffee with cream and sugar: blonde and sweet.

After petroleum, coffee is the second most traded product in the world.

Norwegians drink the most coffee per person in the world.

Starbucks spends more on employee health insurance than it does on coffee beans.

By brewing your own coffee instead of buying a $3 latte each day for 30 years, you'd save $55,341.

Freeze-dried coffee was created for the military.

Long before screenwriters in cafés became a cliché, Francis Ford Coppola wrote large portions of *The Godfather* in Caffe Trieste, San Francisco's first coffee shop.

According to one study, the most dangerous food item to consume while driving is hot coffee.

The New York Stock Exchange started out as a coffeehouse.

Lloyd's of London, famous for insuring Betty Grable's legs and Bruce Springsteen's voice, didn't start as an insurance company. Edward Lloyd began the business in the 17th century as a coffeehouse near the docks in London, and insurance brokers and other gamblers made it their headquarters.

The writer Voltaire drank between 50 and 70 cups of coffee every day.

In 1657 a doctor wrote that coffee was good for "miscarriage, hypochondria, dropsy, gout, and scurvy. Makes skin exceedingly clear and white…it quickens the spirits, and make the heart lightsome."

Coffee sometimes works wonders if your plants are turning yellow. Its acidity helps them to absorb iron.

Decaf coffee was invented accidentally after a storm at sea soaked a shipment of coffee beans in saltwater.

The Supply Room

Yukio Horie invented felt-tip pens in 1962, trying to replace ink brushes for Japanese writing.

Norwegians claim that their own Johan Vaaler invented the paper clip in 1901. We hate to rain on their lutefisk, but two years earlier, an American inventor named William Middlebrook had already patented a machine to make wire paper clips.

Walt Disney World buys 3.8 million pens each year.

A paper clip is about the size of a newborn kangaroo.

Bic estimates that it has sold more than 50 pens every second since 1950.

About 100 people choke to death on ballpoint pens every year.

On October 7, 1806, Ralph Wedgwood patented an "apparatus for producing duplicates of writings" (carbon paper).

The bottom part of a stapler, where the ends of the staple get pressed under, is called the "anvil."

Finnish scissors-maker Fiskars has been in business since 1649—but they've been making scissors only since the 1880s. According to the company, its first products were "nails, thread, knives, hoes, iron wheels, and other things."

Clock Wise

Who should we curse on Monday morning?
Levi Hutchins of Concord, New Hampshire. In
1787, he invented the alarm clock.

Every day, the atomic clocks on GPS satellites
gain 38 microseconds on their earthbound
counterparts. This is a confirmation of Einstein's
theory of relativity, which predicted that time
will run faster when you're located away from
gravity or while moving at a high speed.

Paul Revere made clocks, and Henry Ford
repaired them.

In 2007 President Hugo Chávez ordered
Venezuela's clocks permanently set back 30
minutes. The upside: Venezuelans got more
light in the day. The downside: The move put
the country halfway between two time zones
and its clocks out of sync with those everywhere
else on earth.

The earliest known clock, similar to a sundial,
dates from about 3500 BC.

A cuckoo clock is nearly an exact reproduction
of the sound of the male European cuckoo.

Clocks run ever so slightly faster on
mountaintops than they do at sea level.

77s

The first Talking Heads album, released in 1977, was called simply *77*.

Football jersey #77 has been retired by both the University of Illinois and the Chicago Bears. In both cases, the number was worn by halfback and Hall of Famer Red Grange.

The nuclear aircraft carrier *CVN 77* is also known as the USS *George H.W. Bush*.

Interstate 77 runs from Ohio to South Carolina.

The United States Code, Chapter 77, makes it a federal crime to engage in "peonage, slavery and trafficking in persons."

77 square inches is the combined area of two seven-inch pizzas.

The Group of 77 is part of the United Nations. The original members numbered 77, but today the group includes representatives from more than 130 developing countries who meet to discuss ways of improving their economies.

77 percent is the amount of light blocked by a typical lamp shade.

World "Capitals"

Cow Chip Throwing Capital of the World: Beaver, Oklahoma
In preparation for their annual competition in April, the folks of
Beaver collect, flatten, and dry cow poop into Frisbee-sized throwing
chips. No points for style or choreography; only distance.

Artichoke Capital of the World: Castroville, California
The town comes by its giant fiberglass artichokes honestly:
California grows more artichokes than any other state in the union,
and Castroville's one of the most prolific.

Barbed Wire Capital of the World: La Crosse, Kansas
La Crosse is home to the Barbed Wire Museum—it's either the
world's largest, or one of the top three, depending on how you count.
Regardless, its collection contains 2,000 different samples of barbed
wire, as well as fence posts, books, and educational films.

Bourbon Capital of the World®: Bardstown, Kentucky
The residents of Bardstown are so protective of their title that they
even registered the phrase. Making the stuff since 1776, the area
produces 69 percent of the world's bourbon.

Halloween Capital of the World™: Anoka, Minnesota
The trademarked title comes from the town's claim that it threw the
first town-wide Halloween celebration. In 1920, tired of finding their
"cows roaming Main Street, windows soaped, and outhouses tipped
over," Anoka residents created an annual party with costume parades,
pillow fights, fireworks, snake dances, and "celebrity appearances."

Fruitcake Capital of the World: Claxton, Georgia
Two bakeries pump more than four million pounds of fruitcake out
of Claxton every year. The cake batters and fruits are tumbled 375
pounds at a time in what looks a lot like a cement mixer. Fruitcakes
last six months at room temperature, twice as long refrigerated.

Loon Capital of the World: Mercer, Wisconsin
You know we're talking about the bird, right? The people of Mercer are no more crazy than the rest of us. Well, maybe a *little* crazier, as evidenced by the fact that they proclaimed themselves the World's Loon Capital.

Moonshine Capital of the World: Franklin County, Virginia
Technically, this title has since been retired, but in the 1920s, about 99% of the working residents of Franklin County were involved in a massive bootleg liquor trade. The county museum still honors the nickname with historic stills and other exhibits.

Horseradish Capital of the World: Collinsville, Indiana
Claiming to produce 85 percent of the world's horseradish, Collinsville is a treasure trove of condiment riches. Once the home of the G. S. Suppiger Catsup bottling plant, a 170-foot replica ketchup bottle also serves as the town water tower.

Factory Tour Capital of the World: York, Pennsylvania
Many towns have factory tours, but York has 25 in all—from Harley-Davidson to Bluett Bros. Violins, Snyder's of Hanover Pretzels, the York County Solid Waste Authority, and Hershey's Chocolate World, which contains a 10-minute faux factory-tour ride through a replica chocolate factory. (No chocolate bars are actually made there.)

Fire Hydrant Capital of the World: Albertville, Alabama
Home of a major fire hydrant company, Albertville took on the title proudly and features a nickel-plated hydrant downtown.

Snowshoe Baseball Capital of the World: Lake Tomahawk, Wisconsin
There's nothing like long winters to give you some crazy ideas. Take Snowshoe Baseball, invented by Lake Tomahawk's town chairman Ray Sloan in 1961 as a way of entertaining summer tourists. "Snowshoe baseball" is exactly what the name implies—baseball made comical by playing it in snowshoes in a field covered in sawdust.

Hubcap Capital of the World: Pearsonville, California
Tiny town, one obsessed collector, thousands of hubcaps on display.

An Absorbing Subject

Sponges depend on water flowing through their bodies to provide oxygen and food and to wash away waste.

Most sponges eat bacteria and small food particles. A few are carnivores, eating small crustaceans.

Although apparently fixed to one place, adult sponges can creep very slowly along the ocean floor. How slowly? The fast ones travel one inch in six days.

Fragments of a sponge can grow into a full sponge, like cuttings from a plant.

Thousands of sponge species live in saltwater, but only a few live in freshwater.

Some sponges live 200 years, maybe longer…maybe *much* longer, like thousands of years.

Some dolphins off western Australia use sponges to pad their snouts while digging around for food on the sandy ocean floor.

A sponge on a stick was what ancient Romans used for toilet paper.

Don't confuse loofah "sponges" with marine sponges. Loofahs are the dried shells of a gourd. Natural kitchen sponges, on the other hand, are essentially animal skeletons.

A living sponge doesn't have blood, a heart, veins, or arteries. It also doesn't have a digestive system, a brain, or any sort of nervous system.

Sponges reproduce a lot like plants: each is both male and female, releasing sperm into the water in the hope that some of them wash into the eggs of other sponges. Fertilized eggs turn into larvae that can swim, looking for a good place to put down roots.

Sponges can regulate the flow of water through their bodies, and can even shut it down completely if the water contains too much sand or silt.

MAD Magazine

IT'S A MAD, MAD WORLD

From 1952 until 1955, MAD was a full-color comic book called *Tales Calculated to Drive You Mad*. But in 1954, an inflammatory book titled *Seduction of the Innocent*, written by anti-comics crusader Dr. Fredric Wertham, hit stores, and public hysteria that comic books might be causing juvenile delinquency rose to a fevered pitch. The result was a congressional investigation and a "voluntary" set of guidelines that the industry adopted to avoid more onerous government regulations. The Comics Code Authority (CCA) contained prohibitions that would've made *Tales Calculated to Drive You Mad* impossible to continue as a comic book. The CCA prohibited not just sex, drugs, crime, depravity, lust, monsters, and vampires, but also anything that might promote "disrespect for established authority," something that *Tales Calculated to Drive You Mad* did regularly.

There was a loophole, however: the CCA covered only "comic books." So *Tales Calculated to Drive You Mad* decided on a makeover and MAD "magazine" was born.

MAD FACTS

- In 1961 MAD made copyright history when music publishers—representing all-star songwriters like Cole Porter, Richard Rodgers, and Irving Berlin—sued the magazine. The issue? A songbook of parodies that included words with the instruction that they could be "sung to the tune of" a specific song. The musicians' claim that only the original authors could legally parody their own songs was dismissed by judges all the way up to the U.S. Supreme Court.

- The magazine's peak circulation was 2,132,644. This occurred in 1974, despite intense competition from a (slightly) more grownup satirical magazine, the *National Lampoon*.

- The magazine's mascot—the round-headed boy with an idiotic grin—went unnamed until a staff member noticed the name of Alfred Newman in the credits of a movie. That Newman was a well-regarded film composer (and, incidentally, the uncle of composer Randy Newman). Hoping to forestall a lawsuit, the staff changed the spelling of Alfred's last name and added E as a middle initial.

- 485 MADison Avenue was *MAD's* headquarters for decades. But in the magazine's heyday, one envelope that contained a picture of Alfred E. Neuman was successfully delivered to the right address.

- Between 1955 and 2001, *MAD* ran no real ads. They ran plenty of parody ads, though, viciously mocking nearly every product you could name.

- *MAD* inspired so many imitators that founder/publisher Bill Gaines had a voodoo doll for each competitor labeled with a pin that was removed only when the imitator stopped publishing. Some of mostly short-lived imitators included *Cracked*, *Sick*, *Nuts!*, *Crazy*, *Whack*, *Riot*, *Flip*, and *Madhouse*. By the time of Gaines's death in 1992, only one pin remained, representing *Cracked*, founded in 1958. It stopped publishing in 2007, but still exists as a popular Web site.

- Artist Sergio Aragones has contributed more than 12,000 wordless gags running in the margins and other blank spaces of the magazine. Once called "the world's fastest cartoonist," Aragones's art has appeared in every issue since 1963, except one in 1964 when his drawings were lost in the mail.

*   *   *

THAT'S A LOT OF BOOKS!

The Library of Congress is the largest library in the world. It has more than 638 miles of shelf space to hold its 155 million items. It holds 35 million books and other print materials, 68 million manuscripts, 6.5 million pieces of sheet music, 3.4 million recordings, 13.6 million photographs, 5.4 million maps, and 100,000 comic books. Only about half of the Library of Congress's collection is in English. The rest includes materials in 470 languages.

The Writer's Desk

Mark Twain was the first author to submit a typewritten manuscript to a publisher. The book was *Life on the Mississippi* in 1883. Twain, who loved new gadgets, was also one of the first owners of a typewriter.

During the 33 years that author Anthony Trollope worked for the British post office, he wrote several novels by rising early and writing 1,000 words before work. Within postal circles, he's best known as the guy who invented the street-corner mailbox.

In all of his writings, Shakespeare mentioned the Americas only once, in *The Comedy of Errors*.

Before becoming a world-famous author, Kurt Vonnegut wrote press releases for General Electric.

Author Alissa Rosenbaum is better known as Ayn Rand.

Children's author Margaret Wise Brown—who wrote *Goodnight Moon, The Runaway Bunny*, and *The Bunny's Birthday*—loved to hunt rabbits. She collected their feet as trophies.

First-published authors range in age from four (Dorothy Straight, author of *How the World Began*) to 102 (Alice Pollock, author of *Portrait of My Victorian Youth*).

Most historians now believe that Aesop, the Greek slave and author of fables, probably never existed.

Author Roald Dahl was married for 30 years to actress Patricia Neal.

Spy novel writer Ian Fleming was also a birdwatcher. He named his most famous character after a bird-guide author, ornithologist James Bond.

*　　*　　*

In 1994 Supreme Court Justices Antonin Scalia and Ruth Bader Ginsburg appeared as costumed extras in the Washington Opera's performance of *Ariadne auf Naxos* by Richard Strauss.

Police & Thank You

On average, more fast-food workers are murdered on the job than are police officers.

U.S. police officers are exempt from federal jury duty.

TV cops shoot their guns several times an hour, but the average for a real cop is once for every nine years of service.

New York City's first female police officers—dubbed "police matrons"—went to work in 1891.

The first U.S. city to use police cars was Akron, Ohio, in 1899. The cars were electric wagons that could go 16 mph and cover 30 miles before they needed to be recharged.

America's most successful police dog was Trepp, a Florida golden retriever, with more than 100 arrests to his credit.

Traffic police in South Korea are required by law to report all the bribes they receive.

40 percent of Americans believe police shows are "fairly accurate." Only 14 percent of real police officers agree.

The average IQ of police officers is 104...just a little above the average of 100.

Uncle John's
Page of Lists

4 WORDS THAT READ THE SAME UPSIDE DOWN
1. Mow
2. iPod!
3. SOS
4. Suns

4 HOLES IN ONE
1. Youngest: Jake Paine, 3 years old, 65 yards
2. Oldest: Harold Stilson, 101 years old, 108 yards
3. Longest: Robert Mitera, 444 yards
4. Most: Norman Manley, 59

3 BEST-SELLING ICE CREAM FLAVORS
1. Vanilla
2. Chocolate
3. Butter pecan

TOP 5 U.S. BOY BABY NAMES, 2012
1. Jacob
2. Mason
3. Ethan
4. Noah
5. William

TOP 5 U.S. BOY BABY NAMES, 1912
1. John
2. William
3. James
4. Robert
5. Joseph

6 FAMOUS REDHEADS
1. Genghis Khan
2. Christopher Columbus
3. Elizabeth I
4. Thomas Jefferson
5. Vladimir Lenin
6. Malcolm X

TOP 5 U.S. GIRL BABY NAMES, 2012
1. Sophia
2. Emma
3. Isabella
4. Olivia
5. Ava

TOP 5 U.S. GIRL BABY NAMES, 1912
1. Mary
2. Helen
3. Dorothy
4. Margaret
5. Ruth

6 ACCIDENTAL INVENTIONS
1. Velcro
2. The Slinky
3. Microwave ovens
4. Superglue
5. Teflon
6. X-rays

State Songs

OKLAHOMA: When the state government needed a state song, it settled on an obvious choice: "Oklahoma!" from the musical *Oklahoma*.

FLORIDA: Florida's state song is "Old Folks at Home" by Stephen Foster, but it's not because of all the retired people who live there. The song's famous first line mentions a major waterway that runs through the state: "Way down upon the S'wanee River…" (The river's name is technically spelled "Suwannee.")

The problem with "S'wannee River" was that Foster wrote it for a 19th-century minstrel show, and the original lyrics—complete with ethnic slurs—were sung in a phony black dialect about an African American longing to go back to the plantation where he had been "happily" enslaved. That's how the song was sung during state functions until the 1970s, when embarrassed singers started changing the lyrics to make them less offensive. In 2008 the state legislature finally made the lyric changes official.

KENTUCKY: Another Stephen Foster tune that became a state song was "My Old Kentucky Home," and it suffered from similar racial issues. In 1986 Kentucky legislators voted to revise "darkies," the most objectionable word in the lyrics, to "people."

MARYLAND: The state's official song, "Maryland, My Maryland," is sung to the tune of "O Tannenbaum."

ARKANSAS: Arkansas claims two state songs, one state anthem, and one state historical song, "The Arkansas Traveler," written in the mid-1800s by Colonel Sanford Faulkner. In the 20th century, a state committee rewrote the lyrics to make them less offensive: the original was about a bumpkin fiddle player who wouldn't fix his leaky roof. Few people know either set of lyrics, but many know the melody—it's the kids' song "I'm Bringing Home a Baby Bumblebee."

LOUISIANA: One of Louisiana's official state songs is "Give Me Louisiana." The other is "You Are My Sunshine," a song long associated with Governor Jimmie Davis, who led the state from 1944 to 1948 and again from 1960 to 1964. Also a popular singer, Davis is the only governor of any state who has been inducted into the Country Music Hall of Fame. And he may be the only governor-songwriter who took credit for a song he didn't actually write. Depending on who's telling the story, Davis either bought the music rights for $35 or just plain stole the uncopyrighted song from Oliver Hood (the mandolin player who wrote it) and credited himself as the songwriter.

GEORGIA: Hoagy Carmichael's "Georgia on My Mind" makes sense as Georgia's state song…though the lyrics have always been open to interpretation and could be about the state or about a woman by that name. In 1979, almost 20 years after Georgia native Ray Charles made the song famous, the state legislature claimed it as its own, and Charles performed it on the legislative floor.

*　　*　　*

WHY BLUE FOR BOYS?

A century ago, babies of both genders wore white most often. Otherwise, though, pink symbolized boys and blue (long associated with the Virgin Mary) girls. After World War I, America's clothing industry began pushing those gender-specific colors, perhaps to make handing down baby clothes more complicated than buying new ones. Said a trade publication in 1918, "The generally accepted rule is pink for the boys, and blue for the girls. The reason is that pink, being a more decided and stronger color, is more suitable for the boy, while blue, which is more delicate and dainty, is prettier for the girl."

But then in the 1940s, the fashion industry abruptly reversed course and changed that tradition, in part because it was pushing pink as a way for women to reclaim their femininity as they moved out of wartime factories and fields. From then on, blue became a "boy" color and pink a "girl" color.

The Great 88

88 is considered a doubly lucky number in China because the Mandarin word for eight sounds like the word for "wealth."

The International Astronomical Union recognizes 88 constellations in the sky.

Oldsmobile began using the Rocket 88 high-compression engine in 1949, giving the brand a cooler image. Ike Turner even recorded a rock tribute to the engine in 1951: "Rocket 88."

88 is the only number between 11 and 101 that reads the same forward, backward, upside-down, in the mirror...and even in the mirror upside-down.

Eighty-Eight is the name of a town in Kentucky, named when the postmaster checked his pocket change and found 88¢.

88,000 barrels of oil per hour is the maximum capacity of the Trans-Alaska Pipeline.

88 years is the amount of time that White Sox fans had to wait between winning the World Series in 1916 and 2004.

You Dirty Louse!

Anteaters, armadillos, bats, and platypuses are the only land mammals that don't get lice.

Westerners mostly consider lice to be more an annoyance than a danger, but the bugs carry lots of diseases, including trench fever, relapsing fever, and typhus, which have killed millions around the world. One victim of lice-passed typhus was diarist Anne Frank, who picked up the disease in a crowded concentration camp and died in 1945.

There are about 3,000 species of lice in the world.

A "nitpicker" was originally somebody who picked nits (the eggs of head lice) from people's hair.

People get three kinds of lice: head, body, and pubic. Body lice evolved from head lice after humans lost their lush body hair about 107,000 years ago.

Body lice live in clothing—primarily in the seams—and commute onto the skin mostly to feed. That's why one nickname for body lice is "seam squirrels."

The British military originally coined the nickname "cooties" from *kutu*, the Polynesian word for pubic lice.

One type of specialized lice is *Haematomyzus*, a sort of industrial-strength louse that infects only elephants and warthogs. What makes this louse special is that it has a long, drill-like snout that can penetrate thick hides.

Lice that feed on mammals generally eat blood; lice that feed on birds eat dead skin and feathers.

Human lice must feed every 24 hours or they will starve to death.

The Building with the Most Stories

Before computers, libraries often had a room where patrons could use typewriters. That's how Ray Bradbury wrote *Fahrenheit 451*—at the UCLA library on a typewriter he rented for 20¢ an hour.

The record for the most-overdue library book is 288 years. In 1955 England's University of Cambridge library received a book that was taken out in 1667.

During the Middle Ages, the House of Wisdom was a massive library in Baghdad. It survived until 1258, when it was destroyed by a Mongol invasion.

In 1814, after the British invaded Washington, D.C., and burned the Library of Congress, Thomas Jefferson sold the government 6,487 of his personal books to restart its collection.

Ben Franklin founded America's first public library in Philadelphia in 1731. It's still open to the public.

Harvard University's libraries contain at least three books bound in human skin.

The Library of Congress adds about 20,000 new items every day.

United States libraries lend about 3 million items a day.

Libraries have been around a lot longer than books. Early Egyptian libraries included materials that had been pressed into clay tablets and baked.

Among the books in the prison library at Guantánamo Bay are the Harry Potter and Twilight series.

*   *   *

The U.S. Postal Service owns the world's largest collection of rubber stamps.

Trash Talk

Floating garbage gets trapped in the Great Pacific Garbage Patch, a huge floating island mostly composed of plastics that get caught in the center of the giant, circular Pacific current. Because of the distance and currents, it takes about six years for garbage from the West Coast of the United States to reach the patch, but trash from Asia takes only a year.

If someone says your home is "midden" style, don't take it as a compliment—a "midden" is an ancient garbage pit.

Americans throw out about 4.5 pounds of garbage a day, enough stuff to fill 63,000 garbage trucks.

Americans call it a garbage truck, but the British call it a "dustbin lorry."

Ancient city ruins are usually found many feet underground because of garbage. In ancient times, it was too hard to move the trash out of town or build enough garbage pits to bury it. So people spread it around and covered it with a layer of soil. Almost all ancient cities were built and rebuilt many times on progressively higher layers of layered garbage and dirt.

80 percent of the waste produced by humans on shore ends up in the oceans.

Dolphins with a Porpoise

Whales, dolphins, and porpoises are close relatives. They're all descendants of a hoofed animal related to pigs and cattle that gradually adapted to full aquatic life about 40 million years ago. Dolphins divided fully from the others only about 10 to 12 million years ago.

Dolphins have been observed using tools—such as sponges to protect their snouts—and teaching the knowledge to their young.

Male dolphins fight each other fiercely over mates.

Six of the animals we call "whales" are really dolphins: melon-headed whales, long-finned and short-finned pilot whales, killer whales (orcas), pygmy killer whales, and false killer whales.

Dolphins sometimes attack people. Tilikum, an orca at SeaWorld Orlando, holds the record: three people in three incidents in 1991, 1999, and 2010. He killed trainers the first and third time. The second death was a man who sneaked into the orca tank after hours.

Generally, though, dolphins are friendly to humans and sometimes help us out. In Santa Catarina, Brazil, dolphins drive fish toward fishermen on the shore and signal when to cast the nets. They eat what the nets miss.

Music to My Ears

The Russian composer Igor Stravinsky attended law school, but didn't like it much. In four years he attended fewer than 50 class meetings.

Mozart belonged to the Order of Freemasons and wrote several compositions for their meetings. Masonic legends also inspired his fantasy opera *The Magic Flute*.

An anonymous Marine wrote the words for the "Marine's Hymn," but for the melody, he used composer Jacques Offenbach's 1867 comic opera *Genevieve de Brabant*.

Sixteen-year-old Briton Euphemia Allen wrote "Chopsticks" in 1877. She called it "The Celebrated Chop Waltz" because you played it by "chopping" with your hands.

There are musical notes on every street sign in Mozart, Saskatchewan.

On October 12, 1609, young English composer Thomas Ravenscroft published a collection of folk songs called *Deuteromelia*. Within its pages was a new song that's still around today: "Three Blind Mice."

Legends claim that composer Johannes Brahms hated cats so much that he spent leisure time shooting arrows at them. But it turns out that this wasn't true; it was just a nasty rumor circulated by his rival, composer Richard Wagner.

Despite the plot of the movie *Amadeus*, composer Salieri was not Mozart's bitter rival. They were actually colleagues, and Salieri admired Mozart a great deal.

Wolfgang Amadeus Mozart started playing the harpsichord when he was four, and gave concerts for royalty a year later. He published his first piano piece at the age of seven.

News of the Nose

Your nose (and your ears) will continue to grow throughout your lifetime.

Osmophobia is the fear of smells. *Osphresiolagnia* is the love of smells.

A tortoise drinks through its nose.

In 2008 Dutch winemaker Ilja Gort insured his nose for $8 million.

The lowest part of your nose, the skin that separates your nostrils, is called your *columella nasi.*

Physician Amynthas of Alexandria, Greece, performed the first known nose job in the third century BC.

American plastic surgeons remove about 5,469 feet of noses each year.

Old homicide detective trick: Smearing a menthol rub under the nose helps a lot when dealing with decomposing bodies.

The *nasturtium* is such a nasty-smelling flower that its name in Latin means "a twist of the nose."

Q: What is "digital emunction"? A: It's a fancy way of saying "picking your nose."

Most Expensive...

...**Reality show:** *The X Factor* (the American version). The show costs about $3.5 million per episode to produce.

...**Spice on your grocer's shelf:** saffron. It takes the stamens of nearly 5,000 blossoms just to get one ounce.

...**Divorce:** Australia's Rupert and Anna Torv Murdoch ($1.7 billion in 1999).

...**Etch-A-Sketch:** The 1985 Executive model was made of silver and gemstones ($3,750).

...**Car to insure in the United States:** Cadillac Escalade. (Least expensive: Ford Taurus.)

...**State in which to play golf:** Nevada. (Cheapest: Nebraska.)

...**Wedding:** Prince Charles and Lady Diana ($48 million, 1981).

...**Coffee:** Kopi Luwak ($300 per pound). Its beans are handpicked out of the poop of the *Paradoxurus*, a tree-climbing marsupial. Coffee connoisseurs say it has a unique flavor. (We're sure it does.)

...**Commercial:** $33 million for a 2004 Chanel ad starring Nicole Kidman.

...**Motorcycle:** The MTT Turbine Superbike, powered by a Rolls-Royce Allison engine ($185,000).

...**Video game:** Grand Theft Auto IV, which cost $100 million to develop.

...**TV pilot episode:** *Lost* ($11.5 million in 2004).

...**Aircraft:** The military bomber Northrop Grumman B-2 Spirit, at $2.2 billion per plane.

* * *

QUOTE ME

"There is no more expensive thing than a free gift."
—Michel de Montaigne

Shocking!

If you're ever stuck in a dark room with only a fluorescent bulb and a cat, rub the fluorescent bulb on the cat. The static electricity created will make the bulb glow.

In AD 46, a Roman doctor first used electricity to successfully fight pain, using an electric fish to provide the juice. The only negative side effect: occasionally a patient got electrocuted.

The rain-resistant fabric Gore-Tex was originally created as a coating for electrical wires.

Nikola Tesla, who invented the alternating current system we still use today, died penniless in a New York City hotel.

Electronic equipment really does get dusty faster than other household furnishings because electrical fields attract dust.

Your brain produces enough electricity to power a lightbulb.

A third of the world's population has no electricity.

Washington State produces about 20% of the world's hydroelectric power.

But China's Three Gorges Dam is the largest producer of hydroelectricity in the world.

If you chew a Wint-O-Green Life Saver in the dark, it will emit blue-green sparks because, when the crystalline molecules fracture, a process called *triboluminescence* creates electrical sparks.

December 20, 1880, was the day that electric lights went on for the first time in Broadway's theater district.

Fire Station #6 in Livermore, California, has a lightbulb that has been burning continuously since its installation in 1901.

Electric eels are the most famous, but about 500 other creatures also generate electricity.

Benjamin Franklin experimented with electric shocks on stroke victims.

Coin Toss

1. Portland, Oregon, got its name from a coin toss. When Asa Lovejoy from Boston and Francis Pettygrove of Portland, Maine, both wanted to name the West Coast city after their hometowns, they flipped a coin. It came up heads, and Pettygrove won.

2. A coin toss also determined that Sheffield, Illinois, would be named after founder Joseph Sheffield instead of cofounder Henry Farnam.

3. When the Wright brothers took their first airplane to Kitty Hawk, North Carolina, they flipped a coin to see who would try to fly it. Wilbur won. He stalled after takeoff, though, spending only a few seconds in the air before crashing. The next day, his brother Orville tried. He got into the air for 12 seconds and traveled 120 feet, making his flight the one recognized as the first.

4. On February 3, 1959, rock pioneer Richie Valens flipped a coin with guitarist Tommy Alsup to decide who was going to ride on a chartered plane instead of the freezing-cold tour bus. Valens won…and then lost. The plane crashed on takeoff, killing him, Buddy Holly, and J. P. "the Big Bopper" Richardson.

The Life of Pie

About 75,600,000 pumpkin pies are baked every fall and winter in the United States.

The Great Fire of London in 1666 started on Pudding Lane in the east end and ended on Pye Street in the west. An old fire monument says that this proves the fire was God's punishment for gluttony.

Pie makers have their own lobbying group, the American Pie Council, sponsored by various pie-related companies. It's "committed to preserving America's pie heritage."

Pies have been honored by four American holidays: National Pie Day (January 23), Pecan Pie Day (July 12), Raspberry Cream Pie Day (August 1), and Pumpkin Pie Day (December 25).

Sing a song of sixpence? They really did put live birds into pies in the 1600s. And the birds did fly out when the pie was broken open. The crusts of live-bird pies were baked beforehand with a hidden hole in the bottom. The birds were placed inside the cooled crust right before being delivered to the table.

Other living things were used in pies, but the most memorable was a "court dwarf"—a little person in a royal court who was often the butt of jokes. In 1626 Jeffrey Hudson, aka "Lord Minimus," burst out of a pie to surprise England's Queen Henrietta Maria.

Keep this in mind when pricing pizza: A 10-inch pie yields a little more than two 7-inch ones (78.5 square inches versus 77). A 14-inch pizza yields a little less than two 10-inch ones (157 square inches versus 154).

The first pies appeared in Egypt around 9500 BC.

The trademark of longtime kid-show host Soupy Sales was getting hit in the face with a pie. He was hit with about 19,000 shaving cream pies since his first show in the 1950s.

The first pie-in-the-face in a movie splattered comedian Ben Turpin in *Mr. Flip* (1909).

To the Bat Cave!

It takes about 100 years for a cave stalactite to grow 1 inch.

Bats always turn left when they exit a cave.

The world's largest sea cave is near Florence, Oregon. It's as tall as a 12-story building.

For the 1960s *Batman* TV series, creators used Bronson Cave in L.A.'s Griffith Park. You can still visit it today. According to chiroptologists (bat scientists), you can find 32 bat species in Texas.

Bracken Cave near San Antonio hosts the largest bat colony in the country. Population: about 40 million.

Ever hear the phrase "as solid as the Rock of Gibraltar"? The actual rock is made of gray limestone…and is not so solid. It's riddled with at least 180 caves.

The world's largest cave system, complete with 400 miles of known passageways, is the aptly named Mammoth Cave; most of it lies under Edmonson County, Kentucky.

Why is the Bottomless Pit in New Mexico's Carlsbad Cavern called that? Because stones tossed in it never made a sound. Turns out, though, that it's only 140 feet deep and lined with very soft dirt.

School Daze

In the American colonies, only about one in ten boys finished school. The rest became apprentices or went directly to work.

In 1852 Massachusetts became the first state to introduce compulsory education, requiring that all children from ages 8 to 14 attend school for at least three months a year. By 1918, all American states had a compulsory education law on the books.

President Andrew Jackson was an elementary school dropout who believed that the world was flat.

Thomas Edison didn't get along with school officials and was homeschooled by his mother. Although his education was superior in many ways—self-directed and centered around his own curiosities—his grammar and spelling were atrocious throughout his life.

College graduates earn about $450,000 more over a lifetime than people who have only a high school diploma.

The average college student also carries about $27,253 in student loan debt.

The Aztecs Said It First

The Aztecs spoke a language called Nahuatl, and it's still spoken today by 1.5 million people who live in central Mexico. Here are some of the words that English speakers "borrowed" from them:

Avocado: from *āhuacatl* ("testicle")

Cocoa/cacao: *cacahuatl* ("cacao plant")

Chicle: *tzictli* ("sticky stuff")

Chili: *xilli* ("hot pepper")

Chocolate: *xocolātl* ("bitter water")

Coyote: *cóyotl*, ("trickster")

Mesquite: *mizquitl* ("mesquite shrub")

Mescal: *metl ixcalli* ("oven-cooked agave," which describes how you get the juice to ferment)

Peyote: *peyōtl* ("caterpillar," from the cactus's fuzzy button)

Quetzal: *quetzalli* ("standing brilliant tail feather")

Shack: *xahcalli* ("wooden hut")

Tamale: *tamalli* ("food of meat and corn")

Tomato: *tomatl* ("swelling fruit")

American Bison Get Buffaloed

What North Americans usually call a buffalo is actually a bison. The only places on earth you'll find wild buffalo are in Africa and Asia.

They're big, but bison can run as fast as 40 mph.

Many bison snore.

Canada's largest park, the Wood Buffalo National Park in Alberta and the Northwest Territories, is bigger than Switzerland. Wood buffalo are a subspecies of the plains bison found in the United States, but the Canadian versions are bigger and heavier.

"Buffalo Bill" Cody killed more than 4,000 buffalo (well, bison) in two years…back when people thought that was something to brag about.

In the 1860s, the Kansas Pacific Railroad often allowed passengers to shoot at bison.

The Canadian city of Regina, Saskatchewan, was originally called "Pile o' Bones" after a large bison burial ground that was found there.

You can tell a bison is irritated by looking at his tail: In general, if the tail is hanging and relaxed, the beast is relaxed, too. The stiffer and higher the tail, the more angry the bison.

Bison and cattle are closely related. You can crossbreed the two if you mate a domestic bull with a bison cow. The resulting calves are a "beefalo" hybrid with fertile females and mostly sterile males.

* * *

In the American West, turkeys were moved like cattle, in "drives" of up to a thousand birds.

The First Woman to...

...climb Mount Everest: Junko Tabei (1975).

...be elected to a U.S. political office: Susanna Salter became mayor of Argonia, Kansas, in 1887. Women in Kansas had won the right to vote earlier that year.

...be elected to the U.S. Congress: Jeannette Rankin, (1916). Rankin was a lifelong pacifist, was one of 50 representatives who voted against entering World War I, and was the only one to vote against entering World War II, declaring, "As a woman, I can't go to war and I refuse to send anyone else."

...earn a U.S. pilot's license: Harriet Quimby (1911).

...die as a pilot in a plane crash: Harriet Quimby (July 1912).

...fly solo across the Atlantic Ocean: Amelia Earhart (1932). She equaled Charles Lindbergh's flight exactly five years after him.

...make the cover of *BusinessWeek* magazine: Brownie Wise (1954). Wise invented the home-party selling model for Tupperware; it's since been copied by Mary Kay Cosmetics and many other businesses.

...be nominated for United States president: Victoria Woodhull, nominated by the Equal Rights Party (1871).

...weightlift four times her body weight: Carrie Boudreau, 490 pounds (1995).

...argue a case before the Supreme Court: Belva Lockwood (1879).

...earn more than $100,000 in a single year as a pro athlete: Billie Jean King (1971).

...swim the English Channel: Gertrude Ederle (1926). She made it in 14 hours, 31 minutes—two hours faster than the male record at the time.

Fear Factor

"We humans fear the beast within the wolf because we do not understand the beast within ourselves."

—Gerald Hausman

"If you talk to the animals they will talk with you and you will know each other. If you do not talk to them, you will not know them, and what you do not know, you will fear. What one fears one destroys."

—Chief Dan George

"Suspicion, the offspring of fear, is eminently characteristic of most wild animals. Courage and timidity are extremely variable qualities in the individuals of the same species, as is plainly seen in our dogs."

—Charles Darwin

"There are very few monsters who warrant the fear we have of them."

—Andre Gide

"The wolf that one hears is worse than the orc that one fears."

—J. R. R. Tolkien, *The Fellowship of the Ring*

"Fear helps me from making mistakes, but I [still] make lot of mistakes."

—Steve Irwin

"A cat bitten once by a snake dreads even rope."

—Arab proverb

"There is no living thing that is not afraid when it faces danger. True courage is facing danger when you are afraid."

—L. Frank Baum, *The Wonderful Wizard of Oz*

"I had a linguistics professor who said that it's man's ability to use language that makes him the dominant species on the planet. That may be. But there's another thing that separates us from animals. We're not afraid of vacuum cleaners."

—Jeff Stilson

"Perhaps the wilderness we fear is the pause within our own heartbeats, the silent space that says we live only by grace. Wilderness lives by this same grace."

—Terry Tempest Williams

Trick or Treat?

Not all things that happened on October 31 were spooky. Martin Luther posted his 95 theses on a church door, beginning the Reformation in 1517. Nevada became the 36th state in 1864. The Lincoln Highway, the first cross-country route in America, officially opened in 1913. The Battle of Britain ended in 1940. And the global population reached 7 billion in 2011.

Americans spend more than $1.5 billion on Halloween costumes each year.

In the ninth century, the Catholic Church established All Saints' Day on November 1. The church service was called *Allhallowmas*, so the ghostly night before became known as *All Hallow's e'en*.

Trick-or-treating likely came from the ninth-century custom of "souling." Christian beggars went door to door, promising to pray for dead relatives if the residents gave them a "soul cake."

Jack-o'-lanterns were originally meant to represent souls in purgatory. In Ireland and Scotland, they were made of turnips.

Georgia On My Mind

Georgia was named after King George II of England, who signed the charter papers for the new colony.

Edward Teach, the pirate known as Blackbeard, is said to have made his home on Georgia's Blackbeard Island.

The World of Coca-Cola museum in Atlanta (the birthplace of the fizzy beverage) gives visitors a chance to taste soft drinks from all over the world.

In 2010 Georgia state legislators claimed that the border drawn between it and Tennessee was accidentally a mile farther south than intended and proposed that the boundary be shifted... which, during a bad drought, would've allowed them to claim water from the Tennessee River. For the 10th time since 1887, Tennessee said no.

James Pierpont, who wrote "Jingle Bells," hailed from Savannah...a place that almost never gets any snow.

The first newspaper published in a Native American language was the Cherokee *Phoenix*. It first appeared in New Echota, Georgia, in 1828.

Georgia was the last state to be allowed back into the United States after the Civil War; it didn't return officially until 1870.

In 1842 Georgia's Dr. Crawford W. Long was the first to successfully use ether as an anesthetic. He put a patient to sleep, and then painlessly removed a tumor from the man's neck.

More than 3,000 unknown Confederate soldiers are buried in Atlanta's Oakland Cemetery. The mass grave is marked by a marble sculpture of a dying lion lying on a Confederate flag.

The Okefenokee Swamp near the Florida border has very little solid ground, so it makes sense that it got its name from a Native American word meaning "trembling earth."

Is Nose Mucus Phlegm? No, It's Snot

Mucus in your nose catches harmful dust, fungi, viruses, and bacteria before they can get to your lungs.

The body generates about a quart of mucus a day.

Mucus glands also add protective mucus to your stomach, lungs, eyes, ears, and urogenital systems.

In animals, mucus protects the slimy skins of amphibians, the gills in fish, and the bodies of snails and slugs.

Almost all of the nasal mucus your body produces gets swallowed, mostly unconsciously.

What's *rhinorrhea*? The medical term for a runny nose.

"Mucus" covers about everything slimy in your body, but in the respiratory tract, it's often called "phlegm."

Yellow or green mucus usually means a bacterial infection, but too much clear, watery mucus can be a sign of virus infection or allergies.

Human tears have three layers: an oily layer, a liquid layer, and a mucus layer.

Phlegm keeps your lungs from drying out and catches pollutants that your nose misses. It even fights pollutants, which is why smokers' bodies produce more phlegm and the coughs to expel it.

The German word for mucus is *nasenschleim* ("nose slime").

As a young man, Steve Jobs followed a vegetarian, "mucus-free" diet, in which he avoided foods that supposedly contained or stimulated mucus. He believed doing so would mean he'd rarely have to bathe. (His coworkers disagreed.)

All About Peanut Butter

The earliest peanut butter patent went to Marcellus Edson of Montreal, Canada, in 1884. But centuries before, the Aztecs used a peanut paste made from mashing peanuts.

One acre of peanuts produces enough peanut butter for 30,000 sandwiches.

There are approximately 1,080 peanuts in a 24-ounce jar of peanut butter.

The JIF plant in Lexington, Kentucky, is the world's largest peanut butter factory, squeezing out 190 million pounds of the stuff every year. That's enough to coat 55 football fields one foot thick.

The average American eats 3.3 pounds of peanut butter per year.

Peanut butter really is good for removing chewing gum from your hair.

In the Netherlands, peanut butter is called *pindakaas* ("peanut cheese").

One study says that peanut butter is the second most recognizable scent to Americans. (Coffee came in first.)

Periscope Up

Cornelius Drebbel built the first submarine in 1620 for England's Duke of Buckingham. It was propelled by oars.

America's first functioning submarine was the *Turtle*, a hand-cranked, one-person craft built in 1775, capable of traveling underwater for 30 minutes at 3 mph. Shaped like an acorn, it was used during the Revolutionary War to affix explosives to the bottoms of British ships, but it didn't work very well. When operators couldn't get the timed bombs affixed, they had to release them into the harbor, where they exploded without causing any injuries.

In 1856 the Russians built a 56-foot-long submarine and, during coronation ceremonies for Tsar Alexander II, a small orchestra played the Russian national anthem inside it underwater. The music was likely deafening within that tight space.

In use from 1969 to 1999, the USS *Narwhal* was famous for being the quietest submarine of its time.

In 1966 the submarine USS *Albacore* was clocked at just over 40 mph, an unofficial underwater speed record (for machines, anyway—actual tuna can beat it by 3 mph).

Peanut oil is used for cooking on submarines because it's nearly smokeless, an important consideration in an airtight setting.

"U-boat" is an abbreviation of the German word *unterseeboot*—an "undersea boat," or submarine.

During World War II, the German submarine *U-1206* sank after a "toilet operator error."

In naval tradition, submarines are not ever called "ships." They are "boats," whatever their size.

Volcanic Activity

Earliest known picture of a volcano: an 8,000-year-old wall painting in Turkey.

In Iceland, there are volcanoes beneath glaciers.

Hawaii's Kilauea volcano has been erupting nonstop since 1983.

A Hawaiian legend says that Pele, the volcano goddess, curses anyone who takes lava rock out of Hawaii.

The tallest volcano on Mars is 17 miles high—that's 85 times taller than the Eiffel Tower.

The still-smoking Mount St. Helens volcano, which last erupted in 2008, is the worst air polluter in Washington State.

Highly volcanic areas have some of the most fertile farmland in the world.

An erupting volcano can shoot ash 30 miles into the atmosphere.

The word "volcano" comes from Vulcan, the Roman god of fire.

Oregon's Crater Lake, the deepest in the United States, was formed from the deep crater of a volcano that erupted about 7,700 years ago.

Portland, Oregon, is the only city in the United States to have a volcano within its city limits. (Luckily, it's not currently active.)

The 1815 eruption of Mount Tambora in Indonesia was the deadliest for humans. It killed 92,000 people: about 12,000 from the eruption and 80,000 from starvation worldwide because few crops grew that year. It's still called the "year without summer."

*   *   *

William Henry Harrison was the only U.S. president to attain a degree in medicine.

Jimsonweed and Jamestown

GETTING CRAZY WITH LOCOWEED

Jimsonweed, sometimes called "locoweed," is a scary drug related to the deadly nightshade. Used for asthma, pain relief, and anesthesia in the past, the jimson's leaves and seeds are also a powerful hallucinogen. The problem with using it, or abusing it, is that a toxic dose is only a little higher than a medicinal dose. That makes it dangerous.

Originally native to Asia, jimsonweed is now found all over the world. It grows in bushes that are about five feet tall and has pale yellow-green stems, bitter-tasting leaves that look a little like wrinkled maple leaves, and trumpet-shaped flowers that range in color from white to light lavender. The blossoms smell sweet and open at night, attracting nocturnal moths.

The effects of jimsonweed usually wear off after a day or two, but they can last up to two weeks. In one famous case of mass hallucination—the one that gave the plant its name—the effects lasted for about 11 days. "Jimsonweed," it turns out, is a corruption of the name settlers gave it in the late 1600s: "Jamestown weed," for the town where its dramatic effects were first witnessed by the new Americans.

ITS BETTER WITH BACON

In 1676 Jamestown, Virginia, settlers became disgruntled with their colony's governor, William Berkeley, whom they felt was not doing enough to protect them from the area's Native American tribes. Led by 29-year-old Nathaniel Bacon, the settlers decided to kill—or at least drive out—Native Americans in the area after repeated appeals to their governor to guarantee their personal safety were ignored. Bacon's men ultimately attacked several tribes, provoking what looked like it might become a war. In response, Governor Berkeley sent in troops to put down the uprising, which is now known as Bacon's Rebellion. The soldiers did eventually suppress the rebellion…but only after the rebels burned down Jamestown and a number of Berkeley's soldiers became unwitting guinea pigs in demonstrating the powerful effects of "Jamestown weed."

"ONE OF THE GREATEST COOLERS IN THE WORLD"

Here's what early American historian Robert Beverley, Jr., wrote about the situation in 1705:

> The James-Town Weed (which resembles the Thorny Apple of Peru, and I take to be the plant so call'd) is supposed to be one of the greatest coolers in the world. This being an early plant, was gather'd very young for a boil'd salad, by some of the soldiers sent thither to quell the rebellion of Bacon (1676); and some of them ate plentifully of it, the effect of which was a very pleasant comedy, for they turned natural fools upon it for several days: one would blow up a feather in the air; another would dart straws at it with much fury; and another, stark naked, was sitting up in a corner like a monkey, grinning and making mows [grimaces] at them; a fourth would fondly kiss and paw his companions, and sneer in their faces with a countenance more antic than any in a Dutch droll [comedy].
>
> In this frantic condition they were confined, lest they should, in their folly, destroy themselves—though it was observed that all their actions were full of innocence and good nature. Indeed, they were not very cleanly; for they would have wallowed in their own excrements, if they had not been prevented. A thousand such simple tricks they played, and after eleven days returned themselves again, not remembering anything that had passed.

FYI

Jimsonweed comes under many other names, including stinkweed, thorn-apple, prickly burr, devil's trumpet, devil's weed, hell's bells, moonflower, burundanga, and mad apple.

And the Winner Is...

About 12,000 music industry insiders pick Grammy winners; 5,800 people vote for the Oscars; 868 choose Tony winners; 15,000 award Emmys; and about 90 (the total membership of the Hollywood Foreign Press Association) choose Golden Globe winners.

Gandhi was nominated for the Nobel Peace Prize five times, but he never won it.

It costs about $100 to make a Pulitzer Prize (a gold medal), and $500 to make an Oscar.

The perfume industry's annual awards are called the FiFis.

Panorama magazine once awarded J. Fred Muggs Awards to "people who made monkeys of themselves on TV."

The Rolling Stones, Jimi Hendrix, Janis Joplin, the Who, and the Beach Boys never won a Grammy Award.

Winner of the most Junos, Canada's music award: singer Anne Murray (24).

First American to win the Nobel Peace Prize: Theodore Roosevelt (1906).

Only person to win an Emmy, an Oscar, and a Tony in the same year: Bob Fosse (1973).

Only two actors have won an Emmy and an Oscar in the same year: George C. Scott (1971) and Helen Hunt (1998).

60 Minutes won a Golden Globe Award for Best Drama Series in 1979.

The Red Cross has won more Nobel Prizes than anybody. All three were for peace, awarded in 1917, 1944, and 1963.

In 1904 Cy Young pitched the first official perfect game—no batters reached first base. The Cy Young Award for pitchers has been awarded since 1956.

The Pillsbury Bake-Off has a higher grand prize cash value ($1 million) than the Olympic gold medal for U.S. winners ($25,000) and the Pulitzer Prize ($10,000) put together.

It's in Your Jeans

Credit California's gold rush for American-style blue jeans. In 1853, 17-year-old Levi Strauss arrived in San Francisco and realized that he could earn more money making durable pants than digging in the gold fields.

The stiff blue fabric that Strauss used for the pants came in crates labeled *Serge de Nîme*. Americans didn't realize that *de Nîme* just identified the French city of origin, and started calling the cloth "denim."

Nevada tailor Jacob Davis invented the pants rivet, those metal cylinders that hold pants together at stress points. Davis couldn't afford $68 to patent the idea himself, though, so he made a deal with Strauss to pay for the patent and share the profits.

The back-pocket rivets were covered with cloth in the 1930s after persistent complaints that they gouged wooden furniture.

Denim's characteristic look, especially after it fades, happens because some of the threads are deep blue and others are white.

The first jeans with zippers came out in 1926, made by the Lee Jeans Company. Before that, it was buttons only.

As late at the 1970s, many American school dress codes banned jeans because the pants were believed to be worn mostly by juvenile delinquents.

The biggest boost to jeans-wearing by teens was James Dean in *Rebel Without a Cause* (1955).

"Stone-washed" jeans really are. The garments are tumbled with large pumice stones during washing. Some manufacturers also sand-blast them.

North America buys 39 percent of the world's jeans.

The Canadian province with the fewest pairs of jeans per capita: Quebec.

Percentage of British women who have kept a pair of too-tight jeans, hoping they will fit again someday: almost 60.

Open Wide!

In 1843, J. B. Beers developed America's first gold tooth in Rochester, New York. Then Frank Ritter designed the first dental chair there in 1887.

Until the 18th century, dentists believed that tooth decay was caused by a worm burrowing into a tooth. Dropping sulfuric acid seemed to kill the worm and cure the toothache, but all it really did was kill the tooth's nerve.

Dentists quickly learn the trick for keeping their little mirrors from fogging up inside your mouth—warming them to body temperature in warm water.

The earliest dentists practiced in Egypt around 3700 BC.

Denis Bouguignon, an Orlando dentist featured in the movie *Trekkies*, calls his space-themed office "Starbase Dental" and wears a *Star Trek* uniform while he works.

The ancient Etruscans of northern Italy were the first to use gold in dentistry. This was back in about 500 BC.

"Dentistry" is one of the more than 120 Boy Scout merit badges.

The Emmys

Courteney Cox was the only cast member of *Friends* never to earn an Emmy nomination.

First cartoon to win an Emmy: *Huckleberry Hound*, in 1960.

The prime-time show that has won the most Emmys is *60 Minutes*. As of 2013, they've won 95 Emmys, or roughly 1.6 Emmys per *Minute*. Beloved kid show host Captain Kangaroo won five Emmys during the show's run from the 1950s to the 1980s.

Mister Rogers' Neighborhood won four Emmys, and Fred Rogers himself won a lifetime achievement award in 1997.

M*A*S*H and *Cheers* were nominated for Best Comedy Emmy all 11 seasons of their runs. M*A*S*H won once, *Cheers* won four times.

The first African American to win an Emmy was Harry Belafonte, in 1960 for *The Revlon Revue*.

Only one person has won Emmys for acting, writing, and directing: Alan Alda (for M*A*S*H).

In its nine-year run, *The Facts of Life* received three Emmy nominations: for hairstyling, technical direction, and lead actress in a comedy series (for Charlotte Rae). It lost each time.

The Emmy Award was created by sculptor Louis McManus. He based the female figure on his wife Dorothy.

Charles Douglass was honored with an Emmy for lifetime achievement in 1992. What was his contribution? He invented the laugh track.

*　*　*

First American to vote from space:
Astronaut David Wolf, in 1997.

Delaware

About 200,000 companies are incorporated in Delaware. That's because the state's business laws favor corporations, so it's easier and less expensive to incorporate there than in most other states.

Delaware has only three counties: New Castle, Kent, and Sussex.

Delaware is the second smallest state in the U.S., after Rhode Island.

In 1880, Rehoboth Beach held the first beauty contest in the United States. The Miss United States pageant was the forerunner of today's Miss America contest, and Thomas Edison was one of the judges.

Two towns straddle the border between Delaware and Maryland, and both are named by combining parts of both states' names: Marydel, Maryland, and Delmar, Delaware.

Delaware's state insect is the ladybug.

Delaware was the site of the first log cabins built in North America in 1638. They were the work of Swedes and Finns who had been living in log cabins in their home countries for many years.

Delaware is called the "First State" because it was the first to ratify the U.S. Constitution on December 7, 1787.

The Methodist Church was founded in Frederica, Delaware, in 1784.

You could probably walk across Delaware in a day or two. The state's widest part is 35 miles—the narrowest, just 9 miles.

Eleven concrete observation towers are spaced along Delaware's beaches. They were constructed during World War II to look out for German ships and submarines.

Dr. Henry Heimlich, who invented the Heimlich maneuver, was born in Wilmington.

Crickets Make Chirp Dates

Crickets may look like grasshoppers, but they're only somewhat related. They're closer to katydids.

Crickets eat almost anything, including other crickets. Not just dead ones, but also weak or sick ones.

A few of the 900 kinds of crickets are big enough to bite humans.

A cricket hears with its front knees. Each has a hollow structure that picks up vibrations like our eardrums and turn them into electrical impulses to the cricket's brain.

Only male crickets chirp.

Crickets can sing and eat at the same time.

It's a common myth that crickets chirp with their legs. Crickets play ridges on their wings like a washboard. Making sounds by rubbing body parts together has its own name: Scientists call it "stridulation."

Chirping is the primary use for a cricket's wings. Most can't fly.

The loudest cricket chirp is a "come hither" song to attract females and warn other males away. When a female comes close, the sound changes to a very soft courting song.

Crickets make decent thermometers. The most accurate temperature bug is the snowy tree cricket, a light green cricket that lives in trees. If you count its chirps for 13 seconds and add 40, you'll get the temperature in Fahrenheit.

In the original *Pinocchio* story, the title character smashes an unnamed talking cricket with a mallet. In the Disney movie, of course, Jiminy Cricket took on a starring role.

In parts of Asia, crickets are considered good luck and are sometimes kept as pets in cages.

In America, chirping crickets are seen as a sign that a joke fell flat.

Time for Breakfast

By weight, many packaged cereals have more salt than potato chips, and more sugar than a can of soda.

The average American kid eats more than 15 pounds of cold cereal per year.

In Quebec, Cap'n Crunch cereal is called Capitaine Crounche.

Women who regularly ate cereal in the months before getting pregnant were more likely to have boys.

The first football player on a Wheaties box was Bronko Nagurski of the Chicago Bears, in 1937.

Post Toasties were originally named Elijah's Manna, but quickly changed in 1908 after religious groups protested the name as offensive.

In South Africa, Rice Krispies said "Knap! Knaetter! Knak!" In Sweden, "Piff! Paff! Puff!"

Cheerios was first named Cheerioats in 1941, but Quaker Oats threatened to sue about using "oats" in the name. The new name appeared in 1945.

Up in Smoke

Native Americans used tobacco to make tea and jelly.

President Woodrow Wilson had a pet ram named Ike that grazed on the White House lawn and loved to chew tobacco.

The Puritans considered tobacco to be a dangerous narcotic.

Before a huge rise in cigarette smoking in the 1930s, lung cancer was uncommon, even among workers in mines and sooty factories.

Lucky Strike got its name in 1871, inspired by stories from the gold rush about miners making lucky (gold) strikes.

One additive to cigarettes is ammonia, which dissolves nicotine from the tobacco and releases a more addictive dose to smokers. Others include theobromine and glycyrrhizin, bronchodilators that expand the airways and increase smoke intake.

Cigarette smoke contains at least 40 known carcinogens.

Winston Churchill smoked about 300,000 cigars in his lifetime.

In the 1920s, Listerine produced its own brand of "medicated" cigarettes.

Proverbs, Naturally

Every animal knows far more than you do.
—**Nez Perce**

The heart is but the beach beside the sea that is the world.
—**Chinese**

When a man moves away from nature, his heart becomes hard.
—**Lakota**

No matter how long the winter, spring is sure to follow.
—**Guinean**

The earth is mankind's only friend.
—**East African**

The best time to plant a tree was 20 years ago. The second best time is today.
—**Chinese**

When elephants fight, the grass gets hurt.
—**East African**

Man is preceded by forest and followed by desert.
—**French**

All riches come from the earth.
—**Armenian**

Everyone must pay his debt to nature.
—**German**

Nature without effort surpasses art.
—**Latin**

The tiger depends on the forest; the forest depends on the tiger.
—**Cambodian**

Nature does nothing in vain.
—**Romanian**

Listen to the voice of nature, for it holds treasures for you.
—**Huron**

Just let there be a forest, and there is sure to be a forest spirit.
—**Russian**

In nature, there is no such thing as a lawn.
—**Albanian**

In a moment the ashes are made, but the forest is a long time growing.
—**Senecan**

When the last tree has been cut down, the last river has been polluted, and the last fish has been caught, only then do you realize that money can't buy everything.
—**Native Amer.**

Fake Food

SCIENCE WILL SAVE US!

The decades during and after World War II were an exciting time to be a food chemist. The field was wide open for big, scientific improvements: new artificial colors and flavors to invent, longer shelf lives, and, in some cases, if a natural disaster wiped out an entire crop, a scientist could just invent a substitute. It was an exuberantly naive time, when the slogan might well have been "If life hands you chemicals, make lemonade anyway." Up and down the food chain, the old way of doing things—growing food on farms with manure and crop rotation—gave way to a brave new world of synthetic fertilizers and miracle pesticides like DDT. Pigs, cows, and chickens that once ran wild were now safely contained inside a food factory where they could be managed efficiently, with no wasted feed or space. Today it all sounds a little like a dystopian nightmare, but back then, food chemists thought they were using science to solve big problems like world hunger, malnutrition, and too much waste.

Into that environment strode a superman of creativity: William A. Mitchell, who received 70 patents for fake foods between 1941 and 1976. Here are four of his biggest contributions to American cuisine:

1. ARTIFICIAL TAPIOCA

Shortly after Mitchell was hired at General Foods in 1941, he received his first assignment: save tapioca pudding. During the Great Depression, tapioca became a popular dessert, a lumpy, sweet comfort food that was cheap and easy to make. The problem was that cassava, the starchy root that was its main ingredient, came from Java, Indonesia. When the Japanese invaded the island, the supply was cut off. Mitchell saved the day by figuring out that a combination of food starches mixed with gelatin made a pretty convincing substitute.

2. POP ROCKS

Not all of Mitchell's inventions were soft and squishy; some were granular and full of carbon dioxide. Pop Rocks were a wonderful mistake—they were originally designed to be mixed with water to make a carbonated soft drink.

3. TANG

Contrary to popular opinion (which was helped along by a misleading ad campaign), the powdered artificial orange drink Tang wasn't developed for the space program. Mitchell created it, General Foods introduced it in 1959, and…it flopped. Tang limped along for a few years, until NASA, looking for something to mask the unpleasant flavor of space capsule water, selected it for John Glenn's 1962 space mission. That did it. With a "breakfast of astronauts" advertising campaign, Tang zoomed to success.

4. COOL WHIP

Although it now contains (a little) milk and cream, Mitchell's original 1967 Cool Whip recipe was made up of water, hydrogenated vegetable oil, sugar, corn syrup, high-fructose corn syrup, artificial flavors and colors, and a bunch of other chemical stuff. It didn't taste like whipped cream, but it also didn't require as much refrigeration as the real stuff, making it ideal for picnics and church potlucks.

*　　*　　*

WORDS OF LOVE

Pogonophilia: Love of beards.

Wiccaphilia: Love of witches.

Frigophilia: Love of cold things.

Cyberphilia: Love of the Internet.

Xylophilia: Love of things made of wood.

Pteronophilia: Love of being tickled by feathers.

Hippopotomonstrosesquippedaliophilia:

Love of long words.

Bookstore Bits

The Babylonians started writing down stuff more than 5,000 years ago, and were the first people (that we know of) to leave written records. However, the first bound, modern-style book, called the *Codex*, dates from 4th-century Greece.

The first book printed in North America was a hymnal called *The Whole Booke of Psalmes Faithfully Translated into English Metre*, published in Massachusetts in 1640.

In 1953 the books of John Dewey, Edna Ferber, Dashiell Hammett, and others were banned from the U.S. State Department's overseas libraries because the government decided the authors weren't sufficiently anticommunist.

A single page of a first-edition Gutenberg Bible is worth $25,000.

81 percent of Americans think that they could write a book.

The Greek titan Atlas holding up the world became a popular front illustration for bound collections of maps. That is how the "atlas" got its name.

You can copyright the contents of your book, but you can't copyright the title.

If you lined up every Harry Potter book sold, they'd circle the Earth twice.

San Francisco's City Lights Bookstore was the first in the U.S. to sell only paperbacks.

John Steinbeck experienced writers' self-doubt as much as anyone. While writing *The Grapes of Wrath*, he said, "If I could do this book properly, it would be one of the really fine books and a truly American book. But I am assailed by my own ignorance and inability."

In 2004 a grade-school book report written by Britney Spears sold for $1,900 at auction.

Sweating the Smell Stuff

SMELL LIKE AN EGYPTIAN

Humans have been hiding their stinkiness by dousing themselves with fragrances for ages. The ancient Egyptians came up with a number of fresh and fruity scents. Some floral scents lasted as long as 20 years, and incense was also heavily used. (It had the benefit of masking not just the smell of a single user, but everybody in the room.) And in ancient Asia, people discovered that applying finely ground salt to the underarms worked wonders. When reapplied regularly during the day, the salt killed bacteria.

That's the thing—sweat by itself is odorless. Bacteria on the skin are what release smells when they start to break down sweat's trace amounts of fats. Diet, gender, age, hygiene levels, and genetics all give everybody a slightly different smell. Meat-eaters, for example, release more fats and proteins in their sweat, so they tend to smell stronger than vegans. Women's sweat tends to contain more sulfur, creating an oniony smell when bacteria go at it. Men, on the other hand, release more fatty acids that end up smelling cheesy. And shaved armpits are more likely to be smelly than hairy ones because the hair often wicks out enough moisture to help keep bacteria in check.

DRY UP

By the turn of the 20th century, deodorant manufacturing was in full swing. For example...

- The first modern antiperspirant was called Everdry, introduced in 1903. It had some problems, though. With an active ingredient of aluminum chloride, Everdry was acidic enough to irritate the skin and shorten the life of shirts by slowly eating holes under the arms. (That's still a problem: Even today, those embarrassing yellow armpit stains come from the ingredients of antiperspirants, not the sweat itself.)

- Mum, however, was the first commercial deodorant ever, introduced in Philadelphia in 1888. Bristol-Meyers bought the brand in 1932, and in the 1950s, playing off of the gimmick of the newly invented ballpoint pen, marketers created Ban Roll-On using the same rolling-ball design.

- A chemist in Chicago named Jules Montenier reduced some of the damage in 1941 by adding a chemical called nitrile, which neutralized the acidity of aluminum chloride. He created Stopette, the best-selling deodorant of the 1950s. When Montenier's patent ran out in the late 1950s, Stopette was eclipsed by several new brands, including Gillette's Right Guard, the first spray deodorant.

- Today, aluminum choloride remains the active ingredient of choice in many antiperspirants. How does it work? Its tiny particles get wedged into the sweat glands, creating a plug that keeps sweat from coming out. And because, technically, it alters your natural body functions, the FDA classifies antiperspirants as "drugs."

BENEFITS OF BO
Most people in the United States today use deodorants to mask their smell, but there are actually some positives to BO.

- Humans' unusually stinky BO gives them a disadvantage in hunting, of course, requiring a downwind approach to prey. But it may have also helped early humans to survive by making them unappetizing to predators.

- Researchers at the University of California, Berkeley, found that a compound in male underarm sweat activates brain areas that improve women's mood and sexual receptiveness.

- The smell of your sweat may be an early health warning. If your sweat smells a little like bleach, it can be a sign of liver or kidney disease; if it smells fruity, a sign of diabetes.

*   *   *

Juliette Gordon Low founded the first Girl Scout troop
in Savannah, Georgia, in 1912.

Whale Tales

Humans absorb only about 15 percent of the oxygen they inhale. Whales absorb as much as 90 percent.

When traveling as a group, orcas breathe in unison.

A whale caught near Alaska in 2007 had the tip of a harpoon from the 1880s stuck in its skin.

Whales are able to swim backward and can make facial expressions.

The "whale bones" in ladies' corsets during the 19th century were actually whale teeth.

A whale's teeth tell its age. Each year, whales grow a new layer of enamel around their teeth, making rings like those of a tree.

Whale oil was used as a lubricant for car transmissions as recently as 1973.

Many people say that whale blubber tastes like fresh coconut.

The California gray whale has one of the longest migration routes of any mammal (12,000 miles).

Rhyme & Reason

How much does the job of United States poet laureate pay? Just $35,000 for a one-year term, plus a $5,000 travel budget.

British poets laureate used to serve for life, but now their term is 10 years. Since 1668, there have been only 19 of them.

Canada alternates between an English-speaking poet laureate and a French-speaking one.

President Theodore Roosevelt was a fan of poet E. A. Robinson and arranged a cushy "job" for Robinson in the Customs Department. The poet's official duties consisted of opening his roll-top desk, reading the paper, closing the desk, and leaving the paper on his chair to let his boss know he'd been there. When Roosevelt left office, however, Robinson was told that he'd actually have to start doing a real job. He quit immediately.

Nearly all of Emily Dickinson's poems can be sung to the tune of "The Yellow Rose of Texas." If you get tired of that, the Gilligan's Island theme usually works, too.

A study of prominent American writers showed that poets lived an average of 66.2 years, compared to 72.7 years for nonfiction writers.

Of successful poets studied, one in five killed themselves. This compares badly to the 1 percent suicide rate of the general population.

Langston Hughes was a busboy before he became a key Harlem Renaissance writer. When poet Vachel Lindsay was dining at his restaurant, Hughes placed a packet of his poems next to Lindsay's plate. Lindsay liked what he read and helped Hughes launch his career.

* * *

Warning label on French cigarette boxes:
"Smoking may cause a slow and painful death."

On the Air

In 1895, Guglielmo Marconi, one of radio's earliest developers, wrote to the Italian minister of telegraphs, explaining his wireless telegraph experiments. The official scrawled "To the Longara [insane asylum]" on the letter and recommended that Marconi be committed.

How to tell if a radio is North Korean: The tuning dial is soldered in place. It's preset to official government broadcasts.

The first fleeing fugitive captured with the help of radio was in 1910. Hawley Crippen poisoned his wife in England and hopped an ocean liner for Canada with his mistress disguised as a boy. They were recognized onboard, and after a flurry of Morse code messages, he was arrested when the boat docked.

Peter Jennings hosted a radio show on the Canadian network CBC at age nine.

The first radio commercial ran on August 28, 1922. New York's WEAF broadcast an infomercial for Queensboro Real Estate. The 10-minute ad cost $50.

Glow with the Flow

Marie and Pierre Curie first isolated radium on April 20, 1902. Prolonged exposure to radioactivity killed Marie in 1934. (Pierre died in 1906 after being hit by a horse-drawn wagon.)

In the 1920s, radium was mistakenly considered harmless and used liberally in kids' toys to make them glow in the dark. Everyone started to notice the danger after radiation sickness became common among radium workers.

Spas also grew up around radioactive springs and even abandoned radium mines. Tourists could buy a radium-lined jar that came with a guarantee "to make any water placed herein radioactive within 12 hours" and a prescription to "drink at least eight glasses of water daily."

Some foods are slightly radioactive from naturally present radium and/or potassium, including Brazil nuts, white potatoes, carrots, lima beans, red meat, and beer.

The release of radioactivity outside of the Three Mile Island facility was actually minimal. If you lived within 10 miles of the nuclear plant when it partially melted down in 1979, you would have been exposed to only about 8 millirems of radioactivity, the equivalent of one chest X-ray.

Spring Forward

In most early cultures, the New Year began in the spring to mark the start of the agricultural year.

The Gregorian calendar, first adopted by the Catholic Church in 1582, proclaimed January 1 as the beginning of the year. However, many European towns continued to celebrate their traditional spring "new year" holidays into the late 1700s.

Easter takes place on the Sunday after the first full moon of spring. March 22 is the earliest it can be; April 25, the latest.

Groundhog Day (February 2) originated in Germany, where it was part of a larger festival called Candlemas, when all of a church's candles were blessed...but the animal they used was a badger. There were no badgers in the New World, though, so German immigrants substituted a groundhog instead.

Lent comes from *lencten*, an Anglo-Saxon word that meant "long," but it also meant "spring," in the sense of days growing longer. (*Lencten* is also where we get the word "lengthen.")

Easter lilies bloom in spring because people alter their growing environments to keep them warm and force them to open early. On their own, lilies generally bloom in the summer.

Eostre was the pagan goddess of fertility and spring. Festivals dedicated to her were so popular in pre-Christian Europe that early missionaries kept the trappings and name of her holiday, but redefined what it meant, assigning the "new beginning" to Jesus's resurrection. Originally, though, Eostre ruled the roost and celebrations in her honor included lots of eggs and rabbits because both were symbols of spring, fertility, and new beginnings.

The Largest...

...**single business in Italy** is the Mafia.

...**crop in Mississippi** is catfish.

...**swimming pool in the world,** located in Chile, is more than half a mile long.

...**family of birds on earth:** the *Tyrannidae*, or flycatchers, with more than 400 species.

...**use of freshwater in the United States:** thermoelectric power.

...**joint in the human body:** the knee.

...**cyclone on record:** Typhoon Tip (1979). Its diameter: 1,380 miles, about half the size of the continental United States.

...**county in the United States:** San Bernardino County in California covers 20,160 square miles.

...**comic-book collection:** The Library of Congress has more than 100,000.

...**retail box of pasta** was five feet tall and weighed half a ton. Supermarkets in Turkey sold them in 2012 for 999 Turkish lira (about $560), with proceeds going to UNICEF.

...**frog on earth:** The Goliath frog, an endangered species in western Africa that weighs up to 7 pounds and can stretch out as long as 3 feet.

...**fiberglass cow in the world:** "Salem Sue" in New Salem, North Dakota. She stands 38 feet tall.

The Sporting Life

"Pro football is like nuclear war: there are no winners,
only survivors."

—Frank Gifford

"There are only two kinds of coaches: those who have
been fired, and those who will be fired."

—Ken Loeffler

"Sports do not build character. They reveal it."

—Heywood Broun

"My doctor advised me that a man in his 40s shouldn't
play tennis. I heeded his advice carefully and could
hardly wait until I reached 50 to start again."

—Justice Hugo Black

"You can't think and hit at the same time."

—Yogi Berra

"In America, it is sport that is the opiate of the masses."

—Russell Baker

"You can observe a lot by watching."

—Yogi Berra

"Good teams become great ones when the members trust
each other enough to surrender the 'me' for the 'we.'"

—Phil Jackson

"If a man watches three football games in a row, he
should be declared legally dead."

—Erma Bombeck

The Olympic Spirit

It was traditional for ancient Greek Olympic athletes to compete naked. Women weren't invited as competitors or spectators.

An Olympic torch weighs 3½ pounds, a little more than four cans of beer. It's made of wood, aluminum, and gold-plated brass, with a tank hidden in the base that holds 40 minutes' worth of propane. About 10,000 are made so that runners in the intercontinental relay can keep the torches they run with.

Part of the ancient Olympics were also competitions in the arts, so when the games were revived in modern times, sports-themed painting, literature, music, architecture, and sculpture became medal events. This lasted until 1952, when the games downgraded the arts to noncompetitive exhibitions.

The only country to host the Summer Olympics but not win a single gold medal was Canada, in 1976.

The official Olympic five-rings flag was first flown during the 1920 Olympics but disappeared from the flagpole on the last day. Its fate was unknown until 1997 when diver and bronze medalist Haig Prieste admitted to stealing it on a dare from champion swimmer Duke Kahanamoku. Prieste, then 103 years old, returned the flag in 2000.

Dr. Benjamin Spock, renowned pediatrician and best-selling author, competed in the 1924 Olympics as a rower…and won a gold medal.

Kick-start

Motorcycles were around long before cars—an inventor tested his steam-powered *velocipedraisiavaporianna* in Paris in 1818. But it wasn't until 1869 that American Silvester H. Roper built a "steam velocipede" that could outrun a horse.

World's best-selling vehicle? At 60 million-plus, the Honda Super Cub motorcycle.

The Fonz on *Happy Days* famously owned a motorcycle, but Henry Winkler, who played him for a decade, never learned how to ride one.

The Triumph motorcycle that Marlon Brando rode in *The Wild Ones* was his personal bike.

In 2009 Israeli bikers protested motorcycle insurance rate hikes by riding in only their underwear. Their slogan: "Insurance Is Stripping Us."

In the company's early years, there was only one guy named Harley, but there were three brothers named Davidson.

The first Harley-Davidson motorcycle, built in 1903, used an empty tomato can for a carburetor.

Purr-fection

What do one-third of people allergic to cats have in common? They own a cat.

People in China eat cats. They are an ingredient in a traditional dish called "Dragon, Tiger, & Phoenix," which, besides cat meat ("Tiger"), also includes snake ("Dragon") and chicken ("Phoenix").

Each year in the U.S., about 40,000 people get rabies vaccinations after being bitten by cats and other animals.

Cats enjoy TV and computer monitors more than dogs do. That's probably because cats are more visual than dogs.

South Korean scientists have cloned cats that glow red when exposed to ultraviolet light.

In one cat taste test, black-and-white birds were the cats' least favorite.

Cats are not mentioned in the Bible even once.

Witch-burning Europeans believed that cats were the devil's animals, so hundreds of thousands were put to death during the 14th century. Shortly afterward, the rat population exploded, and the bubonic plague, likely transmitted by fleas on black rats, killed about a quarter of Europe's people.

How do cats move their ears like that? They have 32 muscles around each ear that allow each to move independently of the other.

A gathering of cats is called a "clowder" or a "glaring."

In about eight hours of sleep, you dream once every 90 minutes. Cats sleep nearly 16 hours a day and dream every 12 to 15 minutes.

*   *   *

Alarm clocks have been known to trigger heart attacks.

Roadwork

Combined, the lanes of public roads in the U.S. constitute more than 4 million miles.

Half of the cars on U.S. roads are driven 25 miles or less a day.

Ancient Roman roads had rest stops with inns and stables for travelers about every 15 miles.

In 1908 Detroit laid asphalt on the first paved road in America: a stretch of Woodward Avenue between Six and Seven Mile Roads.

A mathematical formula called Braess's paradox shows that adding more lanes to roads can actually lead to more traffic jams.

There are more roads in national forests than in the national interstate system.

Roadside billboards are prohibited in Alaska, Hawaii, Maine, and Vermont.

States with the poorest road conditions: #1) Louisiana, #2) North Carolina, #3) Oklahoma.

Indiana has more miles of interstate highway per square mile than any other state.

Before crash-test dummies, pig cadavers were used to simulate accident victims.

Safest place in the world to drive: Sweden.

In 2008 Ankeny, Iowa, deiced roads with expired garlic salt, keeping it out of landfills.

An icy road becomes less slippery the more below freezing the temperature drops.

*   *   *

IS IT ASPHALT, TAR, OR CONCRETE?

Asphalt, a byproduct of oil production, flexes slightly with the weight of vehicles, reducing cracks. Tar, a byproduct of changing coal to coke (or fuel), is used mostly as a sealant. And concrete, a mixture of limestone, clay, and gypsum, is used on most sidewalks.

Serious as a Heart Attack

A healthy heart weighs about 10.5 ounces. Hearts struggling to pump grow more muscle to do the job. A really bad ticker can weigh more than two pounds.

In 1941, Winston Churchill had a heart attack in the White House while opening a window. He recovered.

Med students remember the most likely triggers of ischemia, cramping of the heart muscles, by the four Es: exertion, eating, excitement, and exposure to cold.

Three Es of prevention: exercise, eating regularly, and eschewing smoking.

In the United States, someone has a heart attack about every 20 seconds.

The real-life survival rate of using CPR outside of a hospital setting: about 15 percent. On TV shows: about 67 percent.

3 to 4 orgasms a week substantially reduce the risk of cardiac arrest.

If you get to the hospital alive after a heart attack, there's a 90 percent chance you'll survive.

Most likely time to have a heart attack: 6:00 a.m. to 10:00 a.m. Most likely day: Monday. (Saturday is #2).

*   *   *

A SWEET STORY ABOUT A FATAL HEART ATTACK

In 1983 Buckminster Fuller, on hearing that his wife Anne's cancer had worsened, rushed back from a speaking tour to be with her, but by then, she was in a coma. He sat holding her limp hand, when he suddenly felt it tighten around his. "She's squeezing my hand!" he told his daughter, jumped to his feet...and then immediately crumpled to the ground. Fuller had suffered a massive heart attack and, according to his daughter, "died with an exquisitely happy smile on his face." Anne, still in a coma, died 36 hours later.

Doggin' It

Only two animals get prostate cancer: male humans and male dogs.

Kublai Khan owned the most dogs in history—he had 5,000 mastiffs.

That poofy poodle haircut comes from when the dogs were water retrievers. They floated better with half their hair shorn, but the tufts on their bodies and joints protected them from injury and cold.

Dogs with pointed faces typically live longer than dogs with flat faces.

According to dog breeders, Afghan hounds are the dumbest breed; border collies are the smartest.

83 percent of dog owners say they'd risk their lives for Fido. 70 percent say Fido would risk his life for them.

In 1859 Belgium became the first country to use police dogs. They protected officers on the night shift.

Not so long ago, a dogsled was the most dependable vehicle for Canadian Mounties patrolling the Yukon's frozen wilderness, but the snowmobile phased them out. The Mounties last used sled dogs in 1969.

I Hear a Symphony

There's only one known opera about native Greenlanders: *Kaddara*, by Danish composer Hakon Borresen, premiered in 1921.

Famed composer Franz Joseph Haydn wrote 340 hours of music in 45 years...about 1 minute and 14 seconds written each day. If you started listening to his collection for eight hours a day, you'd be done in just over six weeks.

April 27, 1749, marked the premiere of George Frederick Handel's *Music for the Royal Fireworks* during an event in London's Green Park. A short time later, the event's fireworks display ignited the spot where the orchestra had been playing, and it burned down.

Franz Schubert wrote music so quickly and effortlessly that he often wouldn't recognize his own compositions when they were set before him.

The first musical superstar to inspire screaming and fainting females was 19th-century pianist Franz Liszt. When he got tired of all the hysteria, he put his talents to composing.

Sandstorm

An *arenophile* collects sand.

The word "arena" comes from the Latin word *harena*, meaning "sand." Roman arenas included a sand floor to absorb and hide blood from gladiator battles.

"Singing sand" is the phenomenon by which sand actually makes noise. Described as barks, whistles, squeaks, roars, or booms, the sounds depend on the sand's composition, grain size and shape, and humidity.

The number of grains of sand on all of the world's beaches is about 7.5 quintillion.

Napoleon plotted many of his battles in a sandbox.

Before dentist William Lowell patented the wooden golf tee in 1924, most golfers hit their first shots from little piles of wet sand.

According to FEMA in the 1960s, six inches of sand blocked atomic radiation. (They were wrong.)

America's tallest sand dunes are located in Colorado's Great Sand Dunes National Park. They're 750 feet high.

19,000 square miles of grass-stabilized sand dunes make up a quarter of the landlocked state of Nebraska.

A 1950s Quaker Oats promotion sent a small packet of "real Yukon sand" to kids who sent in a box top or 25¢. The sand was dug up near Whitehorse in Canada, packed into small pouches, and then trucked to Anchorage, Alaska, for mailing.

There's no actual sand on sandpaper.

Hawaii and the Galápagos Islands contain the earth's only green sand beaches. The sand is composed of olivine, a gemlike volcanic by-product.

Pure sand melts into glass at about 3,500°F. When lightning strikes a beach or sand dune, it can create hollow glass tubes called "fulgurites" (or "petrified lightning").

Animals That Changed History

FLEAS AND RATS

Impact: Plagues, ending the Middle Ages

From 1347 to 1350, the a virulent disease ravaged the populations of Asia and Europe, killing more than 25 million in Europe alone—about a third of the population. Most people died just three days after becoming infected. Scientists remain perplexed by the outbreak, but many agree that the disease was probably the bubonic plague (or the "black death") and it was probably spread all over the world by infected fleas traveling on rats. In those days, rats thrived among people—on ships and in cities. Infected fleas, the thinking goes, simply hopped off of dying rats and onto people.

The disruption to medieval society was immense and the outbreak helped bring about the end of the feudalism. Muslims in Crimea, in what's now the Ukraine, blamed Christians and expelled them from trading cities, spreading the disease deep into Europe. The Christians blamed Jews and burned many of them alive, killing crucial tradesmen and leaving towns without blacksmiths, innkeepers, bakers, millers, and weavers. Many towns and farms were abandoned, leading to food shortages. Ultimately, the nobles couldn't enforce control on their surviving peasant laborers. So, despite laws aimed at keeping serfs' wages low, the desperate noblemen began doubling and tripling wages, encouraging the serfs of other noblemen to jump ship. Over time, the serfs were able to demand and get a higher standard of living and new rights, loosening the binds that kept them enslaved to one estate and bringing an end to the economic system of feudalism.

DOGS

Impact: Hunting, herding, self-defense

Humans began welcoming dogs into their settlements about 14,000 years ago, the first animals to be domesticated. At first, groups of wolves probably began scavenging human settlements, snatching up the scraps, bones, and other perfectly good animal parts that humans threw out after hunting. Eventually, people discovered that dogs also made good watch animals at night. Humans favored the friendlier, less skittish animals and their puppies, unintentionally breeding dogs that were tame. About 3,000 years ago, people began breeding dogs intentionally, choosing specialized hunting and herding functions. The results were affectionate, efficient hunting animals, and the ability for one person to control an entire herd of sheep, goats, cows, or swine. This allowed tribes to own more livestock and freed up shepherds to pursue other needed occupations like hunting, farming, and metalworking.

CATS

Impact: Made agriculture possible, prevented plagues

Historians believe that about 10,000 years ago a few African wildcats decided to adopt humans. Genetic studies indicate that all of the world's 600 million house cats descend from as few as five original cat pioneers. As a result of this very restricted inbreeding, house cats developed all kinds of quirks and defects, including an inability to taste sweetness.

This all happened in the Fertile Crescent—an unusually fertile area in otherwise barren Egypt and Mesopotamia—at about the same time that people began growing wheat, rye, and barley. These crops provided humans with food stability and allowed them to stop wandering and erect permanent settlements. A few wildcats discovered that the barns and homes in these settlements offered sunny places to sleep, protection from larger animals, scraps of food, and huge quantities of big, juicy mice and rats. Humans, bedeviled by rodents that ate and contaminated the crops they stored after harvests, learned to value their feline friends. Ancient Egyptians even grew to worship cats, making it a crime to kill one. The Romans spread cats across Europe, and the Europeans took them to ports around the world.

Cats went through a dark period in Europe during the Middle Ages, when people began seeing them as evil spirits and companions to witches, resulting in widespread extermination of entire cat populations. But the result was a continent overrun with rats and the diseases they brought, which eventually caused humans to forgive cats and welcome them home.

CATTLE

Impact: Food, clothing, tools, and fuel

For about 8,000 years, cows have provided humans with food from meat and milk; clothes, blankets, and tents from their hides; fertilizer and cooking fuel from their dung; tools from their horns, teeth, and bones; and transportation and power. And they do it all by eating grasses that humans can't digest. Like cats, cattle were adopted by humans after people organized into permanent settlements. That's because, unlike sheep and goats (which had been herded for more than a thousand years before), cattle like to graze familiar fields and return to the same shelter each night. So nomadic lifestyles don't really suit them.

HORSES

Impact: Pre-industrial power and transportation, Mongol invasions

People began domesticating horses about 6,000 years ago, and long before the Industrial Revolution, humans discovered that the animals made great workers and companions. The Mongols were master horsemen who, during the 13th century, ruled the largest empire in history, containing 100 million people and 22 percent of the world's total landmass, stretching from Hungary to the Sea of Japan. Mongol soldiers often rode for hours without stopping, drinking blood from their horses as they conquered new lands. Over time, horses became inextricably linked to humans, providing transportation, power, and even tail hair for violin bows and an estrogen supplement called Premarin, whose name honors its source material: "**preg**nant **mar**e urine."

AMERICAN BISON

Impact: Native American settlement of the Great Plains; American roads; consciousness about saving endangered species

Massive bison herds, numbering up to 30 million animals, once grazed the grassy plains between the Rockies and the Appalachians, from the far north of Canada to Mexico. Native Americans used their migration paths as transportation routes that became road and rail beds still used today. And for thousands of years, Native Americans survived on the grassy North American plains by hunting the bison. But then came Europeans.

When white settlers arrived in North America, they were amazed by the number of bison, a seemingly endless supply, and began shooting them for skins or sport, usually leaving the meat to rot in the sun. There are also reports that wholesale bison slaughter was a deliberate tactic to deprive the Plains Indians of their main food source.

By 1889 the American bison population was down to just 1,091 animals. When the government shrugged off that fact, a few prescient ranchers saved a handful of the remaining animals, breeding them for eventual reintroduction into the wild. Those bison now make up the populations of Yellowstone National Park and Canada's Elk Island Park. The ranchers' success inspired attempts to save other endangered species through laws, hunting bans, and captive breeding programs that release animals into the wild.

BEAVERS

Impact: European exploration of North America, destruction of Native American tribes

Like the American bison, beavers were also nearly wiped out for their fur. In the 1700s, 60 to 80 beavers populated every mile of every stream in Canada and the northern United States. But within 100 years, the critters were hunted to near extinction. Why? Because beaver-skin top hats were all the rage in England. Fur traders had finished off the European beavers, so they went searching for the animals in other British holdings. They discovered a vast beaver population in North America that, in the 1790s, allowed them to ship more than 30,000 pelts a year back to Europe. As the beavers along the American East Coast disappeared, fur trappers explored farther west, following the Great Lakes and continuing in all directions. In 1793 Alexander Mackenzie, the first European to travel across the North American continent, did so on behalf of the North West Fur Company.

For Native Americans, beaver-mania was a mixed blessing. On the one hand, they could exchange furs for many goods they needed. But on the other, waves of European interlopers were infringing on their lands. Worse, the diseases the explorers brought were disastrous to many tribes, wiping out most or all of the inhabitants of some villages.

Fortunately, in the mid-1800s, beavers got a reprieve. Silk hats slowly gained favor, leaving the few remaining beavers in North America alone long enough to repopulate.

Shark Treatment

Sharks evolved 200 million years before dinosaurs.

If they're so old, why don't scientists ever find any fossilized shark bones? Because sharks don't have bones—their bodies are supported by cartilage, which doesn't fossilize. Scientists have found many ancient shark teeth, however.

The older the shark, the larger its teeth.

Sharks can hear lower frequencies than humans can, but humans can hear higher frequencies than sharks can.

A shark vomits by thrusting its stomach out of its mouth...and then pulling it back in.

The spined pygmy shark grows to be just 6 inches long.

Measuring up to 50 feet long, the whale shark is the largest fish in the world.

Sharks have no swim bladder (a gas-filled organ that keeps fish buoyant), so they have to swim constantly to stay afloat.

The largest great white shark ever caught was 21 feet long and weighed 7,000 pounds.

When a sea turtle eats a Portuguese man o' war, the jellyfish-like creature gets its revenge. It gives off a scent that attracts sharks...which then come eat the sea turtle.

The lemon shark grows about 24,000 new teeth every year.

Great white sharks can swim at up to 25 mph.

Shark attacks are extremely rare: fewer than 100 a year worldwide, with only 5 to 15 fatalities. In fact, in a typical year, more people are killed by pigs than sharks.

But...nearly 90 percent of shark attack victims are men.

Speak Up!

A young, struggling Walt Disney originally performed the voice of Mickey Mouse himself to save money on production costs. Bill Scott, cocreator of *Rocky and Bullwinkle*, likewise did the voices of Mr. Peabody and Bullwinkle.

Dan Castellaneta's contract with Fox forbids him from doing Homer Simpson's voice in public.

The first voice ever recorded was Thomas Edison in 1877, when he was messing around with his new invention, the phonograph. The historic first recording? "Mary Had a Little Lamb."

Australia's crested bellbird has an odd defense mechanism: It can throw its voice like a ventriloquist.

Your vocal cords vibrate to create the sound of your voice. If you're an average adult, they vibrate 100 (usually male) to 200 (usually female) times a second. A child's, 250 to 400. And a screaming baby, 500.

The vocal cords of a soprano, singing two octaves above middle C, vibrate 1,024 times a second.

To do Smokey Bear's deep voice in commercials, voice man Jack Weaver put his head in a trash can.

Lloyd's of London once insured Bruce Springsteen's voice for £3.5 million.

In *Snow White and the Seven Dwarfs*, Dopey makes just a handful of sounds during the entire movie: hiccups and snoring, rendered flawlessly by Disney sound man Jimmy MacDonald.

Like most of his audience, even author E. B. White became teary-eyed by the death of his fictional spider Charlotte. When he recorded the audiobook, it took 19 takes before he could read that part without his voice cracking.

Hank Azaria has voiced more than 160 characters on *The Simpsons*.

The Sailing Solution

At the latitude 60° south, it is possible to sail around the world without ever reaching land.

Popeye the Sailor is 5'6".

Before it was used for buildings, the "skyscraper" is what sailors called the uppermost sail on a ship.

On a sailboat, "faffle" is the flapping of a sail when you turn too much into the wind.

In ancient Greek, "astronaut" means "star sailor."

Minnesota, the "Land of 10,000 Lakes," is an understatement: The state actually has 11,842 lakes, which may explain why it has one recreational boat for every six people.

Legend claims that the term "hooker" came from "working" women who followed the camps of Civil War general Joseph Hooker, but that's not true. Sailors popularized the term 20 years earlier when discussing Corlear's Hook, a scandalous dockside area of New York City.

What's the difference between a boat and a ship? According to the U.S. Navy, it's a matter of scale: a boat is "a vessel that can be hauled aboard a ship."

A "fathom" was the distance that a sailor could reach from fingertip to fingertip with arms fully extended as if about to give a hug. And that's where the word came from: in Old English, *fathom* meant "embrace."

"Saint Elmo's fire" is a steady discharge of electricity emitted when electrified clouds meet the masts of sailing ships. ("Elmo" is a nickname for Erasmus, patron saint of Mediterranean sailors.)

First known sailing vessel: A pine dugout from the Netherlands that dates from 8040 BC.

The story of Robinson Crusoe was based on a quarrelsome sailor named Alexander Selkirk. After unending conflict with a captain, Selkirk asked to be marooned on a nearby deserted island, where he lived for four years and four months before being rescued.

One Hump or Two?

The camel is vital to the desert Bedouins, who call it *Ata Allah* ("God's gift").

Many camels chew in a figure-eight pattern.

A *bukht* is the result when you mate a one-humped camel with a two-humped camel. A bukht splits the difference between its parents and sports one elongated hump.

Camels will often refuse to carry an unbalanced load.

Riding a camel takes a lot of moving, shifting, and leaning. The gym on the *Titanic* included a mechanical one for the benefit of travelers going on to the Middle East.

Camels can drink up to seven gallons of water per minute.

During warm weather, camels shed about five pounds of fur, what was their winter coat.

Route 66 westbound out of Albuquerque, New Mexico, began as a camel trail in the 1800s when the army was testing the animals for desert warfare.

It's best not to tick off a camel. When angry, they spit a mixture of saliva and regurgitated stomach bile.

A Flock of Facts

The 225 species of pigeons and doves are the same bird group. Whether a particular species has been named a pigeon or a dove seems to have to do with size—smaller species (some as small as sparrows) are more often called "doves" and the larger ones (some as large as turkeys), "pigeons."

Rock pigeons are the ones we think of as urban pigeons. Their adaptation to buildings and window ledges is not that big a change for them: in the wild, they live on cliffs and rock ledges.

Homing pigeons are just rock pigeons that have been bred for specific characteristics.

The phrase "stool pigeon" (someone who acts as an informant for the police) comes from the term "stall," which was the 15th-century British name for a captive pigeon used to lure hawks into a trap.

In 1963 a court in Libya convicted 75 "smugglers" and sentenced them to death. (The defendants were all pigeons.)

A "silver pigeon" can be a vintage motor scooter, a tropical fish, an architecture award, or a hunting shotgun, but it's not actually a bird.

The U.S. Coast Guard began using search-and-rescue pigeons in 1977. Success rate over the ocean: 93 percent. Human success rates (even after seeing the pigeons respond): only 38 percent. Still, budget cuts killed the program in 1983.

Estimated number of New York City pigeons captured and sold to shooting clubs each year: 144,000. In annual pigeon shoots, up to 15,000 are released over three days and shot for fun and prizes.

On September 1, 1914, the passenger pigeon went extinct when Martha, the last known surviving bird, died in the Cincinnati Zoo. The once-abundant, slow-flying birds were an easy target for sport shooters.

The Northern Lights can impair pigeons' navigating abilities.

Rearguard

Although the idea didn't immediately catch on, American Joseph Gayetty invented modern toilet paper in 1857...and printed his name on every sheet.

The very first toilet paper of any kind has been traced back to China in the late 6th century. Back then, scrap paper was crumpled repeatedly to soften it, but not just any paper would do. Wrote artist Yan Zhitui in AD 589: "Paper on which there are quotations or commentaries from the Five Classics or the names of sages, I dare not use for toilet purposes."

Most households have eight toilet paper rolls in reserve to avoid running out.

The average bathroom visitor uses 8.6 sheets of toilet paper per visit, 57 sheets a day, for a total of 20,805 sheets per year.

On average, an American family of four uses two trees' worth of toilet paper every year.

Ever wonder how they wind toilet paper so neatly on cardboard tubes? They don't. They wind wide rolls of paper around long tubes, and then slice them into small rolls.

Lost in Space

All of our solar system's giant outer planets have rings: Saturn has 23, Uranus has 13, Neptune has 9, and Jupiter has 3. Saturn's are so bright that they were discovered almost 350 years ago. The other planets' rings are too dim to be seen with primitive telescopes and weren't discovered until the 1970s.

According to scientists, Saturn's rings will probably drift into space and disappear eventually.

The only planet whose name comes from Greek mythology is Uranus. (The rest are Roman.)

The dwarf planet Pluto was named in 1930 by Venetia Burney, an 11-year-old British schoolgirl.

Coldest place in the solar system: Triton, a moon of Neptune (-400°F).

Neptune takes 165 Earth years to go around the Sun once.

*   *   *

DID YOU KNOW?

There are about 5,000 earthquakes every year in Alaska. North America's strongest recorded earthquake struck there on March 27, 1964. It had a magnitude of 9.2, stronger than San Francisco's famous 1906 earthquake.

Strange as a $2 Bill

John Trumbull's iconic 1818 painting *Declaration of Independence* is so associated with American history that a version of it was reproduced on the back of the $2 bill. But an anonymous somebody in the U.S. Bureau of Engraving decided to make some changes to Trumbull's work, and that's when things got a little strange.

- First of all, six signers of the Declaration of Independence were simply lopped out of the picture: four (George Wythe, William Whipple, Josiah Bartlett, and Thomas Lynch) from the far left side, and two (Thomas McKean and Philip Livingston) from the far right.

- A patterned rug that appears in the Trumbull painting was removed from under the feet of the five men standing in the center.

- In the painting, Thomas Jefferson is twisted about 90 degrees and his leg is outstretched like a ballet dancer in order to stand ever so slightly on John Adams's foot. The two men had a lot of respect for each other, but they were also political rivals for decades, belonging to opposite parties and running against each other for president. In the $2 bill version, though, the two men's feet are touching toe to toe.

- Finally, there is the curious case of James Wilson, who would eventually go on to become an associate justice of the United States Supreme Court. In the place of the smooth-shaven, white-haired gentleman in Trumbull's painting, the $2 bill includes a young man with dark, close-cropped hair and a short goatee.

THE FINE PRINT
Having said all that, it's only fair to note that the original painting wasn't perfect to begin with. Trumbull pictured just 47 congressmen, even though there were 56 signers of the Declaration of Independence. And of the men he did include, several hadn't actually signed the document.

Meow Mix

Cats can hear sounds as high as 50,000 vibrations per second—people can't hear above the low 20,000s.

Cats don't have a great sense of taste, so they make food choices based on texture, scent, and appearance.

Male cats were called rams or boars until 1760, when an anonymous writer published *The Life and Adventures of a Cat*. Its main character, Tom, achieved widespread popularity, and male cats got a new name: tomcats.

Historians say you can probably thank (or blame) the Pilgrims for bringing the first domestic cats to the New World.

Siamese cats are mostly white when they're born. The markings come later.

There are about 77.7 million pet cats in the United States.

Nearly a third of all households have at least one cat. The average cat-owning home has 2.2 cats.

About half of all American pet cats get presents during the holidays.

Lions...

The lion, aka, the "king of the jungle," lives mainly on the savanna grasslands.

In captivity, lions can live 20 or more years. In the wild, 15 years is typical for females and 12 years for males.

Female lions are social and live in stable prides with their cubs. Male lions have to fight constantly to retain their status in a pride.

Between their bulk and their mane, male lions are not good at hunting. The females do most of that work.

The first MGM lion was named Slats. On July 31, 1928, for the studio's very first "talkie" film— *White Shadows in the South Seas*— MGM added sound effects to its once-silent logo, turning the lion into a full-fledged growler.

Lions are sometimes attacked by South African giant bullfrogs.

A nursing lioness will suckle any of the pride's cubs.

The Cowardly Lion's costume in *The Wizard of Oz* was made from two real lion skins.

The leaping lion logo on the Detroit Lions' helmets is named Bubbles.

The world's youngest lion tamer, Jorge Elich, of the Circus Paris, started working unassisted in 2008…at age 8.

How do you cross a lion and a tiger? Very carefully. You can interbreed them, though they'd never do so in the wild. If the mom is a tigress, the result is a "liger"; if she's a lioness, a "tigon."

*   *   *

YOU'RE MY INSPIRATION

For the painting *American Gothic* (the farm couple with a pitchfork), artist Grant Woods's models were his sister and his dentist.

...and Tigers...

The tiger is the largest member of the cat family. Male Siberian tigers often grow to be 10 feet long and weigh more than 400 pounds.

Tiger stripe patterns are as unique as human fingerprints.

Unlike many wild animals, tigers breed easily in captivity. Perhaps too easily. There are so many captive tigers that they are often sold as pets.

The United States has 12,000 caged tigers, about twice the number of wild tigers worldwide.

Tigers are solitary creatures. Males and females get together briefly to mate, but otherwise live apart. They aren't necessarily hostile, though—two tigers meeting at a water hole may stop and rub cheeks like house cats.

Leopards and tigers can both swim, but tigers are the only cats that do it for fun.

A tiger's tongue is so rough that it can lick the paint off of a building.

An adult tiger can usually kill with a single swipe of its paw.

...and Bears...Oh My!

Polar, grizzly, and brown bears had the same ancestor 150,000 years ago. Even after they split into different species, they interbred during warm periods, when their habitats overlapped, and even now, they sometimes still do.

There's evidence that brown bears came from Ireland.

What does a king give another king who has everything? In 1252, Haakon IV of Norway gave England's Henry III a polar bear. Henry housed the animal in the Tower of London, with a chain long enough to let it fish and swim in the Thames.

Sometimes you wonder if scientists are biased against certain animals—the scientific name for the grizzly bear is *Ursus arctos horribilis*.

In the U.S., it's a federal crime to imitate Smokey Bear for profit. You can get six months in jail and have to pay a fine.

Polar bears at the San Diego Zoo turned green in the summer of 1978 because of algae in their enclosure.

At first, the U.S. Forest Service used Bambi the deer to promote forest fire prevention. But in 1944, when their contract ran out with Disney and they lost the right to use Bambi, they decided on something more intimidating and went with Smokey the Bear.

Koalas may look like bears, but they're actually marsupials.

A bear named Voytek helped carry ammunition for Polish troops during World War II.

Car license plates from Canada's Northwest Territories are shaped like polar bears.

They look fat and slow, but a grizzly bear can run faster than a horse for 100 yards or so. Brown and polar bears can run between 24 and 35 mph.

Antipodes

- Every point on earth has its opposite point, starting with the Arctic Pole and its opposite, the Antarctic (which literally means "opposite of arctic"). There's even a name for a location's opposite point—the spot where you'd end up if you tunneled straight down through the earth. That's called the *antipode*, a Greek word that means "opposed foot."

- Antipodes are true opposites. If you're in the Western Hemisphere, your antipode is in the Eastern Hemisphere. If you're in the Northern Hemisphere, it's in the Southern. Your antipode is the farthest place on earth from wherever you are right now.

- Odds are very good that your antipode is under an ocean. In fact, only about 4 percent of the world's entire landmass has a dry antipode. That's partly because so much of the earth is covered by water (about 70 percent). But it's also because most of the dry land is in the Northern Hemisphere and very little of it is in the Southern. But because of that, if you live in the Southern Hemisphere, your odds of getting a dry antipode are vastly improved.

- The British often refer to Australia and New Zealand as "the Antipodes," and their inhabitants as the "Antipodeans." But technically, England and Ireland's antipodes are in the ocean just south of New Zealand. The actual land mass of New Zealand matches up with parts of Spain, Portugal, and Morocco.

- The Antipode Islands, located in the southwestern Pacific Ocean, were named for this phenomenon. First charted in 1800 by British Captain Henry Waterhouse of the HMS *Reliance*, the islands were originally called the Penantipodes ("nearly antipodes") because they were the closest landmasses to London's antipode.

- Most of North America has an antipode in the Indian Ocean between Africa and Australia, but the extreme northern parts of Canada and Alaska are the antipodes to Antarctica. Hawaii is the only U.S. state that has a land antipode: Botswana in southern Africa.

Mixed Nuts

23 percent of psychiatrists in the United States do business in the New York City metro area.

Towering 1,064 feet above sea level, the highest point of Ohio's Hamilton County is the Rumpke Landfill. Locals call the 509-acre pile of trash "Mt. Rumpke."

The backs of your knees are home to more different kinds of microbes than your gut is.

If the Milky Way galaxy were the size of Asia, our solar system would be the size of a penny.

Just in case mummies have to pee, ancient Egyptians included chamber pots in their burial crypts.

First rock band to play at an outdoor stadium: the Beatles at Shea Stadium (1965).

In 2008 psychologists introduced a new diagnosis: Facebook Addiction Disorder.

About one in six pregnant women gets a craving to chew on coal.

The most common birthday in the United States is October 5. (Approximate conception date: New Year's Eve.)

Ralph Teetor, the man who invented cruise control for cars, was blind.

Sterling silver contains 7.5 percent copper.

Americans use enough toilet paper each year to stretch to the sun and back.

Baby Talk

Archie Bunker on *All in the Family* was the first person to diaper a baby on TV.

The average baby cries at 115 decibels...only 10 decibels lower than a firecracker.

The "Cry Translator" iPhone app claims to help people identify five baby cries: hungry, sleepy, uncomfortable, stressed, or bored. (Reviewers likewise cried that the $4.99 app didn't work adequately, leaving them stressed out and annoyed as well.)

Average amount of sleep lost by parents in a baby's first year of life: 200 hours.

Still, experts say infants age 6 to 12 months old sleep about 10 to 11 hours at night and take a couple of one- to two-hour naps during the day.

At birth, babies usually cry in the key of C or C-sharp.

Q. Who was the first Canadian baby born on Canada's centennial (July 1, 1967)?
A. Pamela Anderson.

When a developer of the baby incubator couldn't get financial backers, he hired nurses and exhibited premature "incubator babies" at world's fairs. The exhibits were popular attractions, raising money and putting pressure on hospitals to invest in the life-saving boxes. New York's Coney Island had two incubator baby exhibits. Admission was 10¢...but free to the parents of the babies.

A German study found that newborn babies begin to cry with an accent within two weeks of birth.

What part of a baby's body is almost the same size in adulthood? The eyes. Unlike everything else, they grow only a little.

Sigmund Freud believed that morning sickness represented a loathing of the baby's father... and the woman's desire to vomit up her baby.

Technically, all babies are *galactophagists*. What does that mean? "One who feeds on milk."

Eat Bugs!

"Entomophagy" is the eating of bugs by humans. It's more common than you'd think. And why not? Bugs outnumber humans by about 200 million to one.

In 2013 the Food and Agriculture Organization of the United Nations, noting that food production will have to double to feed 9 billion people in 2050, issued a report about the benefits of bug-eating for a hungry world.

According to the UN, there are more than 1,900 edible bug species worldwide. In order of consumption, the most popular are beetles (31 percent), followed by caterpillars (18 percent); bees, wasps, and ants (14 percent); and grasshoppers, crickets, and locusts (13 percent). Termites and dragonflies tied at 3 percent.

It's currently impossible to make foods absolutely bug-free, so food and health laws allow a certain number of bugs and bug parts. For example, the FDA allows up to 210 insect fragments in a 25-ounce jar of peanut butter.

Many bugs contain large quantities of lysine, an amino acid often deficient in people whose diets are heavy on grains.

A typical American already eats one to two pounds of bugs every year without knowing it.

Cicada connoisseurs say the bugs are good stir-fried or even picked fresh off the tree.

Crickets can be roasted and eaten whole, or they can be ground into a paste for sauces.

In Judaism, most bugs are not considered kosher, except (according to the Torah) four species of locusts.

Many bug growers for human consumption don't want their creatures to be called "bugs" or "insects"—they prefer the term "mini livestock."

People in Thailand eat about 200 insect species, most notably crickets, grasshoppers, and bamboo caterpillars. Cricket farming is a $30 million industry there.

History's Richest Sports Star

FAMOUS LONG AGO

It's unbelievable how much some professional athletes are making these days—for example, Tiger Woods recently hit (pre-tax, pre-expenses, pre-alimony) career earnings of *one billion* dollars. Even rookie baseball players can become multimillionaires before setting foot on a professional field. But highly paid sports figures aren't a modern invention. In fact, history's all-time top earner by far lived many centuries before baseball or golf even existed.

Gaius Appuleius Diocles lived in the second century AD, when sporting events were becoming more popular. Diocles was a chariot racer, a sport that was roughly the equivalent of a NASCAR today. And like NASCAR drivers, charioteers required expensive equipment and a support team. As a result, they depended on sponsorship by the big businesses of the time. The charioteers could become rich during their short careers, but because chariot races were so dangerous, few lived long enough to retire.

GLORIOUS GAIUS

Gaius Appuleius Diocles became a rich celebrity not only for surviving long enough to have a full career, but for consistently being very successful. For an incredible 24 years, he represented Rome's red, green, and white teams against its blue team. Diocles's record was 1,462 wins out of 4,257 races—a ratio better than one victory in every three starts. When he retired at 42 in the year 146, Diocles's fellow charioteers erected a monument to him that said Diocles was the "champion of all charioteers" and had amassed earnings of 35,863,120 sesterces.

RACE PEEL-OFF

So how much is 35,863,120 sesterces worth today? That can be hard to determine, but some historians have tried: One sesterce was defined at its introduction as being worth 2½ highly prized jackasses. ("Sesterce" came from *semis-tertius*, the Latin word for 2½.) We also know from ancient budget records that 35,863,120 sesterces was enough to supply the entire city of Rome with grain for a year, or to pay the wages of the entire Roman imperial army for 72 days. So with those figures in mind, Diocles's net worth may be the equivalent of up to $5 billion in today's money—some historians go as high as $15 billion.

* * *

ARCHAEOLOGICALLY SPEAKING

"Archaeology is the peeping Tom of the sciences. It is the sandbox of men who care not where they are going; they merely want to know where everyone else has been."

—**Jim Bishop**

"An archaeologist is someone whose career lies in ruins."

—**Anonymous**

"I married an archaeologist because the older I grow, the more he appreciates me."

—**Agatha Christie**

"Archaeologists will date any old thing."

—**Bumper sticker**

"If you're an archaeologist, I bet it's real embarrassing to put together a skull from a bunch of ancient bone fragments, but then it turns out it's not a skull but just an old dried-out potato."

—**Jack Handy**

Hearing Voices

About 10 percent of people in the world have, at one time, heard voices talking inside their heads. Here are some of the most famous.

PHILOSOPHERS & THINKERS

Socrates

Pythagoras

Descartes

Goethe

Sigmund Freud

Carl Gustav Jung

Mahatma Gandhi

Jean-Paul Sartre

CREATIVE FOLK

Beethoven

William Blake

Robert Schumann

Lord Byron

Frederic Chopin

Percy Bysshe Shelley

Charles Dickens

Virginia Woolf

Evelyn Waugh

Philip K. Dick

Anthony Hopkins

Zoe Wanamaker

Paul McCartney

Brian Wilson

SPIRITUAL & RELIGIOUS FIGURES

Moses

Joan of Arc

Martin Luther

St. Augustine

St. Francis

Joseph Smith

Martin Luther King Jr.

LEADERS & RULERS

Alexander the Great

Julius Caesar

Attila the Hun

Charlemagne

Oliver Cromwell

Napoleon Bonaparte

Adolf Hitler

Winston Churchill

SCIENTISTS & EXPLORERS

Galileo

Isaac Newton

Christopher Columbus

John Forbes Nash Jr.

Gone Fishing

The ancient Egyptians used electric catfish to treat certain nervous disorders. Since the big ones can generate up to 400 volts, enough to knock a person unconscious or even kill someone, they used only small ones.

There are jellyfish in every ocean in the world. On top of that, there are freshwater jellyfish that live in lakes.

A five-foot wooden codfish hangs over the entrance to the Massachusetts House of Representatives. "The Sacred Cod" commemorates the importance of fish to the state's economy and is actually the cod's third incarnation: the first was lost in a 1747 fire and the second to British troops during the Revolutionary War.

About 500 species of fish can generate electricity.

Oils from the orange roughy, a deep-sea fish from New Zealand, are used to make shampoo.

How did a fish become a symbol of Christianity? Early Christians discovered that the Greek word for fish, *ichthus*, could be used as a loose acronym for *Iesous Christos, Theou Huios, Soter* ("Jesus Christ, Son of God, Savior"). Since Jesus was already associated with fish and fishermen, it made sense.

Pregnant goldfish are called "twits."

Fish go belly-up when they die because oxygen remains in the fish's swim bladder and gases from decay or sickness collect in internal organs located in their belly, making them float.

Maine is the source of 90 percent of the nation's lobsters.

Most fish for freshwater aquariums are farm-raised. However, each year, 20 million fish are captured from the ocean for saltwater aquariums.

The garfish (or needlefish) has green bones.

Halls of Medicine

Infections caught in hospitals kill about 48,000 Americans a year.

A CDC study found that soap and water tackled germs better than disinfectants.

Studies suggest that proper hand washing could reduce hospital infection rates by up to 50 percent.

The U.S. Navy has two hospital ships: *Mercy* and *Comfort*.

About 25 percent of veterans admitted to VA psychiatric hospitals are homeless.

Sick people in Switzerland are hospitalized longer than those in many other countries: more than nine days, on average.

A survey asked nurses if they'd willingly choose to be a patient in their own hospitals—38 percent said "absolutely not."

According to a British study, hospital admissions rise by up to 52 percent on Friday the 13th.

In the 12th century, St. Bernard of Clairvaux, head doctor of the Roman Catholic Church, forbade the monks in his hospitals from studying medical texts and prohibited the use of any remedy but prayer.

Originally, Blue Shield covered doctors' fees, and Blue Cross covered the expenses of a hospital stay. In most states, the two merged in 1982.

In an average year, influenza causes 114,000 hospital admissions in the United States. (Of these, 36,000 die.)

Births in hospitals instead of at home are a relatively new thing. The first president born in a hospital was Jimmy Carter in 1924.

To choose the healthiest location for a hospital in ninth-century Baghdad, physician Muhammad ibn Zakariya al-Razi hung pieces of meat at possible sites. The location where the meat stayed freshest the longest was the one he chose.

Nazi TV

RACING THE ENGLISH CHANNEL

On January 31, 1935, a minor panel within the British government made a routine announcement that had little impact in England, but sent the Germans into panicked frenzy. After half a year of inquiry and spirited debate, Britain's Television Advisory Committee issued a report in which it determined that the BBC should start a regular TV broadcasting service. Those were still the very early days of television, but the decision would make the BBC the first national TV broadcaster in the world.

It's not that the Germans particularly cared about television, but they did care about propaganda. The government had invested heavily in the message that its master Aryan race was more advanced in *everything*, particularly technological achievement. And so Germany's Reich Broadcasting Corporation (RRG) suddenly came under pressure to set up its own broadcasting service before the British got up and running. That way, Germany would get the bragging rights that came with being the first nation to create its own TV network.

THE TORTOISE VS. THE HARE

The British took their time and worked on creating a usable system, but the Germans had no such priorities. Instead, they rushed in to at least simulate that they were ready for prime time. On March 22, 1935, just over two months after the British announcement, the RRG presented a demonstration of its "first television program service on earth." The program was all propaganda—it began with Reich Program Director Eugen Hadamovsky announcing that, no matter what the Americans and British claimed, television had *really* been invented by a German named Paul Nipkow way back in 1884 with his patent for an "electrical telescope."

The claim wasn't completely a lie. Nipkow had come up with a mechanical scanning wheel—a rapidly rotating disk with a spiral of holes in it that "scanned" images. But American Philo Farnsworth made that contraption obsolete when he invented all-electronic scanning in 1927. Nipkow—still alive in 1935, but somewhat senile—went along with the German myth-making, posing in front of TV sets and not objecting as the government created a legend around him. According to one story, Nipkow had invented TV one lonely Christmas Eve as a way for people to see their families from afar.

THE DEMONSTRATION

"Today, National Socialist broadcasting, in cooperation with the Reichpost and industry, starts regular television broadcasting, as the first broadcasting system on earth," announced Hadamovsky in that March 1935 address. "In this hour, this broadcast will bring to fruition the largest and holiest mission: to plant in all German hearts the picture of their führer."

However, there were problems with this "first" broadcast. First, it used equipment that was already obsolete because of the insistence that the technology had to include Nipkow's spinning disk. As a result, the image was muddy and had few details compared to the all-electric video cameras the British were using. Furthermore, Germany's "regular" broadcasts were just the same tests of old feature films and newsreels over and over again.

Plus, because the German technology required huge amounts of light in a small space, the danger of fire was a constant worry...that came to fruition in the summer of 1935, when the studio caught fire and destroyed most of the equipment. This turned out to be a blessing for the Germans because they closed everything down for six months and replaced the Nipkow disk cameras with modern all-electronic ones based on British and American designs. They also named the newly upgraded broadcasting unit the "Paul Nipkow *Fernsehsender*" (TV station).

GERMANY'S GOT TALENT

Like many things, television was only interesting to the Nazi leaders as long as it was useful for propaganda purposes. Once they'd laid claim to the technological triumph, they weren't particularly interested in providing TV sets for viewing or coming up with programs that would attract viewers. But that changed in the summer of 1936 when Berlin hosted the Olympics and mounting a few cameras pointing down at the field seemed like another good propaganda coup. The RRG also set up 28 public viewing rooms in Berlin, each big enough to hold about 40 people at a time. In all, about 150,000 Germans watched the events.

That triumph and the new viewing rooms spurred actual broadcasts. Most were upbeat films, but there were also variety shows, music and dance performances, and the occasional interview with party officials as the war progressed. Since so few people could actually watch the broadcasts, though, Nazi propaganda chief Paul Goebbels didn't bother dictating too much of the content. As interested as he was in television, he still preferred radio as the mass medium for party propaganda.

NOT-SEE TV

The Nazis' broadcast service began unraveling in late 1943. On November 23, Allied bombers destroyed its transmitter and knocked it off the air. Finally, on May 2, 1945, the Soviet army took over the German TV studios and "the world's first broadcasting service" was gone for good.

*   *   *

DID YOU KNOW?

- In California, it's illegal to shoot game from a moving vehicle... unless the target is a whale.

- Historically, teachers were paid in goods and services by cash-strapped townsfolk. For cash, teachers often worked nighttime jobs like bartending, choir leading, and grave digging.

- You can pick up FM radio stations on the Moon. FM signals travel in a straight line through the atmosphere and into space, so whatever Earth stations are right below the Moon at any given time will be available. AM radio waves, on the other hand, bounce around in the atmosphere and cover more of Earth's territory, but don't reach the Moon.

- American dentists use about 13 tons of gold each year for fillings, crowns, and inlays.

Food News

A pound of armadillo meat has around 780 calories, about the same as lean beef.

The meat from giant squids tastes a lot like ammonia. Scientists believe that the ammonia inside their tissue, less dense than seawater, keeps the animals from sinking.

At least one study has shown that vegetarians have higher IQs than meat eaters.

Only two primates are carnivores: chimps and humans.

What's a flexitarian? A person who eats meat only once or twice a week.

One online company once sold laser-etched edible business cards printed on beef jerky…for $7.50 per card.

Weighing more than 440 pounds, one giant clam can provide enough meat for about 100 gallons of chowder.

It takes 300 gallons of water to produce a loaf of bread. A pound of beef? 2,500 gallons.

The average American eats about five cows' worth of ground beef in a lifetime.

For the Love of Beer

An early beer ad claimed that the drink was really good for putting kids to sleep.

Officially, a nip of beer is a half-pint (8 oz.) or less. A flagon is a quart. An anker is 10 gallons. A barrel, 36 gallons. And a tun, 216 gallons.

World's first trademark: the Bass Beer symbol, a red triangle.

The Pilgrims were supposed to land farther south than Massachusetts, but as one passenger put it, "We could not now take time for further search, our victuals being much spent, especially our beere."

The oldest known beer recipe appears on a Sumerian clay tablet dating from about 1800 BC.

Brewing magnate John Carling never drank beer—it disagreed with his system.

In the 1700s, British soldiers stationed in Canada were entitled to six pints of beer a day.

Beer steins have covers because a 16th-century German law required them as a way to prevent diseases that might come from swallowing flies.

A person who collects beer cans is called a can-ologist.

Roasted malt makes dark beer dark. For pale beer, the malt is left unroasted.

Malt liquor is stronger than beer because brewers add another dollop of sugar, giving an extra jolt to the alcohol-excreting yeast.

If people say you're *gambrinous*, they're accusing you of being full of beer.

The Portland, Oregon, metro area has more breweries—68— than any other city in the world.

If a young Tiriki man from Kenya offers beer to a woman and she spits some of it into his mouth, they are officially engaged.

Neither Pine Nor Apple

Dole Pineapple Juice, introduced in 1933, was initially promoted as a mixer for gin.

In a can of fruit cocktail, pineapple lands firmly in the middle: fewer pieces of it than peaches and pears, more than grapes and cherries.

Some wild pineapple plants have flowers that open only in the dark of night because they're pollinated by bats.

Pulped pineapple leaves can be woven into a fabric called *piña*, commonly used in the Philippines.

Although we associate the pineapple with the Polynesian islands, the fruit originated in Southern Brazil and Paraguay. The Aztecs and Incas cultivated them throughout Mexico and south America, Columbus brought some pineapples back to Spain, and the Spaniards planted them in Hawaii and the Philippines.

A pineapple is not closely related to either a pine or an apple. It's not even a fruit, per se—technically, it's up to 200 berries stuck together.

Pineapples stop ripening when they're picked.

Blame pineapple growers for laws against importing hummingbirds into Hawaii. Hummingbirds pollinate pineapple flowers, creating seeds. But growers and consumers want seedless pineapples—so no hummingbirds.

Pineapple has an enzyme that breaks down protein, making it a good meat tenderizer.

For about half a century, pineapple juice appeared on supermarket shelves in cans only. The acid in the juice dissolved some of the metal, though, so Americans were used to a tinny taste and often rejected fresh pineapple juice as "tasting funny."

D-I-V-O-R-C-E

About 50 percent of U.S. marriages end in divorce. But in India, where arranged marriages are common and there's lots of pressure from families for couples to stay together, the rate is 1 percent.

January is the month when the most couples file for divorce. It is also the month when the fewest couples marry.

According to researchers, an American couple with a first-born daughter is 5 percent more likely to get divorced than those with a first-born son.

Ronald Reagan was the only president to have been divorced.

In less complicated days, a Pueblo woman could divorce her husband by leaving his moccasins on the doorstep.

Massachusetts has the lowest divorce rate in the U.S.

Divorce was illegal in Ireland until 1997.

The only two countries that still don't allow divorce are the Philippines and Vatican City.

Eight years is the average length for a first marriage to end in divorce.

Before no-fault divorce became the norm in the United States, one partner had to prove that the other was guilty of a serious offense to the marriage. "Grounds for divorce" included things like adultery, abandonment, desertion, or cruelty.

95 percent of American divorces are uncontested, which means that the parties and their lawyers come to an agreement without a trial.

The median time between a divorce and a second marriage is 3½ years.

Couples of different religious faiths are three times more likely to divorce than couples who share a religion.

Teeeeth!

For several years after the Civil War, the best dentures were advertised as containing teeth yanked out of the bodies of healthy young soldiers who had been killed in battle.

When George Washington was inaugurated, he had only one of his original teeth. His four sets of dentures were made of hippo ivory, elephant ivory, and real teeth from cows and humans. He eventually lost his last tooth by the time he was 60.

In George Washington's time, you took out your false teeth to eat. They weren't designed for eating—they were just there to look good.

In England in the 19th and early 20th century, it was fashionable to give children a full extraction and a new set of false teeth for their 21st birthday.

In the United States, brushing one's teeth didn't become common until World War II when the army issued toothbrushes to all soldiers.

Italian dentists discovered the anticavity effects of fluoride in 1802. They noticed that the citizens of Naples—a town naturally rich in fluoride—had few cavities and started adding it to water in other places.

Ads Infinitum

"The very first law in advertising is to avoid the concrete promise and cultivate the delightfully vague."

—**Bill Cosby**

"The most powerful element in advertising is the truth."

—**William Bernbach**

"Asked about the power of advertising in research surveys, most agree that it works, but not on them."

—**Eric Clark**

"You can fool all the people all the time if the advertising is right and the budget is big enough."

—**Joseph E. Levine**

"Advertising is the poetry of capitalism."

—**Martin Puchner**

"Good advertising does not just circulate information. It penetrates the public mind with desires and belief."

—**Leo Burnett**

"Bad advertising can unsell a product."

—**David Ogilvy**

"You can tell the ideals of a nation by its advertisements."

—**Norman Douglas**

You Gotta Have Heart...Literally

The human heart beats about 3,600 times an hour. For an adult, that's 31,536,000 beats since this time last year.

Your heart is about the size of two fists, but a blue whale's heart is as big as a car.

Generally, the bigger an animal, the slower its heart rate: A gray whale has a pulse of about nine beats per minute...an adult human, 60 to 100...and a hummingbird, up to 12,000.

The human heart completely circulates blood through the body about three times a minute.

In a normal lifetime, a human heart will pump enough blood to fill three supertankers.

People who exercise regularly have a much lower heart rate than sedentary types.

To make room for your heart, your left lung is smaller than your right.

That "thump-thump" a heart makes when it beats is the sound of its valves closing. They open and close with each beat to let blood into each heart chamber and then push it out.

An octopus has three hearts. A slime eel has four.

During soccer's 2006 World Cup, hospitals discovered that Germany's heart attack rate tripled on days the German team played.

The Egyptians considered the heart the seat of all thought. Although they often removed the other organs (including the brain) for mummification, they always left the heart in the body.

Roughly one in every 120 babies is born with some kind of heart problem, making it the part of the body most likely to be affected by birth defects.

Seeing the color red can make a heart beat faster.

You Are Here

The African country of Mali gets its name from the Bambara word for hippopotamus. Its capital is Bamako, which means "place of crocodiles" in the same language.

In 1535 explorer Jacques Cartier landed in what's now Canada and asked an Iroquois man, "What do you call this place?" Thinking Cartier meant the immediate community, the man said *kanata*, meaning "village." But Cartier, believing that he had just been told the name of the entire landmass, dutifully wrote the word on his map.

A spot just north of Lebanon, Kansas, marks the exact center point of the contiguous United States.

About 25 percent of the Netherlands is below sea level.

Montana, Nevada, Illinois, and Kansas each contain a town called Manhattan.

31 American towns have the word "liberty" in them.

Chicago is closer to Moscow than it is to Rio de Janeiro.

The world's longest nonmilitarized international border runs between Canada and the United States: a total of 5,525 miles.

The U.S. lake with the longest name is Lake Chargoggagoggmanchauggagoggchaubunagungamaugg in Massachusetts.

The World's Longest... (Animal Style)

...**Horse mane:** 18 feet, grown by a California mare named Maude. The longest horse tail: 22 feet on an American palomino named Chinook.

...**Bug:** Chan's megastick, an insect that, not unexpectedly, looks like a large stick as long as 22 inches. (Oddly, it wasn't discovered until 2008.)

...**Beak (on a bird):** The Australian pelican's bill can grow to 19 inches.

...**Alligator:** 19'2", found in Louisiana in 1890.

...**Migration route (bird):** The arctic tern, which flies from the Arctic to Antarctic and back again every year, travels about 24,980 miles.

...**Migration route (mammal):** The California gray whale travels up to 10,000 miles every year—from its summer feeding grounds along Alaska's coast to winter breeding grounds off Mexico's Baja California peninsula.

...**Life span (land animal):** The giant tortoise. Captain James Cook gave the oldest tortoise on record to the Tongan royal family in 1777. It died in 1965 at 188 years old.

...**Life span (birds):** The Laysan albatross can live for 42 years.

...**Time without water:** Giraffes can go several months without a drink.

The Sweet Life

It takes about 12 pounds of sugar beets to make one pound of sugar.

In 1890 the average American consumed five pounds of sugar per year. Today, it's about 140 pounds.

The sole ingredient of both rock candy and cotton candy: pure sugar, sometimes with coloring.

It takes three feet of sugarcane to fill a single-serving sugar packet.

Sugarcane not only provides 78 percent of the world's sugar supply, but it's also the source of a fiber called *bagasse* that's used in wallboard, plastics, and heating fuel.

A two-pound bag of sugar contains about 5 million individual grains.

The first person to add sugar to gum was a dentist: William Finley Semple, in 1869.

In 1893 sugar producers called in a few favors and got the U.S. military to help them overthrow Lili'uokalani, the last queen of Hawaii.

Brown sugar isn't a healthier, more natural, or less refined sugar. It's just white sugar with a little molasses mixed in.

Very Hungry Caterpillars

Caterpillars hardly ever sleep. It gets in the way of their eating, which is how they spend nearly every minute of their active life.

Caterpillars have mouths, but moths and butterflies don't. (They have a proboscis for sniffing up moisture instead.)

Moths don't eat clothes—their caterpillars do.

It takes about 2,000 to 3,000 silkworm cocoons to make a pound of silk. The caterpillars inside are usually killed.

A silkworm wraps itself in one long thread of silk from its salivary glands. That thread can measure a mile long.

Caterpillar feces is a major find for the fungus grower ants of Central and South America. They gather the droppings to grow mushrooms in huge underground chambers.

There are more than 1,000 species of Eupithecia caterpillars worldwide, and all were thought to be vegetarians. That was until scientists took a good look at the species in Hawaii and discovered that 15 of them gobble down other bugs...including other Eupithecia caterpillars.

A caterpillar has three times as many muscles as a human: about 2,000 to a human's 650.

"Peyote" came from the Aztec word *peyutl*. That means "caterpillar's cocoon," which may refer to the woolly white tufts on a cactus.

Caterpillar means "hairy cat" in Old French.

Silkworms, domesticated at least 5,000 years ago, no longer occur in the wild. Over the years, their moths have lost the ability to fly and have become dependent on humans.

Unfamiliar Circles

The small town of Circle, Alaska, got its name from gold miners, who christened the town in 1893 and believed that they sat squarely on the Arctic Circle. They were wrong, though—the circle that inspired the name lies 50 miles north.

The ring for a sumo match consists of a 15-foot circle made of rice-straw bales. The goal is to stay on your feet and inside the circle while muscling the other wrestler down or out.

The oldest existing letter in the English alphabet is O.

If you drew a circle around the equator and another around the poles, the equatorial circle would be 68 miles larger.

The classic monk haircut—which involves shaving the top of the head so that a near-perfect halo of hair encircles the cleared area—is called a "tonsure." It's long been a symbol of humility…or sometimes humiliation. In the ancient Byzantine empire, deposed kings and their sons were tonsured, and, as if a bad haircut weren't enough, castrated.

Circuses are usually performed in one, two, or three rings because the word *circus* meant "circle" in Latin.

What's Your Eke Name?

The term "eke name" in early English meant "additional name." It eventually morphed into "nickname."

In 1896 Leo Hirshfield named his chewy chocolate rolls after his daughter, whose nickname was "Tootsie."

Writer Thomas Lanier "Tennessee" Williams wasn't from Tennessee. He was born in Mississippi, but he chose "Tennessee" as a nickname because his father was from there.

Q: Who nicknamed Conan O'Brien "Coco"? A: Tom Hanks.

As a child, Brazilian soccer player Edson Arantes do Nacimento hated being called by the nickname Pelé.

Virginia Woolf's childhood nickname was "Goat" because, her brothers claimed, she was eccentric and "prone to accidents."

World War I ace the Red Baron wasn't really a baron. Manfred von Richthofen was called that only by his enemies. The Germans called him *Der Rote Kampfflieger* ("the Red Battle Flyer").

Albert Einstein was so slow to learn to talk that his family's maid called him "the dopey one."

When nerdy Tiger Woods played on Stanford University's golf team, he picked up a new nickname: "Urkel," after the accordion-playing nerd on TV's *Family Matters*.

Ancient Greek philosopher Diogenes of Sinope chose to live on the streets and ignore societal norms (like hygiene and good manners), so people nicknamed him "the Dog." In Greek, *kunikos* means "doglike," and his followers became known as "cynics."

Charles Dickens nicknamed his wife "Dearest Darling Pig."

Where Love Means Nothing

Someone invented tennis in France, during the 12th century. It was called *jeu de paume*, or "game of the palm," because you played it like handball. Later, when racquets were added, the game got a new name: *tenetz* ("get and hold").

Although the French invented tennis, the British refined it into the game we know today.

According to the Oxford Dictionary, the term "love" (meaning zero points) is probably short for "to play for love of the game" instead of for a reward.

An official tennis rule: "The racquets must not provide any kind of communication, instruction, or advice to the player during the match."

Between 1908 and 1960, tennis rules said that a server had to keep one foot on the ground at all times.

Tennis ball felt is usually made of wool.

When dropped onto concrete from a height of 100 feet a regulation tennis ball must bounce 53 to 58 inches.

Tennis balls are fuzzy to slow down the game. The fuzz increases wind resistance, reduces bounce, and grips the racquet strings slightly for ball control.

In Vino Veritas

Red wine has about 25 calories per ounce.

One ton of grapes will make 160 gallons of wine.

California's first winemakers were Spanish missionaries.

French chemist Louis Pasteur first developed pasteurization to preserve wine.

Historians say that the *Mayflower* had a sweet, sticky smell from transporting wine.

It can take up to two years to remove all the solid impurities (grape skins, dead yeast cells, and other debris) from wine. This step, called "racking," consists of draining out the gunk at the bottom of the barrel every now and again.

What's a vineroon? It's another name for a winemaker.

A standard oak barrel holds enough wine to fill about 300 bottles.

Stomping grapes for wine may *look* fun, but it was exhausting and could be dangerous. Grape skins are slippery, and the juice gives off carbon dioxide. Grape stompers sometimes died of asphyxiation... or fell and drowned.

A Space Odyssey

Food on the space station comes from plastic or foil packages and requires no cooking. That saves energy, which comes from solar panels.

Spacecraft from Earth sometimes bring fresh fruit and vegetables.

Urine is collected, purified, and recycled into drinking water.

Solid waste is collected in individual plastic bags and stored for transfer back to Earth. This is an improvement over previous space stations where hundreds of bags of excrement were jettisoned into space and still orbit Earth to this day.

The International Space Station has wi-fi.

Crews are typically made up of six members, each staying about six months, with arrival and departure times staggered.

Crews bathe with wet wipes, a water jet, rinse-less shampoo, and soap from a toothpastelike tube. Toothpaste is edible to save water.

Sleeping quarters have to be well-ventilated with fans or else a bubble of carbon dioxide forms around the sleeper's head, causing oxygen deprivation.

Foot Notes

Your feet contain about a quarter of the bones in your body.

Scientists have found 350,000-year-old fossilized human footprints.

Saint Servatus is the patron saint of people suffering from foot injuries. (He's also the guy who protects us from rats.)

Aristotle believed that going barefoot diminished the libido.

That numbness when your foot goes to sleep is called "obdormition."

On average, your feet hit the floor 7,000 times a day.

Paris Hilton's feet are so big (size 11) that she has designers custom-make her shoes.

What is "epidermophytosis"? That's the technical name for athlete's foot.

Food of the Gods

Chocolate comes from the cacao tree, *Theobroma cacao*. It's a fitting name because *theobroma* comes from the Latin words for "food of the gods."

Mayan emperors were often buried with jars of chocolate. The average American consumes approximately 11.7 pounds of chocolate each year, but only 29 percent choose dark chocolate over milk.

Chocolate comes from the ivory-colored seeds of the cocoa tree's fruit. Each melonlike fruit contains 20 to 50 seeds. About 400 seeds are required to make a pound of chocolate.

In 1974 a Pepperidge Farm employee in a Downington, Pennsylvania, plant died after falling into a vat of chocolate. His name: Robert C. Hershey.

The chemical theobromine is what makes chocolate fatal to pets—many animals don't metabolize it well. Generally, the darker the chocolate, the more theobromine.

People who are depressed eat about 55 percent more chocolate than people who aren't.

The Mars Candy Company is not named for the planet, but for its founder, Frank Mars.

Cocoa butter liquefies at a temperature slightly below 98.6°F, which is why it melts in your pocket. M&Ms were invented to provide sugar shells that had a higher melting temperature.

The Aztecs discovered and named *chocolatl*, but they used it as a beverage for its feel-good effects, not its flavor. In fact, *chocolatl* meant "bitter water."

British candy maker Cadbury made the world's first heart-shaped box of chocolates in 1861.

White chocolate has all the fat and sugar of chocolate, but none of the healthy flavonoids…and no solid cocoa. It does contain cocoa butter, though.

In 2004 interviewers asked British office workers if they would reveal their computer passwords in exchange for a chocolate bar—71 percent said they would.

Cocoa usually starts losing flavor after about six months.

Kid Stuff

Saint Sebastian is the patron saint of unruly children.

According to Crayola, American children between the ages of two and eight spend 28 minutes a day coloring.

Worldwide, the average child receives $32 worth of toys per year. The average American kid: $328.

Two out of three people admit that they had imaginary friends when they were little.

Unintentional consequence of those "this is your brain on drugs" commercials: some young kids refused to eat fried eggs, fearing that they were laced with drugs.

"You have 'em, I'll amuse 'em." That's what Theodor Geisel (Dr. Seuss) said about being a parent. He never had any kids of his own.

Thomas Edison burned down his father's barn when he was six, "just to see what it would do."

Each year, the average American child eats more than 15 pounds of cold cereal.

One in 200 kids is a vegetarian.

70 percent of American daycare centers use TV to keep the kids entertained.

On average, American parents spend twice as much time in their cars as with their kids.

One in three British kids says their mum prefers the cat to their dad.

Children need twice as much oxygen as people over 80.

John Locke help mold the modern world's view of human rights, but his essay "Some Thoughts Concerning Education," published in 1690, suggested bathing kids in cold water, dressing them in thin-soled shoes (so that healthy water can leak in), and quenching their thirst with beer.

Reflect on This

The Mesopotamians figured out how to make glass in about 3500 BC.

Specialized workers who add layers of color to clear glass are called "flashers."

Most car safety-glass windshields block up to 97 percent of UV rays.

In the 1880s, doctors made the first glass contact lens. It was designed for somebody who'd had an eyelid removed, and it covered the whole eye.

Ben Franklin invented bifocals by cutting his two sets of glasses in half and gluing the mismatched pieces together.

The energy saved from recycling a glass bottle could power a lightbulb for four hours. Otherwise, a glass bottle can take as long as 4,000 years to decompose.

The New York Botanical Garden has the world's largest Victorian greenhouse.

Window glass slows the speed of light by about 66,000 miles per second.

The oldest surviving stained-glass windows are in Germany's Augsburg Cathedral, built in the 12th century.

Going Postal

The first permanent airmail routes began on May 15, 1918, when U.S. Army pilots started shuttling mail between New York City, Philadelphia, and Washington, DC.

Sending packages through the mail—known as Parcel Post—was new in 1913, and it was fast and cheap. People sent produce, eggs, tobacco, and even live animals. Then, in 1914, the parents of five-year-old May Pierstorff mailed her 75 miles across Idaho to her grandparents' house. (Her postage totaled 53¢.) Other parents started doing the same thing, so in 1920 the postal service forbade mailing kids.

In 1916 Will Coltharp of Vernal, Utah, sent an entire bank building's worth of bricks (80,000) through the mail in 50-pound increments (the heaviest package the postal service would accept). At the time, freight charges for the bricks cost four times *more* than Parcel Post.

William Faulkner once worked as the postmaster of Oxford, Mississippi.

Q. What is the busiest mailing day in the United States?
A. December 14—mail volume nearly doubles.

The only U.S. town where mail arrives by mule: Supai, Arizona, on the floor of the Grand Canyon.

Theodore Hook of London sent the first postcard in 1840. It was a picture he drew himself...and sent to himself.

The U.S. Postal Service processes about 39.7 million address changes a year.

When the postal service came up with ZIP codes in 1963, people thought it had to do with zipping mail along. Actually, though, ZIP is an acronym for Zone Improvement Plan, which divided up regions to help mail be sorted efficiently.

Kid Lit

About 10 percent of all books published each year are aimed at children.

In 1999 *Harry Potter and the Sorcerer's Stone* became the first children's book to top the *New York Times* best-seller list in more than 40 years.

Advice from the first etiquette book written for children, *On Civility in Children* by Desiderius Erasmus, 1530: "Do not move back and forth on your chair. Whoever does that gives the impression of constantly breaking or trying to break wind."

Not all the Winnie-the-Pooh characters were based on Christopher Robin Milne's stuffed animals. Owl and Rabbit were based on live animals often seen in the woods behind the Milne family home.

The word "nerd" first appeared in *If I Ran the Zoo* by Dr. Seuss.

Hugh Lofting's *Story of Doctor Doolittle* inspired a very young Stephen King to become a writer.

Dr. Seuss got this rejection note about his book, *To Think That I Saw It On Mulberry Street*: "It's too different from other juvenile [books] on the market to warrant selling."

In 2001, 84 percent of American children were read to frequently by a family member.

The Eiffel Tower

The tower was controversial from the start. Three hundred artists and architects publicly objected to its design and the fact that it looked "like a gigantic black smokestack."

The Eiffel Tower was originally designed as a temporary entrance arch for the 1889 World's Fair.

Postcard historians credit the Eiffel Tower (and the tourists amazed by it at the fair) with making picture postcards popular in France.

After the Germans captured Paris during World War II, French rebels sabotaged the Eiffel Tower's elevators before a visit by Adolf Hitler, forcing him to climb the stairs. The elevators remained "broken" for the rest of the war.

For 41 years, the Eiffel Tower was the tallest structure in the world. It was surpassed by New York City's Chrysler Building in 1930…and by lots of other buildings since.

In 1925 a con man named Victor Lustig created an apparently convincing story and "sold" the Eiffel Tower to two different scrap metal dealers. Needless to say, when the men arrived with heavy machinery to dismantle their prize, they discovered that they'd been had.

Author Guy de Maupassant hated the tower so much that he ate lunch in its restaurant every day because, he said, it was the one place in Paris where he didn't have to look at the structure.

General and detailed drawings for the tower's 18,038 parts required a third of an acre of drafting paper.

More than 7 million people a year pay about $11 to go up the tower.

Just Plane Tragic

THE RED BARON

When: 1918
Where: Vaux-sur-Somme, France
The bane of Allied aircraft, Manfred "the Red Baron" von Richthofen was a flying ace credited with at least 80 air-combat victories during World War I. But he who lives by the warplane will likely die by the warplane. Richthofen's luck ran out with a single bullet fired from the ground. It pierced his heart and lungs, but he was still able to land his plane. According to the Australian soldiers who arrived on the scene, his last word before he died was "Kaputt!"

WILL ROGERS

When: 1935
Where: Near Point Barrow, Alaska
"I ain't got anything funny to say. All I know is what I read in the papers," was how humorist Will Rogers usually began his comedy routines. In the early 1900s, Rogers was the Jon Stewart of his day, making people laugh with off-the-cuff topical humor about the news, world leaders, politicians, gangsters, and masters of industry. He appeared in 71 movies, wrote more than 4,000 newspaper columns, and was a beloved performer on stage and radio. He even wrote his own epitaph—"I never met a man I didn't like"—and on August 15, 1935, got the chance to use it. While flying through Alaska on a plane piloted by Wiley Post (the first aviator to fly around the world solo), an engine failed. The plane plowed into a shallow lagoon. Both men died.

AMELIA EARHART

When: 1937
Where: Somewhere in the Pacific Ocean
Amelia Earhart was a rebel from the start. Growing up in the early 1900s, she climbed trees, hunted rats, and made a point to defy the gender restrictions of her time. She flew her first plane in 1921, and when she was recruited in 1928 to join a team flying across the Atlantic Ocean, making her the first woman to complete that flight, she jumped at the chance.

Nine years later, she took on another challenge: being the first woman to fly around the world. It was a huge undertaking, 29,000 miles in all, but she set off from Miami on June 1, 1937. Twenty-eight days later, she and her navigator Fred Noonan landed in New Guinea with just 7,000 miles left to go. They never made it to their next stop: Howland Island, a tiny bit of land in the giant Pacific Ocean. Amid bad weather and low fuel, Earhart's plane disappeared over the ocean. A rescue effort launched by the U.S. Coast Guard was the largest in history, but after more than two weeks of scouring the open ocean, the government called off the search, declaring that Earhart, Noonan, and their plane had been lost.

Amelia Earhart's disappearance became one of the biggest mysteries in history, and professional and amateur archaeologists spent the next 70 years searching for her plane. Finally, in May 2013, an aircraft preservation group announced that it had sonar images of the ocean floor showing what it believed to be the remains of Earhart's plane. The location: About 1,800 miles south of Hawaii, near Nikumaroro, a small island in the western Pacific that's nearly 350 miles from Howland Island.

YURI GAGARIN
When: 1968
Where: Near Kirzhach, Russia
In 1961, Soviet fighter pilot Yuri Gagarin was selected for a trip to outer space, mainly because at 5'1", he could fit into the cramped cockpit of the tiny *Vostolk 1* spacecraft. (Also, he was already an accomplished flyer and military man.) On April 12, he made the trip, becoming the first human to orbit Earth. That successful flight made him famous, and as a Soviet space hero, his country banned him from participating in future space flights because they feared a plunge in public morale if he died. So Gagarin went back to the Soviet air force. That proved to be a fatal mistake. In 1968, during refresher training in a MiG, he and his flight instructor entered a spin and crashed. Both men died.

THE OLD CHRISTIANS RUGBY TEAM
When: 1972
Where: The border of Chile and Argentina
In October 1972, the plane carrying the Old Christians rugby team from Uruguay crashed in the Andes Mountains en route to a match

in Chile. Twenty-five of the 45 people on board survived the crash…
and then were stranded in the freezing mountain wilderness for 10
weeks before help arrived. Another eight people died from starvation
and cold.

While on the mountain, after exploring all other alternatives
and nearing starving, the survivors reluctantly succumbed to
cannibalism, eating the frozen bodies of the people who had died.
Their story was immortalized in the 1993 movie, *Alive*.

*   *   *

DID YOU KNOW?

- The Hells Angels motorcycle club took its name from the crew
  of a World War II bomber squadron , the *Flying Fortress* Hell's
  Angels. (The crew got its name from 1930 movie.)

- Unlike most mammals, camels don't have a constant body temperature. Their bodies fluctuate from 94.1°F to 104°F, depending
  on the temperature outside. A camel doesn't even start perspiring
  until its body temperature reaches about 107°F.

- Since 1889, Cornell University has had a tradition of asking
  professors to donate their brains after death. Not many of the professors do it anymore, but in the late 19th century, the program's
  heyday, the school had 1,200 brains in its collection.

- About two of every three U.S. dollars have circulated outside of
  U.S. borders.

- The Moon's gravity affects everything from the tides to temperatures and storms all over the world. Without it, Earth's climate
  would be so volatile that the planet would be uninhabitable.

- Despite legends, nobody knocked the nose off of Egypt's Great
  Sphinx of Giza. Carved out of sandstone, the statue has eroded
  from water and wind-borne sand over the years. Its nose, being
  the thinnest part, disappeared first.

Birds Do It...
Bees Do It

Beavers, some penguin species, and geese mate for life.

The only mammals that lay eggs are the platypus and the echidna.

Ant queens never leave the ground except to mate once. They fly in the air and mate with males. When they come back, they're grounded for good: queens even pull off their own wings.

Lobsters can mate only when females molt and shed their shells, which they do every two years, leaving them naked and defenseless. Males protect the females in their lairs for one week until the new shells come in.

Mating mosquitoes synchronize their wing beats.

Walruses mate in the water—males float patiently near ice floes, waiting for a female to dive in.

Female kangaroos don't get pregnant during droughts.

When the female hornbill is nesting, she and her mate seal her up in a hollow tree trunk with mud, chewed food, and their own droppings, leaving a small hole to feed her through. That's to protect her from snakes and monkeys. When the eggs hatch, she breaks out and reseals her chicks inside the tree trunk, allowing both parents to hunt food for their young.

Male porcupines get into fierce battles over females—the winner chooses his prospective mate by urinating on her.

*   *   *

The guillotine got its name from French physician Joseph-Ignace Guillotin, who promoted it as being a more humane way of beheading than the traditional axe method.

Cat Haters

IVAN THE TERRIBLE
Claim to fame: Czar of Russia from 1547 to 1584

Sixteenth-century Russian czar Ivan IV Vasilyevich ("the Terrible"), was known for his rage-filled outbursts, including one in which he killed his eldest son. In childhood, the story goes, he liked to toss cats off of high balconies and out windows, simply for sport.

AMBROSE BIERCE
Claim to fame: Author and satirist

Ambrose Bierce's *The Devil's Dictionary* defines "cat" as "a soft indestructible automaton provided by nature to be kicked when things go wrong in the domestic circle."

NOAH WEBSTER
Claim to fame: Word enthusiast and dictionary writer

Webster was a closet cat hater. No stories exist of him kicking a cat, but an entry in his second dictionary belies a deep-seated mistrust. Ascribing wicked intentions to normal cat behavior, he defined "cat" thusly: "The domestic cat is a deceitful animal and when enraged extremely spiteful."

SIR WALTER SCOTT
Claim to fame: 18th and 19th century novelist and poet

In Sir Walter Scott's defense, he ended life as a cat lover, but he wasn't always that way. He wrote, "The greatest advance of age which I have yet found is liking a cat, an animal which I detested, and becoming fond of a garden, an art which I despised."

DWIGHT D. EISENHOWER
Claim to fame: Five-star General and 34th U.S. president

Dwight Eisenhower hated cats so much, he ordered that any cat found wandering onto his Gettysburg farm be shot on the spot.

GEORGES LOUIS LECLERC DE BUFFON

Claim to fame: 18th-century naturalist

Leclerc de Buffon had a special place in his heart for many animals, but he seemed to believe the cat held some sort of deliberately evil intent. He wrote that felines had "an innate malice and perverse disposition which increases as they grow up" and that they "easily assume the habits of society, but never acquire its manners."

PIERRE DE RONSARD

Claim to fame: 16th-century French poet

Pierre de Ronsard may be the poet laureate of cat haters. As evidence, all we need to do is point to a translation of the poet's own words:

> *There is no man now living anywhere*
> *Who hates cats with a deeper hate than I;*
> *I hate their eyes, their heads, the way they stare,*
> *And when I see one come, I turn and fly.*

*　　*　　*

ROCKET SCIENCE

By the early 1800s, rockets were all the rage, and Italian tinkerer Claude Ruggieri turned his attention toward creating a rocket that could launch people into the air. The rockets of the time were too small by themselves, but Ruggieri imagined a "rocket necklace"—clusters of rockets attached to a metal chamber that all went off at the same time. In 1806 in Paris, Ruggieri launched a sheep 600 feet into the air and landed it safely using a parachute. But then he went too far: When the French government learned that Ruggieri was planning to send up a small child next, it immediately stopped his experiments.

The Witches of Stalingrad

IT HAPPENED ONE DARK NIGHT...

Imagine you're a German soldier, fighting your way deep into the Soviet Union during the summer of 1942. During the time you're not actually on the front lines, you feel pretty safe and get a chance to rest, let down your guard, even sleep a full night without constant vigilance. After all, the Soviet army is retreating fast, and you're just 19 miles from Moscow.

Still, you can't relax completely. There have been whispered rumors of *nachthexen*, "night witches" who fly silently after dark and drop bombs into previously safe areas, destroying military targets and fraying nerves. You don't completely believe it, but like a lot of rumors, you wonder if there's likely some grain of a truth.

Then, while on guard duty one night, you hear a rustling sound above, almost like wind through a broomstick. Before you can investigate, the darkness lights up with a blinding flash and a deafening explosion. The Night Witches have struck again!

TOIL AND TROUBLE

By 1942, the Soviet armed forces were reeling. Millions of men had been killed defending their homeland, often with antique rifles and inadequate defenses. Three million more had been taken prisoner. What to do? Well, there were always the women. Already working in fields and factories, some Soviet women were recruited as pilots, mechanics, navigators, and officers of a new all-female unit, the 588th Night Bomber Regiment. They were assigned to hit specific German military targets and to scare its forces with unpredictable, random attacks.

Some in the Soviet air force was resistant to the idea. The "bomber" planes that the women were given to do the job seemed absurdly inadequate: obsolete biplanes made in 1928 of wood and canvas and designed for crop dusting and training. Each plane could carry only two 220-pound bombs. And they were slow—with a top speed of 97 mph—and so flammable that they could ignite if hit by flares or tracer bullets. The planes' tiny engines were also noisy and tended to stall easily, requiring the pilot to climb out and turn the propeller by hand to get it started again. And because they flew so low, the women weren't issued parachutes, which just added weight and wouldn't open in time anyway. And radios? Forget about it. The women navigated in the dark using a map, penlight, compass, and stopwatch to figure out where they were.

WITCHY WOMEN

The female flyers, all between the ages of 17 and 26, turned most of these serious drawbacks into virtues. Their top speed was slower than the stall speed of German fighters, so if the female pilots maneuvered into sudden dives or tight turns, the little planes were hard to shoot down. Their low-altitude and wood-and-canvas construction also didn't normally make a blip on radar. And the women's skill at restarting their planes' noisy little engines inspired the best tactic they could use against German antiaircraft defenses: The women would increase altitude until they came close to their well-defended targets, and then cut their engines and glide, making little noise beyond a light rustling until they released their payload. As the bombs exploded, the pilot would restart the engine and hightail it out of there, just barely above the Germans on the ground. And so the "Night Witches" became a nickname that the 588th borrowed proudly from their enemy.

BURN THE WITCH!

German fighter pilots mostly gave up trying to catch the Night Witches, but ground troops redoubled their efforts. The flimsy Russian planes often came back riddled with bullets from ground fire. (After a particularly harrowing raid, one pilot counted 42 new bullet holes in her plane.) The Germans also developed a new tactic, setting up a circle of hidden antiaircraft guns and spotlights around likely targets. Knowing that the Witches flew in two-plane formations, the spotlight operators tracked them across the sky while the antiaircraft guns ripped the flimsy aircraft into pieces.

In response, the 588th added a third plane behind the other two. As soon as the spotlights hit the first planes, they'd pretend to give up on bombing the target, splitting off in opposite directions while the spotlight operators scrambled to follow them. Meanwhile, the third plane glided in to deliver its load. At the next two targets, they'd switch places until all three planes had dropped their bombs.

From 1942 until the war's end in 1945, the 40 two-person crews flew more than 30,000 missions, sometimes as many as 18 in a single night. By the end of the war, they'd dropped 23,000 tons of bombs. Twenty-three of the Witches earned the Hero of the Soviet Union medal (the highest honor available), and about 30 died in combat.

* * *

HISTORY'S DEADLIEST VOLCANIC ERUPTIONS

1. Mount Tambora, Indonesia
When: April 1815
Killed: 90,000

2. Krakatoa, Indonesia
When: August 1883
Killed: 36,000

3. Mount Pelée, Martinique
When: May 1902
Killed: 30,000

4. Nevado del Ruiz, Colombia
When: November 1985
Killed: 25,000

Whales...

...have earwax.

...have a blowhole instead of nostrils.

...suck in about 525 gallons of air with each breath.

...have tails that move up and down; fish tails move from side to side.

...are the biggest creatures in the ocean, but most feed on some of the smallest: plankton.

...usually have single births, and pregnancy lasts anywhere from 9 to 16 months.

...are protected by the U.S. government. Bothering a whale in American waters nets a federal fine of $10,000.

...sing songs. The songs of blue whales can last as long as 30 minutes and can travel more than 100 miles.

...have no vocal cords. They probably sing their songs by circulating air through the tubes and chambers of their respiratory system.

The Piano Is My Forte

Originally, the piano was called the pianoforte, before people shortened its name. (*Forte* means "play loudly" in Italian.)

Italian harpsichord maker Bartolomeo Cristofori built the first piano sometime before 1700.

When Johann Sebastian Bach first heard a piano around 1726, he didn't like it. But by 1747, Bach was playing one, composing with it, and selling pianos to fellow musicians.

Some early pianos reversed which keys were white and black, making the sharps and flats white, and the main keys black.

Modern pianos have 18 more keys than the pianos used by Beethoven.

A piano's total string tension can exceed 20 tons.

Sting wrote the Police hit song "Every Breath You Take" on Noel Coward's piano.

Pounding the keys of a piano can knock it out of tune.

The Write Stuff

The best-selling fiction author of all time is William Shakespeare. #2: Agatha Christie.

Writer Lewis Carroll coined the word "chortle." It means a cross between a chuckle and a snort.

It took author J. R. R. Tolkien 12 years to write the Lord of the Rings trilogy.

Author Norman Mailer claimed to have invented thumb wrestling.

Novelist F. Scott Fitzgerald was born Francis Scott Key Fitzgerald. The name was meant as a tribute to his second cousin three times removed, who was the composer of "The Star Spangled Banner."

What did the initials in e. e. cummings's name stand for? "Edward Estlin." (Or "edward estlin," if you prefer.)

In 1901 author Jack London ran for mayor of Oakland, California, on the Socialist ticket. He got just 245 votes and beat only the Prohibitionist candidate (60 votes).

After almost being killed by a minivan in 1999, author Stephen King bought the vehicle and beat it with a baseball bat.

Dr. Seuss didn't become a real doctor until 1955 when Dartmouth University gave him an honorary degree.

Louisa May Alcott was on a committee that banned *Huckleberry Finn* from the Concord Library in Massachusetts. Of the book and its famous author, she said, "If Mr. Clemens cannot think of something better to tell our pure-minded lads and lasses, he had best stop writing for them."

* * *

By the time actor Steve McQueen died, he had collected 210 motorcycles.

The Average...

...**American** walks about 2.5 miles a day. (The health community recommends doubling that.)

...**person's cholesterol level** in China: 127. In America: 200.

...**Hell's Angels biker** will ride about 20,000 miles this year.

...**person** speaks about 165 words per minute.

... **American worker** admits to wasting two hours of work time on the Internet each day.

...**American CEO** earns more in one workday than the average worker earns all year.

...**woman** spends one week per year looking in mirrors.

...**American** used five gallons of water a day in 1900. In 2013: 100 gallons.

...**person** has a vocabulary of 20,000 words.

...**woman** apologizes 5.2 times per day; man, 3.6 times a day.

...**person** takes 32 seconds to pull out of a parking space.

...**adult** is exposed to 100 chemicals a day...just by using personal care products.

...**American** eats twice as much protein as the human body needs.

...**Facebook user** has 130 "friends."

Pipe Up

A typical church organ has hundreds of pipes. The world's largest, in Atlantic City's Convention Hall, uses 33,112 pipes.

The earliest pipe organ comes from the third century BC.

Early organs used water to power them, but that changed in the mid-1800s when steam, gasoline, and eventually electricity took over.

The organ pipes used for bass notes take up a lot of space. Some newer pipe organs, called hybrids, "cheat" by using traditional pipes for most notes, but generate the lower tones electronically to save money and space.

Organ makers often add "facade" pipes that don't make a sound, but look nice. Most of the pipes of an organ are hidden behind the ones you can see. Some are less than an inch long.

Warmer temperatures than normal will make an organ go slightly sharp; colder temps make it slightly flat.

Dead at 27

Rock 'n' roll is a dangerous business…and a superstitious one.
All of these stars died at the age of 27.

Janis Joplin

Jimi Hendrix

Jim Morrison

Robert Johnson

Amy Winehouse

Dave Alexander (The Stooges)

Ron "Pigpen" McKernan (Grateful Dead)

Alan "Blind Owl" Wilson (Canned Heat)

Pete de Freitas (Echo and the Bunnymen)

Malcolm Hale (Spanky and Our Gang)

Jeremy Ward (The Mars Volta)

Brian Jones (Rolling Stones)

Kurt Cobain (Nirvana)

Pete Ham (Badfinger)

Kristen Pfaff (Hole)

Rudy Lewis (Drifters)

Freaky Tah (Lost Boyz)

Gary Thain (Uriah Heep)

Bloodsuckers

There are more than 3,500 species of mosquitoes. Only a couple hundred bite people.

It would require 1.12 million mosquito bites to completely drain your blood.

Only female mosquitoes bite. They need blood to lay viable eggs. Male mosquitoes live on flower nectar.

Citronella, catnip, rosemary, lemon oil, eucalyptus oil, and marigold all have a reputation for repelling mosquitoes. They don't exactly keep the bugs away, but they mask the smell of carbon dioxide, rendering humans invisible to the pests. Mosquitoes find us by smelling our exhaled breath, so if you can confuse them with scents, you're less likely to get bitten.

The best way to avoid mosquitoes is by draining any standing water, no matter how small, every week. That includes birdbaths, kid's pools, tree holes, rainwater drains, and even little-used drains in and around your house. Mosquito larvae need to live 7 to 14 days in water.

Mosquitoes normally travel no more than half a mile from their point of origin.

A mosquito's wings beat 300 to 600 times per second.

Unsung Space Travelers

FRUIT FLIES

The first travelers in space were not humans, dogs, apes, or monkeys, but plain, everyday fruit flies. In 1947, at the beginning of the space race, the United States launched a V-2 rocket carrying seeds and fruit flies from White Sands, New Mexico, in an effort to study the effects of radiation beyond the Earth's atmosphere. The rocket went up 68 miles to the edge of outer space. Then the capsule detached, the parachute engaged, and the capsule fell back to Earth. The bugs and seeds survived the journey.

IBERIAN RIBBED NEWTS

In 1985 Soviet scientists operated on 10 newts, amputating one of their front limbs and an eye lens before launching them into space. Why would they do such a thing? The Soviets wanted to know if the missing limbs would regenerate in zero gravity in the same way they regenerated on Earth. In fact, the newts healed significantly faster when in space than similarly amputated control groups back on Earth.

ROUNDWORMS

When the space shuttle *Columbia* disintegrated over Texas in 2003, its seven crew members died. So did the silkworms, garden orb spiders, carpenter bees, Japanese killifish, and harvester ants that had been on the shuttle with them as part of various experiments. The only known survivors were roundworms called nematodes that were found intact in the debris.

All Aboard!

Before steam engines, trains were pulled by horses or mules. But before that, they were powered people. The first railroad was built in Greece in the sixth century BC and was pushed along by slaves.

The shortest and steepest railroad in the U.S. is at Dubuque, Iowa. It rises at an incline of 60 degrees and is only 296 feet long.

The first coin-operated toilet was unveiled in a train station in Terre Haute, Indiana, in 1910. At that time, most people had never seen an indoor toilet and came to gawk, making it hard for travelers to actually use them.

Every July since 1979, thousands of people have gathered along the railroad tracks in Laguna Niguel, CA, and dropped their drawers for "Moon Amtrak Day."

In railroad lingo, to "buckle the rubbers" meant to connect the pneumatic air, steam, or signal hoses that ran between cars.

Two common phrases that began as railroad terms: "Making the grade" referred to getting to the top of a steep slope. And "getting sidetracked" meant moving trains or cars off the main track onto a short auxiliary track for loading, unloading, or temporary storage.

The hobby of trainspotting entails tallying every rail engine that you see. The champion of all time is England's Bill Curtis, who, over 40 years, "tracked" more than 85,000 different locomotives in 31 countries.

The first steam-powered railway was built in England in 1825.

India has the most railroad stations in the world: 7,083.

Tourists on trains stopping in Palisade, Nevada, in the 1870s often complained that the Wild West wasn't very wild. So the townspeople staged gunfights to make things more exciting.

Olympic Facts

The first U.S. city to host the Summer Olympics was St. Louis in 1904. In a scandalous turn of events, the apparent winner of the marathon, American Fred Lorz, was disqualified after riding in a car for most of the run.

Tug of war was an Olympic event from 1900 to 1920.

The oldest medalist was Oscar Gomer Swahn of Sweden, who won the 1920 "double-shots team running deer" shooting competition at age 72. The oldest female gold medalist was American Eliza Pollock, a 63-year-old who won at archery in 1904.

From 1968 to 2000, all female Olympic competitors were required to take a "gender verification exam." All except one: England's Princess Anne, who competed in an equestrian competition in 1976, got a royal exemption.

At first, the exams just required groups of women athletes to parade unclothed past medical experts who made sure they didn't have male genitalia. Eventually, the Olympics added a blood test for the male hormone androgen, since it is what is responsible for the increased size and muscle mass advantages in men.

The tests were needed, said Olympics officials, because men were cheating and competing as women to gain an unfair advantage. During the 1936, for example, German high jumper Dora Ratjen was revealed to be a man named Hermann Ratjen. He came in fourth. The very masculine "Press sisters" from Russia each won a gold medal in the 1960s. And North Korea's Sin Kim Dan broke records in sprinting at the 1964 Games...until "her" father recognized her as his long-missing son.

*　　*　　*

The temperature of the lit end of a cigarette when the smoker is inhaling is about 1,652°F.

Uncle John's Page of Lists

3 EARLY JAPANESE ANIME SHOWS ON AMERICAN TELEVISION
1. *Astro Boy*, 1963
2. *Gigantor*, 1966
3. *Kimba the White Lion*, 1966

2 BODY PARTS THAT PEOPLE HATE THE MOST
1. Thighs (women)
2. Rear (men)

5 EARLY VIDEO GAMES
1. Nim: a counting/math game, 1951
2. OXO: tic-tac-toe, 1952
3. Tennis for Two: like Pong, 1958
4. Mouse in a Maze: a labyrinth chase for cheese, 1959
5. Spacewar: two spaceships battling, 1961

2 REDUNDANT PLACE NAMES
1. Pago Pago
2. Walla Walla (Washington)

5 U.S. CITIES THAT PEOPLE SAY THEY MOST WANT TO MOVE TO
1. Denver, CO
2. San Diego, CA
3. Seattle, WA
4. Orlando, FL
5. Tampa, FL

6 CHILD ACTORS WHO BECAME MORE FAMOUS AS ADULTS
1. Ryan Gosling
2. Jason Bateman
3. Leonardo DiCaprio
4. Elizabeth Taylor
5. Neil Patrick Harris
6. Ron Howard

4 FOUNDING FATHERS WHO WERE FREEMASONS
1. George Washington
2. Benjamin Franklin
3. John Hancock
4. Paul Revere

THE 4 MOST-RECYCLED PRODUCTS IN THE U.S.
1. Asphalt (99%)
2. Steel (88%)
3. Paper (66%)
4. Aluminum cans (65%)

THE FIRST 4 *ROLLING STONE* MAGAZINE COVER IMAGES
1. John Lennon
2. Tina Turner
3. The Beatles
4. Jimi Hendrix, Donovan & Otis Redding

Annoying Musical Instruments

VUVUZELA

The facts:

The 2010 FIFA World Cup in South Africa brought the vuvuzela to the attention of the world. Loud enough to cause hearing loss, the long plastic horn typically plays a single tone in the hands of a novice. But you didn't even have to be in the soccer stadium to be annoyed by this instrument—TV viewers also complained about the continuous buzz coming from their screens.

- A vuvuzela can generate 144 decibels of sound. The U.S. National Institute for Occupational Safety and Heath recommends that the maximum exposure to a sound at 100 decibels be less than 15 minutes a day.

- Besides causing ear pain, a study by a British doctor found that the instrument also launched microparticles of saliva that can stay suspended in the air for hours, making it a near-perfect mechanism for spreading colds and flu.

- Since the 2010 World Cup, many sports events and venues have banned the horns.

Why it deserves (at least a little) respect:

- Some South Africans consider vuvuzelas to be a symbol of national pride.

- They can be the sound of freedom. Vuvuzelas were used in several demonstrations in 2010: against British Petroleum's headquarters in London after its massive oil spill in the Gulf of Mexico, and in Wisconsin against Governor Scott Walker's antiunion laws.

- Since a vuvuzela is essentially a bugle without curves, brass, or a purity of tone, skilled players can wrestle harmonic tones out of a vuvuzela, making it possible to play "Taps," "Reveille," and other bugle calls.

JEW'S HARP

The facts:

The only thing harplike about the Jew's harp is that you pluck it. This small metal instrument includes a reed that players hold against their lips and pluck. It's got a metallic wang-wanga-wanga sound—sometimes heard on world music or really old country and bluegrass records—and changes in pitch come from moving your mouth, opening your throat passage, and altering your breathing slightly.

There are lots of theories about why it's called a Jew's harp, but no one is really sure where the name comes from. Some say it came from "jaw harp" or the French word *jeu* ("toy") or the Dutch name *jeugd* ("youth") harp.

Why it deserves (at least a little) respect:

- Some historians claim it's the oldest non-drum instrument in the world, with pictorial evidence from a Chinese drawing from the fourth century BC.

- It's one of the few instruments that uses a person's skull, cheeks, and head cavity as its sounding board, amplifier, and pitch changer.

- Between 1769 and 1771, composer Johann Albrechtsberger wrote at least seven concertos for Jew's harps and strings, of which only three are still known to exist.

- Twelve Jew's harps were included among the gifts explorers Meriwether Lewis and William Clark brought to make peace with Native Americans as they traveled across America from 1804 to 1806.

ACCORDION

The facts:

The squeezebox had a heyday during first half of the 1900s, but these days, it's most often scorned as a fixture of polka and zydeco bands or Lawrence Welk types in bowties. True, goofball Weird Al Yankovic and the band They Might Be Giants have used accordions since the 1990s, but they were generally being sarcastic.

Despite its pariah status, a small corps of accordion lovers still carry on the tradition, gathering in annual conventions all over the world. In 1998 several hundred accordionists gathered in Menlo Park, California, to try to break the world record for most accordions playing "Lady of Spain" at one time. Unfortunately, the Guinness World Records ultimately declared that there weren't enough players to warrant a world record.

Why it deserves (at least a little) respect:
- The instrument's design is pretty interesting. Invented in Vienna, Austria, in the early 1800s, the accordion has evolved into a bellows that can play notes while blowing either in our out. Using a bellows was a good decision, because the other options to create that kind of sound had limitations: Multiple reeds playing at the same time would have required either a mechanical pump or a dangerously hyperventilated player, for example. And a foot pump (or an electric air pump, which hadn't been invented yet) would have destroyed the player's ability to stand, walk, and wander around while playing. The lucky result is that accordionists can deftly manipulate the speed and force of the hand-powered bellows, giving emphasis and oomph to certain notes, while smoothing and quieting others.
- The flashy keyboarding of the player's right hand is what most people notice, but the left hand is doing a lot of work. It's not only pushing the bellows, but quietly pressing a bank of 120 buttons, each of which plays a complete chord.

*   *   *

WHY'S IT CALLED "STARBOARD"?

Blame the Vikings. Their ships' rudders were on the right side, so that became known as *styrbord* (steer side). They called the left side *larbord* (loading side). The two names sounded enough alike to cause lots of confusion, though, so the British jettisoned "larboard" for "port." That term came from the fact that sailors docked their ships on the left side at ports so as to prevent the rudders or steering oars (which were on the right sides) from being crushed.

Who's Your Daddy?

The ancient Greeks believed that orchid roots could determine a child's gender. Prospective dads ate large orchid roots if they wanted a boy; moms ate small ones for a girl.

John Wilkes Booth's father once sent a death threat to President Andrew Jackson.

A McGill University study found that kids who grow up having frequent interactions with their dads develop more empathy for others.

In ancient Rome, a father or husband had the right to sell any member of his family into slavery.

Younger fathers have a higher proportion of sons than older fathers.

In the U.S., dads make up 2.7 percent of the stay-at-home parents. In the UK, it's 14 percent.

All U.S. presidents have had kids except three...and all three were named James: James Madison, James Polk, and James Buchanan. George Washington didn't have biological children, but he raised his widowed wife Martha's children.

Pot Luck

During the 1890s temperance movement, marijuana was recommended as a substitute for alcohol.

In one study, spiders given marijuana started to spin webs but quit halfway through.

About 75 to 80 percent of all marijuana grown outdoors in the United States is on state or federal land.

The earliest known use of marijuana comes from the Bronze Age (3000–1000 BC).

Charred cannabis seeds have been recovered from an ancient burial site in present-day Romania.

Pot was also found in a 2,700-year-old shaman's grave in China.

A study determined that long-term cannabis users were 62 percent less likely to develop cancers of the head and neck than nonusers.

Cannabis users are also less likely to obese than nonusers.

Reference Book Duos

FUNK & WAGNALLS

Significance:
From the early 1900s until the 1980s, Funk & Wagnalls published reference books: dictionaries and a series of encyclopedias. The encyclopedias, in particular, found their way into millions of American homes because of the way they were marketed: the 29 volumes were sold one volume per week in supermarkets, meaning if you bought the book with aardvarks on January 1, you wouldn't learn about zygotes until the middle of July. Consumers liked Funk & Wagnalls because the arrangement spread the cost of a complete encyclopedia set over 29 weeks; supermarkets liked them because consumers were motivated to come back to the same store for seven months so they wouldn't miss any volumes.

Who Were They?
In 1876 a Lutheran minister named Isaac Kaufmann Funk started a company that would publish works that reflected his interest in religion, psychic phenomena, and temperance. In 1877 Funk took on clergyman Adam Willis Wagnalls as a partner, and they began publishing reference works, starting with a dictionary in 1893. The first *Funk & Wagnalls Standard Encyclopedia* came out in 1912, the same year that Funk died.

What Happened Next?
It wasn't until 1953, after Funk's son Wilfred sold the company to Unicorn Publishing, that its unique supermarket marketing strategy emerged. Using the "loss leader" sales technique—selling something for a loss and making the money back when consumers buy more to complete a set—Unicorn sold the first volume for just 99¢ and then raised the price to $2.99 for subsequent volumes. (That's about $25 each today.) A full set of encyclopedias eventually cost $84.71 (about $712 today). Although many people abandoned their sets before reaching the last volume (some after that first cheap book), many parents considered the price affordable and worthwhile when it was spread over seven months.

Fun Footnote: When Microsoft tried to license content from well-known encyclopedias for its electronic *Encarta Encyclopedia*, it was repeatedly rebuffed, so the company used Funk & Wagnalls content until it could create its own.

MERRIAM-WEBSTER

Significance:
During the early 1800s, Connecticut-born Noah Webster created the 70,000-word *An American Dictionary of the English Language,* the first comprehensive dictionary of American English. After Webster's death, George Merriam bought the rights to republish and adapt the dictionary.

Who Was Webster?
Decades after his schooling began at age six in 1764, Noah Webster despised his teachers because they concentrated on teaching religion above everything else. While at Yale, the American Revolution broke out, and Webster was an ardent supporter. After college, he taught school, creating a successful series of textbooks and spellers designed to push the curriculum toward a more rigorous, secular approach and away from cultural dependency on England. A believer in simplifying spelling, he removed the u's from the British spellings of words like "colour" and "humour," and decided that the newly established United States needed a dictionary that reflected its use of the language and rich influx of words adopted from immigrants, enslaved Africans, and Native Americans.

His textbook income allowed him to publish the first truly American dictionary in 1806, followed by two decades of intensive labor on the comprehensive version, during which he learned 26 languages in order to better track down the origins of individual words. Released in 1828 when Webster was 70, *An American Dictionary of the English Language* contained 70,000 words, of which 12,000 had never appeared in a dictionary before. He revised and expanded the dictionary, adding another 5,000 words for an 1841 reissue that was published two years before his death at 84 years.

What Happened Next?
As far as we know, Noah Webster never met George Merriam. When

Merriam bought the rights to reprint and revise Webster's dictionary, he also inherited a massive headache. For one thing, Webster's official version of his dictionary, priced at a budget-breaking $20 (about $450 today), had sold fewer than 2,500 copies. American copyright law was weak at the time, and other publishers had reprinted Webster's work word-for-word in cheaper and more popular editions.

Noah Webster had successfully leaned on government officials to reform the copyright laws in 1831, but it was too late to do much good. In fact, court cases in the early 20th century established that "Webster's Dictionary" had become a generic term and could be used by any publisher. So Merriam decided the best way to compete was to go the infringers one better: print cheaper dictionaries in large quantities, cutting the cost below that of competitors. The first edition of *Merriam-Webster's* came out in 1847 with a $6 price tag (about $150 today)—still pricey, but within the budget of many libraries, schools, and businesses. In fact, the Massachusetts government ordered one for each school in the state, and New York ordered 10,000 copies.

Fun Footnote: Poet Emily Dickinson was the proud owner of an original *Webster's Dictionary*. For many years, it was, in her own words, her "only companion." Dickinson scholars consider many of her poems to be "definition poems" that borrowed heavily from the dictionary for inspiration.

STRUNK & WHITE
Significance:
In 2011 *Time* magazine called *The Elements of Style* (also called *Strunk & White*) one of the best and most influential nonfiction books since the 1920s. It boils down the demands of good writing to a succinct 105 pages, with such pithy advice as "Omit needless words!"; "Do not break sentences in two"; and "Use the active voice." In its first year, *Elements* sold two million copies. By its 40th anniversary in 1999, it had sold 10 million, and the slender volume is still required reading in many writing classes.

Who Were They?
As with Merriam and Webster, William Strunk Jr. (1869–1946)

and E. B. White (1899–1985) were collaborators who didn't actually work together, with White starting his work on the project long after Strunk had died. The two did know each other, though. Strunk was an English professor at Cornell University, and White took his writing course in 1919. White later became famous as a contributor to the *New Yorker* magazine and the author of the children's books *Charlotte's Web* and *Stuart Little*. In 1957 he wrote a piece for the *New Yorker* about his writing professor's lasting influence on him, particularly a pamphlet Strunk had written that White characterized as an attempt to "cut the vast tangle of English rhetoric down to size and write its rules and principles on the head of a pin."

What Happened Next?
When White's editors at Macmillan read his praise of Strunk and the book, they asked White to update his professor's tome for publication. In an ironic twist, one of the things they asked was that White make it *less* succinct, since it was awfully hard to get a good price for a pamphlet of 12 pieces of paper folded in half and stapled in the middle. White more than doubled the book's bulk, but it remained short. And perhaps its length was the key to its success: Unlike most reference books, *The Elements of Style* was short and easy enough to read in one sitting and then put on a nearby shelf for future reference. English teachers loved it, and made it a must-have item for aspiring writers.

Fun Footnote: Strunk, an expert in classical literature, was hired as a literary consultant for MGM's 1936 production of *Romeo and Juliet*, directed by George Cukor and starring Norma Shearer and Leslie Howard. Before he even arrived, though, the scriptwriters unwittingly took Strunk's succinct writing philosophy to heart and cut out about half of Shakespeare's script.

*　　*　　*

The amount of garbage and recycling collected on an average day in New York City is nearly 12,000 tons.

Bridging the Gap

Construction on the Golden Gate Bridge began during the Great Depression, on January 5, 1933. It opened four years later, ahead of schedule and under budget.

During construction, chief engineer Joseph Strauss had a net placed below the bridge for safety, a new idea for the time. It saved 19 workers' lives.

The "Golden Gate" was what people called the narrow strait that connects San Francisco Bay to the Pacific Ocean. The bridge took its name from that.

The bridge's official color is "international orange."

In 1994 the American Society of Civil Engineers named the Golden Gate Bridge as one of the Seven Wonders of the Modern World.

California law bans the scattering of cremated remains from the Golden Gate Bridge.

Octopuses

The plural of octopus is octopuses.

Octopuses play games like catch, releasing objects into currents and catching them. They also use coconut shells for tools.

Octopuses can break out of their own aquariums and climb into others in search of food; they also sometimes board fishing boats.

The average octopus mates only once in its lifetime, a few months before its death.

Octopus mothers are especially self-sacrificing: they guard their eggs without eating for 6½ months until they hatch, starving themselves to death.

Octopuses have no bones, so they can squeeze into very small openings.

The only hard part of an octopus's body is its beak.

There are about 100 octopus species.

Octopuses have three hearts: one pumps blood through the animal's entire body; the other two pump blood into its two gills to better absorb oxygen from the water.

Octopuses swim fast by jet-propelling themselves by squirting water through a funnel-like body part called a *hyponome*.

Octopuses live only one to three years.

They are pretty smart—they have good long- and short-term memory, and excel at mazes and problem-solving.

*   *   *

DID YOU KNOW?

It wasn't until the 1940s that the U.S. Supreme Court ruled that state governments (not just the feds) had to guarantee religious freedom. Before that, a number of states specifically prohibited anybody but Protestants from holding office, and Connecticut and Massachusets even had state churches.

The Comic Book Code

In 1954 the U.S. government enacted a "code" for the comic book industry to regulate violence, language, and other issues that might come up in the stories. Comic book creators lived by that "code" for almost half a century. Marvel finally became the first to renounce it in 2001, and in 2011 DC Comics and Archie Comics were the last publishers to use it. Here are some of government's rules:

CRIME AND CRIMINALS

"Crimes shall never be presented in such a way as to create sympathy for the criminal, to promote distrust of the forces of law and justice, or to inspire others with a desire to imitate criminals...If crime is depicted it shall be as a sordid and unpleasant activity...Criminals shall not be presented so as to be rendered glamorous...In every instance good shall triumph over evil and the criminal punished for his misdeeds."

RESPECT FOR AUTHORITY

"Policemen, judges, government officials, and respected institutions shall never be presented in such a way as to create disrespect for established authority...Respect for parents, the moral code, and for honorable behavior shall be fostered."

VIOLENCE, GHOULS, AND WEREWOLVES

"All scenes of horror, excessive bloodshed, gory or gruesome crimes, depravity, lust, sadism, masochism shall not be permitted...All lurid, unsavory, gruesome illustrations shall be eliminated...Scenes dealing with, or instruments associated with walking dead, torture, vampires and vampirism, ghouls, cannibalism, and werewolfism are prohibited...Inclusion of stories dealing with evil shall be used or shall be published only where the intent is to illustrate a moral issue and in no case shall evil be presented alluringly, nor so as to injure the sensibilities of the reader."

PROFANITY, SLANG, AND GOOD GRAMMAR

"Profanity, obscenity, smut, vulgarity, or words or symbols which have acquired undesirable meanings are forbidden...Although slang and colloquialisms are acceptable, excessive use should be discouraged and, wherever possible, good grammar shall be employed."

SEX

"Suggestive and salacious illustration or suggestive posture is unacceptable...All characters shall be depicted in dress reasonably acceptable to society...Females shall be drawn realistically without exaggeration of any physical qualities...Passion or romantic interest shall never be treated in such a way as to stimulate the lower and baser emotions...Seduction and rape shall never be shown or suggested...Sex perversion or any inference to same is strictly forbidden."

THE SANCTITY OF MARRIAGE

"Divorce shall not be treated humorously nor represented as desirable...Illicit sex relations are neither to be hinted at nor portrayed...Sexual abnormalities are unacceptable...The treatment of live-romance stories shall emphasize the value of the home and the sanctity of marriage."

TITLES

"No comic magazine shall use the word(s) 'horror' or 'terror' in its title...Restraint in the use of the word 'crime' in titles or subtitles shall be exercised...The letters of the word 'crime' on a comics-magazine cover shall never be appreciably greater in dimension than the other words contained in the title. The word 'crime' shall never appear alone on a cover."

*   *   *

Is it an insult or a compliment to be called a "nasute"? Hard to say. The word can mean that you have a quick intellect, a critical attitude, a good sense of smell...or a big nose.

Change the Channel

The first president to appear on television was Franklin D. Roosevelt. The year was 1939, and the place was the New York World's Fair.

Koko, the first signing gorilla, loved to watch *Mister Rogers' Neighborhood*. When she finally met Rogers in person, Koko wrapped her long arms around him and then—as she'd seen him do on TV—she gently removed his shoes.

TVs had a channel 1 until 1948, when that frequency was taken back from the broadcasters and given to radio services.

A study from England's Nottingham Trent University found that watching TV news triggers depression, confusion, irritation, anger, and anxiety.

St. Clare of Assisi (1194–1253) was designated as the patron saint of television based on a reported miracle that once, too ill to attend Mass, she was able to hear and see the service on the wall of her room.

Humans burn one to two calories a minute watching TV, about the same amount as while sleeping.

The 1960 Winter Olympics in Squaw Valley were the first to sell exclusive broadcast rights to a TV network. ABC paid $50,000 to broadcast the Olympics coverage.

TV's Emmy Awards aren't named for a person, but for the "Immy," short for "image orthicon," the main piece of a 1950s TV camera.

*   *   *

"If it weren't for Philo T. Farnsworth, we'd still be eating frozen radio dinners."
—**Johnny Carson, on Philo T. Farnsworth, the inventor of television**

Baby Animals

Baby dolphins must hold their breath while nursing.

Despite the picturesque clocks, the European cuckoo has a dark side. The cuckoo mother doesn't ever make a nest—she lays one egg at a time into the nests of other species. When the cuckoo baby hatches, it busies itself with shoving the other hatchlings and eggs out, and the unsuspecting mother raises the murderous young cuckoo as her own.

Newborn rabbits are helpless for at least 10 days, but baby hares can hop around within minutes of being born.

Seals sometimes eat baby sharks.

Alligators don't have sex chromosomes. A baby's gender is determined by the temperature around the egg. If it is 86°F or below, the baby probably will be a girl; 93°F and above, a boy. A nest that hovers around 88°F will produce both sexes.

A baby platypus is born with a full set of teeth that fall out after a few weeks. Adults are toothless.

The green tree python isn't green when it's a baby—it's yellow, red, or brown.

Baby mice are called *kittens*, *pups*, or *pinkies*.

New lobsters emerge from their eggs as microscopic larvae. After floating on the surface of the ocean for two weeks, they settle to the bottom to grow into lobsters as we know them. For every 100,000 baby lobsters, only about four will survive.

Baby alligators bark to signal to their mothers that they're ready to emerge from their eggs.

In 1863 British scientist John Davy pumped air into empty eggshells and placed them underwater. By watching tiny bubbles form on the surface of the eggs, he proved his theory that baby birds can breathe because of thousands of microscopic air holes in their shells.

A baby robin can eat up to 14 feet of earthworms a day.

Monkey babies suck their thumbs, too.

Hairs to You

An *acrocomic* is a person with long hair.

Humans and chimpanzees have the same number of hair follicles.

At one time, Roman law decreed that all prostitutes had to bleach their hair blonde.

1 in 3 U.S. Caucasian women has blonde hair—but 1 in 20 is natural.

Hair on your scalp will grow approximately half an inch per month.

The average person grows 6.5 feet of nose hair in a lifetime.

The scientific name for hairs standing on end because of fright: *piloerection*.

In India, hairy ears are a measure of a man's virility.

A Yale study found that having a "bad-hair day" really does negatively affect many people's moods.

At any given time, 15 percent of a person's hair follicles are resting.

There are about 550 hairs in one of your eyebrows.

Lice can change their body color to match a person's hair.

On average, an adult human has about five million body hairs.

Get Along, Little Dogies

Wagon trains heading west averaged only about 1 to 2 mph.

Almost half of all cowboys in the 1800s were white; a quarter, Mexican; and a quarter, black.

Usual pay for a cowboy in the Old West was food, a bed in the bunkhouse, and a dollar a day.

In 1882 a Texas cattle association banned cowboys from carrying six-shooters. The *Texas Live Stock Journal* explained the ban in 1884: "The six-shooter loaded with deadly cartridges is a dangerous companion for any man, especially if he should unfortunately be primed with whiskey. Cattlemen should unite in aiding the enforcement of the law against carrying of deadly weapons."

Former Wild West gunfighter Bat Masterson became a sports writer for the *New York Morning Telegraph*. After two decades of word-slingin', he died in 1921 with his boots on…in front of his typewriter at work.

The average cowboy in the Old West was 24 years old; his career lasted about seven years.

Stetson cowboy hats were created way back in 1865…and way back East in Pennsylvania.

The first rodeo took place on July 4, 1888 in Prescott, Arizona.

Used for Texas-to-Denver cattle drives, the Goodnight–Loving Trail got its name from cattlemen Charles Goodnight and Oliver Loving, who were pioneers in using long-distance cattle drives as a way to get their livestock to the market.

A herd of cattle in the Old West traveled about 15 miles a day. A trail drive from Texas to a railroad town in another state could cover a thousand miles and take a whole summer.

Why did cowboy boots have such high heels? To better hold the stirrup, and to put some extra distance above the mud, muck, and poop from horses and cattle.

Can You Hear Me Now?

The word "noise" comes from the Latin word *nausea*, as does "nauseous."

About 28 million Americans have at least some hearing loss. Excess noise is the cause in a third of the cases.

The denser a material, the faster a noise will move through it. For example, noises travel 15 times faster through steel than through air.

Underwater ocean noise has increased by 300 percent since 1969. That can confuse ocean animals like dolphins and whales that depend on sound over long distances to navigate and locate each other.

Loud noises can scare away evil spirits, too. At least, that's the premise behind the tradition of setting off large numbers of firecrackers at Chinese celebrations of all sorts, from New Year's to weddings to funerals.

Noise can disrupt normal behavior in the smallest creatures. For example, when exposed to persistent traffic noise, zebra finches are more likely to cheat on their mates.

"White noise" is the sound of static that is pretty much equal at all sonic frequencies. But there are also other "colors" of noise—pink, blue, brown, green, etc.—that audio engineers generate with some frequencies more accentuated than others.

Besides hearing loss, high noise levels can contribute to stress and cardiovascular disease. Studies show that even moderately high levels of noise during an eight-hour workday raises blood pressure.

Loud noises can cause parakeets to lose feathers.

An African cicada can produce 106.7-decibel noise—as loud as a chainsaw.

* * *

Odds of a golfer hitting a hole in one: 1 in 40,000.

Running on Empty

In the first few modern Olympics, a marathon's length was 24.85 miles (or 40 kilometers), the distance from the Marathon Bridge to historic Athens. After 1896, the distance varied. Then, at the London Olympics in 1908, organizers wanted the race to start at Windsor Castle and run to the White City Stadium—that was an even 26 miles. Then, kowtowing to the royal family, organizers extended the course another 385 yards into the stadium and around most of the track so that it finished right in front of the royal box. In an effort to standardize the distance for future marathons, the Olympic Committee adopted that distance permanently.

In 1970, 126 men and one woman started at the first New York City Marathon...and only 55 (all men) finished. In 2011, 30,200 men and 17,563 women started, and only about 478 of the runners *didn't* finish.

Legend has it that the first marathon, held in 490 BC, had one contender, a Greek messenger who ran from the Battle of Marathon back to Athens to announce a victory over the Persians.

Susie Hewer of the United Kingdom knits five-foot-long scarves...while running in a marathon. Hewer has done it *several* times to raise money for Alzheimer's awareness. A recent run-and-knit was the London Marathon in April 2013. Hewer's time was 5:05:23, and her scarf was 6½ feet long, a personal best.

Guinness World Records keeps track of lots of marathon records, including finishers dressed as an astronaut (3:19:37), in a wetsuit (3:25:00), carrying an 80-pound pack (5:58:58), in a gorilla or other full-body animal suit (3:31:36), and costumed as an insect (3:24:10).

*   *   *

A baby turkey is called a "poult."

231

The Name Is Smith, John Smith

In the United States, more than 2.3 million people are named John Smith. But who were the most notable John Smiths in history?

- The most famous John Smith (1580–1631) was an adventurer who helped found the Jamestown colony in Virginia and who wrote vividly of being saved by Pocahontas.

- John Smith (1661–1727), nicknamed "Thrice-Hanged," was a burglar who was unsuccessfully hanged three times in England before finally being exiled to Virginia.

- John Smith (1750–1836) composed the tune of "The Anacreontic Song," which America stole for its national anthem.

- John Smith (1798–1888) was one of the first curators of Kew Gardens in London and oversaw its transition from a private to a public space.

- John Smith (1837–?) invented shorthand, went to jail for tax resistance, and created his own system of utopianism.

- Two John Smiths won the Medal of Honor, and two others won the Victoria Cross.

- John Smith, an Australian minister who goes by the nickname "Bullfrog," founded the God's Squad, a scruffy Christian biker gang that ministers to bikers.

- John Smith was a pro wrestler in the 1990s who went by the name of J. T. Smith. His gimmick was that he suffered a head injury and woke up thinking he was Italian. He founded a tag-team named the Full-Blooded Italians that was notable for the fact that none of them were really Italian.

- John Smith, better known as Ranger Smith, was Yogi Bear's foil in cartoons.

- John Smith, played by George Peppard and nicknamed Hannibal, was the leader of TV's *A-Team*.

Land of Lincoln

Illinois boasts that its the Land of Lincoln, but it was just one of his homes. He also lived in Kentucky, Indiana, and Washington, D.C.

Chicago was the site of one of America's first private detective agencies. Cook County sheriff Allan Pinkerton started the Pinkerton Agency in 1851. The agency acted as guards for presidents, but also as infiltrators, spies, and hired goons for corporations wanting to stop unions.

The world's first Dairy Queen opened in Joliet, Illinois, in 1940.

Chicago was home to the first 24-hour drive-in funeral home. Video cameras and a 25-inch color TV allowed people to drive up and view a dead loved one without leaving their cars.

The original Morris the Cat, spokes-feline for 9Lives cat food, was discovered by animal talent agents in the Hinsdale, Illinois, animal shelter and adopted shortly before he was supposed to be euthanized. Maybe that's why Morris's *real* name was Lucky.

It's against the law to offer a dog or other domesticated pet a cigar in Zion, Illinois…but no mention is made of cigarettes or pipes.

Really Dead, or Just Mostly Dead?

BURIED ALIVE

In the 17th and 18th centuries, there was a widespread phobia among Europeans and Americans about being mistaken for dead and waking up in a coffin, buried alive. Books and the popular press spread lurid stories of people waking right before the coffin was nailed shut and of corpses in morgues with their fingers chewed off—a sign, it was said, that the panicked people awoke and chewed their own hands in hunger (although rats were more likely).

There was (at least a little) reason to worry. As anatomist Jacques Bénigne Winslow admitted in 1740, "The onset of putrefaction is the only reliable indicator that the subject has died."

In response to the panic, inventors got busy creating coffins with ropes attached to signal bells aboveground. Writer Hans Christian Andersen used his own method—before going to sleep each night, he'd place a sign on his bedstand that read, "I only APPEAR to be dead."

HOW TO TELL IF HE'S REALLY DEAD

Helpful doctors also came up with reassuring procedures to revive people who only "appeared to be dead." For example, using a special pipe to blow tobacco smoke up a suspected corpse's anus was thought to be a solid way of separating the quick from the dead. If the person was alive, the smoke was supposed to stimulate breathing.

Winslow himself suggested measures to decide whether a person was really a corpse. "The individual's nostrils are to be irritated by introducing sternutaries, errhines, juices of onions, garlic and horse-radish.... The gums are to be rubbed with garlic, and the skin stimulated by the liberal application of whips and nettles. The intestines can be irritated by the most acrid enemas, the limbs agitated through violent pulling, and the ears shocked by hideous Shrieks and excessive Noises. Vinegar and salt should be poured in the corpse's mouth and where they cannot be had, it is customary to pour warm Urine into it, which has been observed to produce happy Effects."

If the "happy effects" didn't appear, it was time for extreme action like cutting the bottoms of the feet, thrusting needles under the toenails, and pouring hot wax on the forehead. If none of these abuses actually elicited a response, doctors assumed that they could safely pronounce the person dead. And as a general rule, they did— as far as history knows, none of these methods ever revived anyone.

*   *   *

PRINCE OF POPPERS

- Bubble wrap's official name—given by the Sealed Air Corporation, which owns the trademarked title—is "Bubble Wrap® Brand Cushioning material." (The company's offices provide boxes of bubble wrap for stressed employees to pop.)

- *Puchipuchi*, the Japanese word for bubble wrap, came from the sound that the bubbles make when you pop them.

- The bubbles in the wrap don't have to be round. They can be made in nearly any shape. In 1997 the Torninova Corporation in Italy offered wrap with heart-shaped bubbles.

- Inventors inadvertently came up with bubble wrap in 1957 when they tried to create textured wallpaper by sealing bubbles between two shower curtains. They discovered that it didn't really work as wallpaper, and bubble wrap was born.

- As of 2013, there were more than 250 Facebook pages dedicated to bubble wrap.

Tea Time

Technically, "tea" is only made of water poured over the leaves of the tea plant, *Camellia sinensis*. The herbal and other varieties around today aren't *real* tea.

Dry tea is about 3 percent caffeine by weight.

Black, white, yellow, green, and oolong teas all come from the same plant. The type and color depend on how the tea is processed.

The 10th century BC marks the earliest record of tea drinking in China.

In China, tea was considered a medicine before it was considered a beverage. That transition took place during the Tang Dynasty, between 618 and 907 AD.

Tea grows in India and was used as a medicine there too, but Indians didn't begin drinking tea as a beverage until British colonists introduced Chinese varieties there.

One pound of tea makes about 200 servings.

80 percent of the tea drunk in America is black tea, iced.

The official "hospitality drink" of South Carolina is tea, presumably iced and heavily sweetened. That may be because America's first tea farm was planted in Summerville, South Carolina, in 1890.

The estimated value (in today's dollars) of the 342 chests of tea dumped into the harbor during the Boston Tea Party is $700,000.

TV's talking horse of the 1950s, Mister Ed, had a filming-day diet of 20 pounds of hay and a gallon of sweet tea.

Although the British are now thoroughly associated with tea drinking, it didn't become a popular beverage there until the early 18th century.

Some research indicates a lower rate of cancer among green tea drinkers.

The English, Irish, and Kuwaitis drink more tea per capita than Americans.

Revenge of the Nerds

Electrical engineer Hurley Smith invented the pocket protector in 1943.

Dr. Seuss first used the word nerd—although as a fictitious animal, not in the context of a computer geek—in *If I Ran the Zoo*.

A quiet lonely child, Fred Rogers of *Mister Rogers* fame found solace in a rich fantasy world, brought to life with puppets.

Orville Redenbacher was obsessed by popcorn from his childhood days in the 4H Club, eventually doing crossbreeding experiments in the 1950s and 1960s.

Redenbacher turned down a position at West Point in order to study agronomy at Purdue.

At Atari, Steve Jobs was transferred to a one-person night shift after calling coworkers names and giving up bathing.

Midwestern teenage nerds Jerry Siegel and Joe Shuster created Superman.

Bill Gates scored 1590 on the SAT. His business partner, Paul Allen, scored a perfect 1600.

Shoo Fly, Don't Bother Me

Houseflies have been flying long before there were houses: about 65 million years.

A fly's wings flap at 200 beats a second—that's what makes the buzz.

Female flies lay 75 to 100 eggs at a time, and those eggs hatch in eight to twelve hours. They can repeat the process four to five times in a lifetime (which lasts up to four weeks).

During World War I, doctors accidentally discovered that housefly maggots (the larva stage) clean out open sores and help them heal. Maggot urine even disinfected the wound.

Flies vomit as they land on food, softening it to make the food easy to slurp up.

Alaskans swear that there are no houseflies in their state.

Flies are often the first sign of spring. They survive extreme cold by hibernating and wake up with the first spring thaw.

Female flies are slightly larger than males.

They fly at only about 4.5 mph.

Flies see the world like a wide-angle mosaic. Their two big eyes are really 3,000 to 6,000 simple eyes that give a big picture of what's around them but never let them focus in on details.

Flies have three more simple eyes on the tops of their heads that they use to know which way is up when flying.

* * *

About half of all peanuts grown in the U.S. become peanut butter. The rest go to snack nuts and confectionery.

The Aloha State

The rainiest spot in the world is Kauai's Mt. Waialeale. It consistently records about 460 inches of rain per year.

Hawaii has the highest life expectancy of any state.

McDonald's and Burger King restaurants in Hawaii sell SPAM for breakfast.

Mark Twain was one of the first Americans to try surfing while in Hawaii. He wrote, "I tried surf-bathing…the board struck the shore…without any cargo, and I struck the bottom about the same time."

But it was author Jack London, who visited Hawaii in 1907, who is credited with helping to save the sport from extinction. He wrote an article about his surfing teacher, George Freeth, and that generated enough interest that Freeth was invited to give surfing exhibitions up and down the California coast.

The state's motto is *Ua Mau Ke Ea O Ka Aina I Ka Pono* ("The life of the land is perpetuated in righteousness").

Barking Sands Beach on Kauai is called that because the sand's texture and formations make it sound like a dog barking when the waves roll in.

The native people called their land Owyhee, or Hawaika—early accounts differ. Whatever they said, English settlers heard it as "Hawaii."

The Hawaiian island of Molokai was once a leper colony—sufferers were quarantined there to keep the incurable disease from spreading.

Only two mammals are native to Hawaii: the hoary bat and the monk seal. The rest were imported from somewhere else.

Ka Lae, on the Big Island, is the southernmost point in the United States.

Between 1934 and 1955, there was not a single bank robbery in Hawaii.

75 percent of Hawaii's population lives on the island of Oahu.

First Mates

Early in their marriage, Lou Henry Hoover and her husband Herbert spent several years in China. When in the White House, they sometimes spoke Chinese to thwart eavesdroppers.

Louisa Adams, wife of John Quincy Adams, bred silkworms in the White House to weave her own silk cloth.

Lucy Hayes, wife of Rutherford, was the first First Lady to earn a college degree. This was in the 1850s, when most women didn't even graduate from high school.

Betty Bloomer was a dancer with Martha Graham's dance troupe, a model, and a retail fashion coordinator. We know her better as Betty Ford.

Claudia and Thelma were the real first names of back-to-back First Ladies, but they were known as Lady Bird Johnson and Pat Nixon.

Edith Roosevelt, Teddy's First Lady, was proficient at stilts. In fact, every member of the family had a pair for walking tall in the halls of the White House.

Martha Washington owned a parrot that her husband George couldn't stand. (And vice versa.)

Julia Tyler was John Tyler's second First Lady. His first wife of 29 years died during the second year of his presidency.

Every First Lady since Barbara Bush has appeared on *Sesame Street*.

* * *

THE HANGIN' JUDGE

From 1875 to 1896, Judge Isaac "Hanging Judge" Parker had jurisdiction over western Arkansas and the Indian Territory. Parker was infamous for his severity. During his tenure on the bench, Parker sentenced 160 men to death, and 79 of them were hanged. His courtroom, jail, and gallows were known as "hell on the border."

Expendable Organs

APPENDIX

Only some mammals have an appendix—rodents, rabbits, marsupials and primates (including humans). Located near the junction of the small and large intestines, it is a no-longer-useful stump of a much larger pouch.

What it's for: The appendix was once part of a larger cellulose-digesting pouch left over from ancient times when humans were mostly herbivores.

Why we can do without it: Although some scientists have recently speculated that the appendix might carry a reservoir of useful gut microorganisms, humans can certainly live without it. When an appendix gets infected and bursts, the spread of toxic fluid can kill the patient. It's also possible to get appendix cancer.

Side effects of removal? A small number of patients may develop infections or have reactions to anesthesia, but compared to the risks of not taking out an infected appendix, the risks are pretty low.

TONSILS

Every year about 530,000 kids under the age of 15 have their tonsils removed. It's one of the most common organ removals, and probably the oldest. A Hindi medical guide from about 1000 BC holds the first known instructions for doing a tonsillectomy: "When troublesome, they are to be seized between the blades of a forceps, drawn forward, and with a semicircular knife, a third of the swelled part is removed." Roman doctors in the first century AD also debated whether full or partial removal was best.

What they're for: Tonsils are specialized lymph nodes that help filter bacteria and viruses out of the blood.

Why we can do without them: When they get infected, tonsils can cause sore throats and apnea, but if they're removed, other lymph nodes take over their function.

Side effects of removal? About one in 15,000 patients dies from bleeding, reactions to anesthesia, or airway obstruction. In a few patients, throat problems get worse. A review of 7,765 research papers in 2009 found that the positive effects in kids were generally modest and short-lived.

ADENOIDS

In a way, the adenoids are sort of the tonsils of the nose—they rest in the base of the nose and trap germs. When infected, they can impair nose breathing and increase chronic infections and earaches. They are often removed at the same time as the tonsils.

What they're for: Filtering bacteria and viruses.

Why we can do without them: For babies under one year of age, the adenoids are an important part of the immune system, but after that age, they become increasingly irrelevant.

Side effects of removal? See tonsillectomy, above. Recent studies have also called into question the effectiveness of adenoid removal for preventing respiratory infections. Even for the condition most helped by an adenoidectomy—snoring and near-suffocation caused by sleep apnea—some patients saw no improvement afterward.

GALLBLADDER

The gallbladder sits just under the liver.

What it's for: To store bile from the liver that's released as needed to digest fatty foods.

Why we can do without it: Your gallbladder can get blocked by stones, creating a backup and infection that can be life-threatening.

Side effects of removal? The bile constantly goes directly from the liver to the small intestine without the gallbladder acting as a gatekeeper. Rarely, patients experience frequent or constant diarrhea from that.

* * *

Camel humps don't store water. They store fat, which allows them to go for weeks without food in the desert. As the fat gets used up, the humps get floppy and bounce from side to side.

Five Connecticut Firsts

1. On January 28, 1878, the world's first telephone exchange opened in New Haven. If you had a phone, you could ring the operator to connect you to any of the other 21 phone owners in town.

2. Seeing the number of Yale football players who got injured during practice, a young divinity student at Yale named Amos Alonzo Stagg created the first-ever tackling dummy. No dummy he, Stagg went on to become a college football coach.

3. State residents claim that Connecticut is where cattle branding got its start in the United States. Why? Apparently Connecticut farmers were required by law to mark all their pigs, which led them to do it to their cattle, too.

4. Connecticut was home to the first place where a hamburger was served between two pieces of bread (and oldest still-existing hamburger stand) in the United States: Louis' Lunch, New Haven, opened in 1895.

5. The *Hartford Courant*, established in 1764, is the oldest still-published newspaper in the United States.

Don't Steal Our Butter, Butterfly

People in the Middle Ages in Europe believed that butterflies were fairies in disguise, fluttering by to steal their dairy products.

In the early 1700s, butterfly collector Lady Eleanor Glanville was declared insane after an entomologist testified, "None but those deprived of their Senses would go in Pursuit of butterflyes."

There are 15,000 to 20,000 species of butterflies in the world—4,000 are in the South American rain forests alone.

Like bees, butterflies pollinate plants.

Some butterflies have ears on their wings.

Butterflies suck nectar from flowers using their proboscis, which works like a straw. When not in use, it curls up so it's out of the way.

The scales on a butterfly's wing overlap like roof tiles.

Lolita writer Vladimir Nabokov was also a compulsive butterfly collector and researcher.

Bad Movie Science

THE DAY AFTER TOMORROW (2004)

Premise: The Gulf Stream, an Atlantic ocean current that helps regulate Earth's temperature, has become so affected by global warming that it essentially stops. The ocean suddenly rises and massive icy tidal waves flood New York City. Within days, North America is a frozen wasteland.

Bad Science: Global warming can have a detrimental effect on the oceans, but it can't stop the Gulf Stream that fast. Even if it could, in order for New York City to flood like it did in the movie, the entire continent of Antarctica would have to melt. For that to happen, all of the sunlight that hits Earth would have to be collectively beamed at the South Pole...for three years.

THE MATRIX (1999)

Premise: After the machines take over the world, the human resistance "scorches the sky" to block out the machines' power supply—sunlight. So the machines use the humans for power, keeping them alive in a vegetative state while subjecting their brains to a life simulation. The machines "liquefy the dead so they can be fed intravenously to the living."

Bad Science: Neither the machines nor the humans know much about sustainable energy production. Blocking out the Sun would just destroy Earth's biosphere; the machines could easily build solar panels in space to get all the power they need. Second, human energy is inefficient—only about 35% of the energy from food converts to mechanical energy. And feeding humans to humans can lead to a disease called kuru, which causes insanity—and would screw up the simulation.

THE CORE (2003)

Premise: This big-budget action flick stars Aaron Eckhart and Hilary Swank. After Earth's inner core suddenly stops rotating, the planet's magnetic field collapses. This allows the Sun's microwaves to penetrate the atmosphere and cause havoc on the surface. Humanity's only hope is a ragtag group of scientists who must travel down to the center of the planet in an experimental vehicle. Their plan: detonate several nuclear bombs in the hopes of "jump-starting Earth's engine."

Bad Science: If Earth's core—which spins at 550 mph (although the movie says 1,000 mph)—suddenly stopped rotating, all of its rotational energy would be released up into the mantle, and then to the surface, causing a massive earthquake that would last for years. Also, microwaves couldn't fry the surface; they're too weak, and they aren't even affected by magnetic fields. And as far as building a ship that can withstand the immense pressure inside Earth to detonate nuclear bombs that will jump-start the core…we don't have nearly enough room to go into how impossible that is.

WATERWORLD (1995)

Premise: The surface of Earth has been completely covered in water. In one scene, the Mariner (Kevin Costner) swims around an abandoned underwater city that's revealed to be none other than Denver, Colorado, once known as the "Mile-High City."

Bad Science: If the temperature of Earth increased 8°F, sea levels would rise by three feet due to melting polar ice caps, which would be ecologically catastrophic. But sea levels could never rise to the point where Denver was completely submerged—the city's elevation is 5,280 feet. If all the world's ice melted, the oceans would rise 250 feet, submerging many coastal cities, but not Denver.

THE HAPPENING (2008)

Premise: (If you haven't seen this and don't want to have the "twist ending" spoiled, stop reading!) Throughout the movie, some unknown force is causing people all over the northeastern United States to spontaneously kill themselves. The cause is revealed to be trees—angry, angry trees. Retaliating en masse against humans for polluting the planet, the trees emit neurotoxins called pyrethrins, which scramble the brain and lead to suicide.

Bad Science: Pyrethrins come in very small quantities (in liquid form) in chrysanthemums native to Australia. And the liquid can be toxic, which is why it's used in pesticides. But trees could never emit suicide-causing neurotoxins.

Just Nuts!

In the nut biz, almond meats are categorized by four sizes: light, middling, good, and heavy.

The Bible mentions only two nuts by name: pistachios and almonds.

Buckeyes got their name because early settlers thought the nut looked like the eye of a deer.

The Turks claimed that horse chestnuts cured their steeds of excessive flatulence.

Pecans are the only nuts native to the continental United States.

The almond tree is a member of the rose family.

A chipmunk can store about a teaspoon's worth of nuts in each cheek.

It takes 300 pounds of pressure per square inch to break a macadamia nut's shell.

George Washington Carver, best known for his work with peanuts, also invented 75 uses for pecans.

Cashews are related to both mangoes and poison oak.

Because an unshelled walnut looks a little like a brain, the nuts got a reputation for being a good "brain food."

*   *   *

DID YOU KNOW?

President Franklin D. Roosevelt's portrait is on the dime in part to honor the March of Dimes charity, an organization he helped to found in 1938 as a way of helping victims of polio. The FDR dime was released on January 30, 1946, nine months after the popular president's death and on what would have been his 64th birthday.

I Do...Do You?

In ancient tribal days, kidnapping a woman for a bride was considered an acceptable form of courtship. Groomsmen helped with the kidnapping and then prevented recapture by her clansmen.

Studies show: Married men change their underwear twice as often as single men.

The ancient Egyptians believed that the *vena amoris* ("vein of love") ran directly from the heart to the fourth finger of the left hand. That's why people started wearing wedding rings on that finger.

Polls show that only 7 percent of married women trust their husbands to do the laundry correctly.

In 1928 (male) writer Evelyn Waugh married a woman named Evelyn Gardner. To avoid confusion, their friends called them "He-Evelyn Waugh" and "She-Evelyn Waugh." Mercifully (for everyone but He-Evelyn), She-Evelyn solved the problem a year later by running off with another man.

Sweeping Changes

On June 8, 1869, Ives McGaffey patented the world's first suction vacuum cleaner—he called it the "Whirlwind." It was a manual model—users had to turn a hand crank at the same time that they pushed it back and forth on the floor.

In 1907 a Canton, Ohio, janitor named James Spangler invented the first practical home vacuum cleaner as a way of reducing his asthma when cleaning carpets at his job. He used a broom handle as a rotary brush, an electric fan in a wooden soap box, and a pillowcase as a dust bag. Not having the capital to produce his vacuum for sale, he sold the patent to William Hoover, the husband of a family friend, who refined the externals of the design.

There's not really a "vacuum" in a vacuum cleaner. A vacuum is a space that's completely empty of anything, including air. To be more accurate, the appliance should be called a "suction cleaner."

A typical vacuum cleaner reduces air pressure inside itself, making air from outside come rushing in (along with any dust or dirt that gets caught up in the draft).

There are about 15,000 vacuum cleaner–related accidents in the U.S. every year.

The rock group AC/DC got its name from the power info printed on the back of a vacuum cleaner.

Vacuuming for 92 minutes will burn off the calories in a 360-calorie blueberry muffin.

The Incas Said It First

At the end of the 15th century, the Incas spread the Quechua language throughout South America, and when Spanish explorers arrived, they helped to bring Quechuan words to the rest of the world. Here are some of the ones English borrowed.

Llama

Puma

Kinwa: Quinoa

Kuntur: Condor

Huanu: Guano, meaning "dung"

Inka: Inca, meaning "king" or "lord"

Ch'arki: Jerky, meaning "dried flesh"

Kuka: Coca/cocaine, meaning "coca plant"

*   *   *

VIVE LA FRANCE!

The postrevolutionary French government introduced a metric clock with 10 hours per day—each consisting of 100 minutes of 100 seconds each. Forget "1 alligator, 2 alligator..." to count seconds. To count a metric second (2.4 regular seconds), you'd need to say, "1 alligator, elephant, and aardvark..." But workers who didn't want an eight-day workweek rebelled, and the idea of a metric clock was sent to the guillotine.

Fruit Flies

Male fruit flies deprived of females are more likely to drink alcohol.

Fruit flies are generally harmless to people—since they eat rotting fruit and don't seem to carry many human diseases—but some are dangerous to crops. The Asian fruit fly causes lots of damage to soft summer fruit crops like berries, peaches, and grapes.

Harvard University researchers started experimenting with fruit flies in 1901, and then Thomas Hunt Morgan of Columbia University was inspired to do the same. Over the next 30 years, Morgan and colleagues used what they learned to establish the basic foundation of genetics, for which he won the Nobel Prize in 1933.

Today, about 7,500 scientists work with fruit flies to study fundamental issues of biology.

A fruit fly lives about 10 days at normal indoor temperature, seven days at 82°F.

Adults start mating 8 to 12 hours after emerging from the pupa. Females lay eggs in rotting fruit, up to 500 eggs a day, for up to 10 days.

In 2000 scientists sequenced and published the fruit fly's complete genome.

In the wild, fruit flies are yellow-brown with bright red eyes, but some lab-grown variations have brown or white eyes and dark bodies.

Fruit flies navigate using the earth's magnetic fields.

The common fruit fly originally came from western Africa. Researchers say they arrived in America about 500 years ago, possibly living on rotting fruit on slave ships.

*   *   *

The U.S. shreds 7,000 tons of worn-out paper currency each year. Face value: about $10 billion.

It Happened on Christmas

Christmas Island was discovered and named (1643): Captain William Mynors of the British East India Company stumbled on the island in the Indian Ocean and named it after the holiday.

The West Point Eggnog Riot (1826): Seventy cadets at West Point, including Jefferson Davis, the future president of the Confederacy, engaged in a drunken riot on Christmas Day after large quantities of eggnog were smuggled into their barracks. The rioters made up a third of the student body, but only 20 were court-martialed. (Davis wasn't one of them.)

Pardoning of Confederates (1868): Three years after the end of the Civil War, President Andrew Johnson granted an unconditional pardon to all Confederate soldiers.

The Japanese captured Hong Kong (1941): The Japanese attacked Hong Kong on December 8, 1941, eight hours after they attacked Pearl Harbor. They conquered Hong Kong 17 days later, on December 25, and held the city until the war ended in 1945.

***Apollo* 8 orbited the moon (1968):** On Christmas Day, *Apollo* 8 became the first spacecraft to orbit the Moon, look at the "dark side," and see the sphere of Earth all at once.

Flagging Interest

Vexed by vexillology? No need—it's the study of flags.

The only nation with a plain, solid-colored flag was Libya. (It was green from 1977 to 2011.)

The official Olympic flag was first flown during the 1920 Games.

The X on the Confederate flag is called a St. Andrew's Cross. (It is also featured on the flag of Scotland and of the Russian navy.) It's based on the legend that St. Andrew was crucified on an X-shaped cross.

An ancient British designer laid the Scottish cross of St. Andrew over the British cross of St. George and created the Union Jack, adopted in 1606.

Napoleon designed Italy's national flag.

How many national flags have brown as their main color? None.

The maple leaf on the Canadian flag has 11 "points." Actual maple leaves have 23.

In 2001, post-9/11 patriotism proved to be a boon for flag makers, and not just American ones. We bought 113 million foreign-made American flags, most of which came from China.

The state flag of Alaska shows the Big Dipper and was designed by 13-year-old Benny Benson, an Aleut boy from the small town of Chignik, Alaska, who won a contest in 1926.

Ohio's state flag is a pennant instead of a rectangle, the only state flag shaped that way.

For $13 to $24 (depending on size and fabric), your senator or representative will sell you an American flag with a certificate that says it has flown over the U.S. Capitol Building. It's a popular offer…which is why there are people whose job is to stand on the roof of the Capitol, zipping flag after flag up and down a flagpole all day.

Oregon's state flag is the only one with a different image on each side: the front side has the state seal, and the back a beaver.

First in Space!

First person to run the Boston Marathon while in space: NASA astronaut Sunita Williams aboard the International Space Station. She was an official participant, even though she ran on a treadmill. Her time: 4:23:10.

First monkey in space: Albert II, a rhesus monkey, on a U.S. rocket, 1949. He died, as did Albert III, IV, and V.

First monkey in space to survive: Miss Baker, a squirrel monkey, 1958. She lived another 26 years after landing. Her companion, Able, also survived the flight, but died three days later during an operation to remove an infected medical electrode that had been implanted for the flight.

First fatalities in space: Soviet astronauts Georgi Dobrovolski, Viktor Patsayev, and Vladislav Volkov on June 29, 1971.

First haircut in space: American astronaut Paul Weitz got a trim from Pete Conrad in 1973.

First fish in space: A mummichog, 1973.

First e-mail from space: On August 28, 1991, from the crew of the space shuttle *Atlantis*.

First codger in space: John Glenn, age 77, on October 29, 1998. His space shuttle flight honored his first flight in 1962, when he became the fifth person in space and the first American to orbit Earth. Bonus fact: In 1962 the people of Perth, Australia, turned on their house, street, and car lights to greet John Glenn as he flew over them in the dark. In 1998 they did the same thing.

First video game advertisement from space: Astronaut Don Pettit catapulted stuffed birds at pigs in the International Space Station in 2012 to promote the Angry Birds in Space game, which had been created in cooperation with NASA.

First woman in space: Russian Valentina Tereshkova in 1963. (Sally Ride didn't become the first *American* woman in space until 20 years later.)

First cat in space: Felix, launched by the French in 1963.

Labor Relations

Today, only about 11 percent of U.S. workers belong to unions, as opposed to 35 percent in the 1950s.

On average, American teachers work more hours than teachers in any other country: 1,097 hours per year.

In September 1882, during America's gilded age when the rich were getting richer and their workers becoming poorer, machinist and labor union secretary Matthew Maguire organized a march in New York City to support unionization. Thousands of workers took an unpaid day off to join it, and an annual Labor Day tradition was born. It became an official federal holiday in 1894.

The earliest written record of an organized workers' strike occurred in 115 BC during the building of the tomb of Egyptian pharaoh Rameses III. There was a lot of corruption in high places and continuing wars that drained the treasury. When the workers' rations and pay became overdue, they stopped working and marched, chanting, "We are hungry!" and other slogans. They eventually got their pay.

England's Big Ben

Although most people refer to London's famous and enormous clock tower as Big Ben, that name is really just for the 13-ton bell that chimes every hour. The chime was named after Benjamin Hall, the bell's commissioner. His name is also inscribed on the bell.

The tower is called Elizabeth Tower and was built in 1858. It's the third-tallest freestanding clock tower in the world, standing 16 stories high. It also holds the largest four-faced chiming clock in the world, suspended 180 feet above the ground.

Architect Augustus Pugin designed the tower as one of his last projects. Shortly after submitting the final design in February 1852, Pugin suffered a mental breakdown as a result of kidney disease and working too hard. He couldn't speak or recognize family members and friends, and he died in September of the same year.

The clock mechanism is kept accurate by a 660-pound pendulum. On the pendulum is a stack of old penny coins. If the clock is running slow, adding a penny will increase its speed by 0.4 seconds a day. Taking one away will decrease its speed by the same amount.

Thanks to slightly shifting soil, Elizabeth Tower leans 9 inches to the northwest.

You can climb to the top of the tower and be temporarily deafened by Big Ben, but only if you're a resident of the United Kingdom and are willing to put in a reservation four months in advance.

You also must be willing to climb the 334 limestone steps to the top. There is no elevator.

Each clock face is 23 feet across. The tip of each minute hand travels 72 feet an hour, 1,728 feet a day...for a total of 119.5 miles a year.

On August 20, 1949, Big Ben shocked London by chiming 4.5 minutes late. It turned out that hundreds of starlings had landed on the clock's minute hands, temporarily stopping the time.

Berry Specific

Grapes, persimmons, currants, coffee berries, tomatoes, peppers, pumpkins, and watermelons are all considered berries biologically. They are a class of fruit that is "fleshy and produced from a single ovary."

In 1923 horticulturist Rudolph Boysen crossed several varieties of blackberries and raspberries to create a new variety, but a lack of commercial success made him lose interest in the fruit. A grower named Walter Knott later adopted a few of Boysen's neglected vines and began serving boysenberries fresh and in jams and pies.

Do you ever consume juniper berries? Sure you do, if you drink gin. It's the major ingredient.

Crows, bluebirds, rabbits, and deer can eat poison ivy berries without a problem; humans can't.

Berries bounce—supposedly, they're ready to eat if you drop one from chest height, and it bounces seven times.

In 1883 Calfornia's James Harvey Logan invented the loganberry. He was trying to crossbreed two blackberry varieties, but a nearby raspberry plant also got its pollen into the mix. Of the 50 seeds he planted, one became the loganberry.

In 1882 Canadian John Lake, founder of a Temperance Society commune in Saskatchewan, was contemplating what to call his alcohol-free settlement when a young disciple offered him a handful of berries. Lake liked the sound of the Cree name for the fruit, *misâskwatômin* ("early berries"), which he heard as "saskatoon" in English. It became the name of his new village.

Technically, a strawberry isn't a berry. It's an "accessory fruit," like apples and pears. What we call the "seeds" are actually each an independent dry fruit that contains a microscopic seed inside. The luscious red part is part of the flower that holds dozens of seeds together.

Meet Some Meat

Ham isn't just any old piece of pig meat. It comes specifically off of the rump area.

Most spoiled meat is turned into tallow for pet food, automobile tires, cosmetics, soaps, candles, detergents, lubricants, crayons, and plastics.

Until 1966, Catholics were allowed to eat fish during Lent, but were not allowed to eat meat. For settlers in Africa, though, there was one exception: hippos. The reasoning was that since the animal spends so much time in the water, it could technically be classified as a fish.

Ants can't digest meat, but ant larvae can. So if an ant larva is fed meat, it vomits some of it back up, partly digested, for the adults to share.

According to some foodies, beavers, wombats, and crocodiles taste like pork; hippos and zebras taste like beef; lions and boa constrictors taste like veal; and baby wasps taste like scrambled eggs.

Human meat is also said to taste like pork (but we don't want to verify that).

Hoops, I Did It Again

Disneyland has a basketball court for employees inside the Matterhorn.

Nowadays the basketball team that's scored against gets the ball back. But before 1937, there was a jump ball after every basket.

In 1891 James Naismith invented basketball at a YMCA in Springfield, Massachusetts. He asked the custodian for empty wooden boxes to use as targets, but there were none available. There were two peach baskets, though. Naismith nailed those to the balconies at either end of the gym, and they just happened to be 10 feet off the floor, which is why that is still the regulation height for baskets.

In the first pro basketball league (1898), players on the Trenton, New Jersey, team were paid $2.50 for home games and $1.25 for away games.

Wilt Chamberlain was the first professional basketball star who was more than 7' tall.

Michael Jordan was demoted to the junior varsity basketball team while in high school.

Slam dunks were banned in college basketball between 1967 and 1976.

Basketball is the only major sport invented in the U.S.

The Purefoods Tender Juicy Giants, a basketball team in the Philippines, are named after a hot dog.

Considering the notable shortage of lakes in Southern California, the name "Los Angeles Lakers" makes sense only if you know that the team began in Minnesota, whose nickname is "the Land of 10,000 Lakes."

* * *

Alaska has the honor of being the state with the most outhouses.

Fish Facts

Native American tribes along the Pacific Coast used eulachon, a small ocean fish, as candles. The fish were so oily that people just strung wicks through the bodies and burned them, hence their other name: candlefish.

More than 800 fish species can vocalize sounds.

Men who sold fish were called "fishmongers." Woman in the same occupation were called "fishwives."

What's *ichthyoallyeinotoxism*? LSD-like hallucinations brought on by eating sarpa salpa, little spinefoots, and other kinds of tropical or coastal fish.

Raash is an electric African catfish that grows up to 4 feet in length. In Arabic, the name means "thunder," but its effects are more like lightning. The fish uses electricity to kill or stun its prey and to repel predators.

Most koi fish have a life span of 47 years, but Hanako, a koi from Japan, lived to be 226 years old.

Lungfish can survive out of water for months.

A Slooow List

Snails first slithered the earth about 600 million years ago.

Snails breathe through a thick layer of skin under their shells called the mantle.

Some snails have lungs, some have gills.

What is *heliculture?* The science of growing snails for food.

A snail crawls at an average speed of 0.03 mph...or about one foot every three minutes.

Some snails can hibernate in the winter and live off their fat. They can also hibernate in the summer during severe droughts. To avoid drying out, they seal their shells with a layer of mucus.

If a snail's eye gets severed, it will grow a new one.

The largest species of snail is the giant African land snail: it can weigh two pounds and have a shell that's 15 inches long.

All About Barbie

Totally Stylin' Tattoos Barbie (and her pal Totally
Stylin' Nikki), who came with 40 temporary
tattoos (including a lower back "tramp stamp"),
made a small furor in 2009 among parents who
weren't comfortable with their young daughters
seeing Barbie inked up. (The dolls stayed on the
market, though.)

Barbie's official birthday: March 9, 1959.

Barbie dolls sold in Japan have their lips closed,
with no teeth showing, because in 1995 marketers
from Mattel discovered that in Japan (as the *New
York Times* put it), "women still cover their mouths
with their hands when they laugh so as not to
expose their teeth."

Barbie's hometown, according to Mattel, is
Willows, Wisconsin.

Barbie has a last name, and it isn't "Doll." It's
Roberts.

If Barbie were human, her measurements would be
38-18-28.

Barbie's first car: A pink 1962 Austin-Healey
British sports car.

Mattel's 2010 Collector Barbie was Palm Beach
Sugar Daddy Ken. He wore white pants and a lime-
green jacket, and came with a tiny white lap dog.

Barbie outsells Ken by about two to one.

Don't Play That Again, Sam

- An "earworm" is a song that repeats...and repeats...in the brain. What's the hallmark of a typical earworm? It's most likely to be a song with simple lyrics and a melody that you've heard many times.

- Songs with lyrics were the most frequent tormentors, making up 74 percent of those reported. Another 15 percent were commercial jingles, and 11 percent were instrumentals.

- In 2003 University of Cincinnati professor James Kellaris released a paper on earworms. He interviewed 559 students and found that 98% had experienced the phenomenon.

- Dr. Kellaris, by the way, is credited with popularizing the term "earworm," from a German word, *ohrworm*. However, the German word actually refers to something different: an overnight hit song that appears suddenly and quickly becomes popular.

- Other words suggested for the phenomenon include serious submissions such as "involuntary musical imagery," "obsessive musical thought," "musical meme," or "stuck song syndrome," as well as some less-serious ones: "humsickness" or "repetitunitus."

- Most people have their own idiosyncratic list of songs that get stuck in their heads. In that 2003 study, the professor's personal list of top 10 earworm songs included two jingles (Chili's "Baby Back Ribs" and Kit-Kat's "Gimme a Break") and one instrumental (the *Mission: Impossible* theme).

Other songs that ranked high included "The Lion Sleeps Tonight," "YMCA," "We Will Rock You," "Who Let the Dogs Out," "Whoomp, There It Is," and "It's a Small World After All."

- If the list above accidentally infected you with an earworm, here are some ways that people have used to dislodge them. Mentally switching to another song is very popular—even if it runs the risk of replacing one earworm with another. Trying to pass the earworm on to somebody else by singing or talking about the song sometimes works. Still others finish an earworm off by literally finishing it—instead of repeating a part of the song, they mentally continue all the way to the end, breaking the cycle…sometimes.

- The most comforting news about earworms is that they almost never last more than 24 hours, and usually it's much less than that—typically 27 minutes, according to "earworm diaries" collected from subjects of another study.

*　*　*

HODGEPODGE

- What are ray guns, drag pipes, and pea shooters? Mufflers, to motorcycle buffs.

- At the 1893 Chicago Worlds Fair, Milton Snavely Hershey saw a chocolate-making machine from Germany and decided to go into the business himself. Hershey bars and Kisses are the result.

- Women weren't allowed to run the marathon in the Olympics until 1984.

A Mark of Extinction

On September 1, 1914, the passenger pigeon officially went extinct when Martha, the last known survivor, died in the Cincinnati Zoo. Once the most abundant bird species in the world, its vast flocks became an easy target for hunters.

Hawaii's state bird is a goose called the nene, which evolved from visiting Canada geese about 500,000 years ago. In 1952 its population included just 30 birds, down from 25,000 in 1778. Rescued from extinction by the efforts of conservationists who bred them in nature reserves around the world, there are now about 800 in the wild and 1,000 in zoos.

More than 90 percent of all animal species in earth's history are now extinct.

The mylodon, a gigantic ground sloth the size of a black bear, survived through much of human history. It didn't become extinct until about 5,000 years ago.

Dingoes, introduced to Australia from Southeast Asia about 5,000 years ago, caused the extinction of the thylacine, or Tasmanian tiger, a doglike marsupial. The last thylacine on mainland Australia died during the 19th century, but the animals lasted until the 1930s on the isolated island of Tasmania.

Burned at the Skate

NOBODY EXPECTS THE SPANISH INQUISITION

During the 15th and 16th centuries, the heyday of the Spanish Empire, the country's kings and queens tended to go brutally overboard in their support of the Roman Catholic Church. They forced Jews and Muslims to convert or get out of the country in 1492, and then created the infamous Inquisition to root out atheists, freethinkers, Christians of the wrong kind, and any former Jews and Muslims who were only *pretending* to be Catholic. Torture, forced confessions, and burnings at the stake were common tools used to "save" the souls of those deemed insufficiently Catholic.

In 1566 Spain's King Philip II got some disturbing news about a distant province ruled by his empire. Thanks to the devilish and revolutionary influence of people like Martin Luther and John Calvin, the scourge of Protestantism had taken root in the Spanish-controlled Netherlands. After trying out slightly gentler methods, Philip sent in Spanish troops with orders to scare the devil—or at least the Calvin and Luther—out of the locals. In response, many of the Dutch people rose up in rebellion, and Philip decided that anything, even mass murder, was acceptable in the effort to convince the Dutch to accept Catholicism.

THE SWORD OF THE LORD

Not all Dutch towns resisted or wanted trouble, but even that didn't help them. In November 1572, the city of Naarden tried to negotiate surrender with the Spanish by inviting the invading army to a lavish feast. But after the food and toasts and expressions of friendship and loyalty were finished, the army gathered the 3,000 residents into the town church. Moments after sending in a reluctant priest to tell the people to pray, the army rushed in with swords and began slaughtering the townspeople. Eventually, the soldiers burned the church down to make sure there were no survivors. Other cities and towns were similarly ransacked, and an estimated 100,000 people were killed.

DUTCH THREAT

News of the massacres spread quickly through the rest of the Netherlands, and resistance became the only way the Dutch could see to throw off the Spanish invasion, even for towns that had been loyal to the empire and Catholicism. That wouldn't be easy, though. The Spaniards were marching toward Amsterdam, and the small cities along the way didn't have the armies to resist them. But evacuating thousands of citizens on short notice with winter coming wasn't possible either. Still, they couldn't just wait around to be killed. So what *could* they do?

Further complicating matters was the fact that the Netherlands didn't have any mountains or other high places to use defensively. In fact, because so much of the Dutch countryside had once been swamps, lakes, and ocean floor, 30 percent of its land is actually below sea level and most of the rest, just barely above it. But then, officials in the city of Alkmaar in the central part of the country came up with a plan so crazy it probably shouldn't have worked.

Here's how the plan went: Flood everything. Breach the levees and dikes that kept rivers and the waters of the North Sea at bay. Create a huge lake on farmland around the city, making it difficult for marching armies to reach its gates. The townspeople went to work—opening water gates, digging holes in levees, and damming rivers. Soon there was water everywhere, and it was too deep to cross on foot. Other towns did the same thing, and when the Spanish army arrived, it looked out helplessly over broad waters and stopped dead.

THE ICE BRIGADE

The Spanish then retreated back to their ships and decided to attack Amsterdam by way of its harbor instead. Time was running out, though, because winter was coming. For the Spanish, that looked like it might be a silver lining: When the cold of winter came, all of those lakes would freeze into ice highways.

The first test of that theory came shortly afterward when the ragtag Dutch fleet was frozen into the Amsterdam harbor, making the Dutch unable to confront the Spanish ships head-on. Taking that advantage, Spanish troops began marching across the ice to attack the ships first, and then they planned to head to the coastline on foot.

But as they marched gingerly across the frozen ice, they were confronted by a horrifying apparition. Wave after wave of Dutch soldiers flew across the surface of the ice with incredible speed, flitting into range just long enough to fire a musket before retreating again behind walls of ice and frozen snow. The Spanish soldiers had never seen anything like it: "It was a thing never heard of before today," the Spanish Duke of Alva recounted with grudging admiration, "to see a body of musketeers fighting like that on a frozen sea."

THE AGONY OF THE FEET

The Spanish didn't stay for long. Alva ordered a quick retreat…or at least as quickly as the Spanish soldiers could go with slippery shoes and frostbitten toes. The Dutch skating masters followed, pushing Alva's men back to their ships and picking off several hundred of them in the process.

Alva killed a few Dutch soldiers and finally got his hands on the real cause of their high-speed dexterity: ice skates. He sent a pair back to Spain with a message that his soldiers needed skates of their own. When he received that message, the king of Spain ordered 7,000 pairs of ice skates made, and the Spanish military started offering skating lessons.

EPILOGUE

The Spanish became decent skaters, but as defenders, the Dutch held a significant advantage. They were also able to push the Spaniards onto thin ice by cutting the frozen flooded cities at tactical spots, creating deadly traps that sent their enemies plunging deep into freezing water. The Dutch also doubled their fighting forces by teaching civilian women how to shoot and repair damaged walls (often raiding Catholic churches for statues and using them as building material to taunt and demoralize the Spanish).

The war lasted for 80 years, alternating between stalemates and horrifying brutality, but by 1648, the Netherlands and Belgium had driven out the Spanish once and for all. The Dutch continued to refine strategic flooding as a defensive tactic, adding forts along roads and bridges. The "Dutch Water Line" remained effective as a defensive strategy until the air power of World War II finally made it obsolete.

Giddy-Up!

Men's suit coats have a slit in the back because the slit kept the coats from riding up when the wearer was on a horse.

The outer coverings of major league baseballs have been made of cow leather since 1974. Before that, it was horsehide.

1,100 horses were used during the filming of Gone With the Wind.

Arabian horses have one less rib and one less lumbar bone than other horse breeds.

Horses lie down for only about 43 minutes a day.

Secretariat, the Kentucky Derby's fastest horse, finished the race in 1 minute, 59 seconds in 1973. That's about 37.5 mph.

An adult horse produces 10 gallons of saliva every day.

Out of the 205 bones that make up a horse's body, 80 are in its legs.

The $1\frac{1}{4}$-mile Dubai World Cup, run on a sandy, desert track, is the richest horse race ever. The winner takes home $10 million.

Let's Talk About Love

According to researchers, most people will fall in love seven times before they get married.

It's not surprising that romantic love triggers the *ventral tegmental*, the brain's pleasure center. But it also stimulates the *caudate nucleus*, which is associated with memory and learning.

The maple leaf is a symbol of lovers in China and Japan.

Love and fear cause the same physical reactions: pupil dilation, sweaty palms, and elevated heart rate.

Traditionally, if you receive 13 roses, it means that the flowers have come from a secret admirer.

One poll showed that Americans believe Democrats are better lovers than Republicans.

The technical term for being obsessively infatuated with another person is "limerance."

Male mice sing love calls to females, but don't expect to hear them, unless you record them and reduce the pitch. The songs of mousy love are in tones too high for humans to hear.

*   *   *

LOVELY QUOTES

"One is very crazy when in love."
—**Sigmund Freud**

"Love is the net where hearts are caught like fish."
—**Muhammad Ali**

"The only abnormality is the incapacity to love."
—**Anaïs Nin**

"We had a lot in common. I loved him and he loved him."
—**Shelley Winters**

Gouda Nuff!

There are about 400 varieties of cheese.

The world's worst-smelling cheese is French Vieux Boulogne—supposedly, it smells like a barnyard.

Italy has a thriving black market for an illegal cheese that contains live maggots, the larva of the "cheese fly" (*Pophilia casei*). The traditional Sardinian sheep's milk cheese called *casu marzu* uses the larvae for fermentation. Some people try to remove the larvae before eating it; others don't. Either way, if the maggots are not alive when you buy it, the cheese is considered to be spoiled.

Cheddar cheese came from a village of the same name in Somerset, England. It's naturally white, but often artificially colored orange, using an extract of the annatto fruit.

What does the maggoty cheese taste like? It has an ammonia flavor that can linger as an aftertaste for several hours. Also, when disturbed, the maggots can propel themselves six inches, so it's traditional to cover your eyes.

Goat and cow cheeses are the most common, but there are also horse, llama, zebra, buffalo, camel, reindeer, donkey, and yak cheeses.

He may or may not have been the first person to put a slice of cheese on top of a hamburger, but the trademark name "cheeseburger" was issued in 1935 to Louis Ballast of the Humpty Dumpty Barrel Drive-In in Denver, Colorado.

The holes in Swiss cheese are called "eyes."

For a few months in 1942, the only type of cheese that could be sold legally in the United States was American cheese. But after objections by cheese lovers and America's cheese-making World War II allies (the British), the rule was rescinded.

Great (and Not-So-Great) Lakes

Canada has about two million lakes—more than 60 percent of the world's total.

Of the world's five biggest lakes, three are Great Lakes. In order: Caspian Sea (Middle East), Lake Superior, Lake Victoria (Africa), Lake Huron, and Lake Michigan.

HOMES is the acronym that will help you remember the Great Lakes: Huron, Ontario, Michigan, Erie, Superior.

Michigan borders every Great Lake except Lake Ontario. Any spot in the state is within 85 miles of one of the lakes.

Lake Tahoe isn't huge, but it is deep—it holds enough water to cover all of California with 14 inches of water.

Florida's Okeechobee Lake is about half the size of Rhode Island…but only nine feet deep.

On November 20, 1980, Louisiana's Lake Peigneur suddenly disappeared. A Texaco crew drilling for oil on the lake's bottom struck a salt mine a quarter-mile below, and in just four hours, a whirlpool sucked the entire 1,300-acre lake into the ground. Luckily, no lives were lost, and the lake eventually refilled.

Maryland has no natural lakes. What it has comes from digging and damming.

The world's oldest lake, about 30 million years old, is Lake Baikal in Siberia.

There are no permanent lakes in Saudi Arabia.

Some volcanic lakes—like Mount Pinatubo in the Philippines—have water so acidic from escaping gases that it can burn through human flesh in minutes.

Mousetrap

Mice have had a remarkable career as pests. In fact, they are so successful that, throughout history, people have put an awful lot of effort into keeping them out of their homes, food stores, and businesses. That's tough, though—mice can flatten out their bodies and slide through cracks as thin as ⅜ of an inch, meaning that if a pencil can roll under a door, so can a mouse.

Cats and some dogs make good mousetraps, but to some people, having cats and dogs is almost as bad as infestation by mice. So it's not surprising that thousands of mouse-catching contraptions have been invented over the years. What *is* surprising, though, is that, for hundreds of years, most didn't work very well. They were too complicated, too bulky, and too easy for the rodents to escape from.

HOOKER TRAP

That all changed in 1894 when a brand-new mousetrap came out of Abington, Illinois, patented by a man named William Chauncey Hooker. The design was simple, effective, cheap to manufacture, and—as its name "Out O' Sight" implied (complete with the face of a mouse peeking out from the middle O)—easy to hide. Although revolutionary at the time, the wood-and-wire, spring-snap trap quickly became the leading design, and today it's the most recognizable one.

Hooker and his mousetraps were a huge success. But they might have done even better if it weren't for an Englishman who not only stole Hooker's design, but the credit for it as well.

THE WILY ENGLISHMAN

Even today, if you look up the inventor of the mousetrap, you may run across the name of James Henry Atkinson from Leeds, Yorkshire. A self-described "ironmonger," the wannabe inventor had received patents for various contraptions before, but his mousetrap application to the British Patent Office in 1898 was unique: the trap was small, elegant, simple, cheap to manufacture, and easy to hide.

He called it the "Little Nipper," and it was a near-perfect copy of the design Hooker had patented three years earlier. "It is quite likely that Atkinson had seen the Hooker trap in the shops or in advertisements," admitted British historical writer Stephen Dulkin. Back then, this sort of infringement happened a lot because the British Patent Office didn't begin systematically researching whether a claimed invention had been done before until 1905.

Over the years, other mousetraps were invented besides Hooker's. Some are arguably better than one that kills mice by breaking their spines with a brutal snap of metal. But although some have gained a little bit of traction, the Hooker trap continues to rule the mousetrap kingdom.

* * *

JON STEWART SEZ

"If you don't stick to your values when they're being tested, they're not values: they're hobbies."

"Fatherhood is great because you can ruin someone from scratch."

"I have complete faith in the continued absurdity of whatever's going on."

"You wonder sometimes how our government puts on its pants in the morning."

"I always knew I shouldn't have said that."

America's Old Roads

America's first transportation network was built about 2,500 years ago. Native Americans established land and river routes by 500 BC, allowing for travel, migration, and trade among communities throughout North and South America.

The ancient trade routes spread goods far and wide: seafood and decorative shells from coastal tribes, copper from Michigan, furs from Canada, gold from Mexico, mica from the Appalachians, and obsidian from the Rockies often traveled hundreds or thousands of miles from their points of origin.

One commodity often traded from the Pacific Northwest was candlefish. They had so much body fat that they could be dried and burned like candles. The trading route from the area became known as the Grease Trail because it was slippery with fish fat.

Land routes were common, but rivers were the most popular trade routes, whether traders traveled via dugout canoes or on paths along the shore.

When there were no rivers to follow, prehistoric paths were often created by "nature's bulldozers"—massive herds of bison that migrated along the same routes each year. The animals found the path of least resistance, eating, trampling and knocking down underbrush, bypassing swamps and obstacles, and finding the easiest ways over mountains.

Some paths were used to transport warriors. The Seneca Trail, which stretches from what's now Alabama to New York State, linked so many warring villages that some tribes called it *Athawominee* ("path where they go armed"). The British translated that as the "War Path," and that's where the phrase "on the warpath" comes from.

Many of today's streets, roads, highways, and interstates were laid down over existing Native American trails. For example, the route called the Wickquasgeck Trail is now one of the most famous streets in the world: New York City's Broadway.

Ads Nauseum

"Half the money I spend on advertising is wasted; the trouble is I don't know which half."

—**John Wanamaker**

"Advertising is a valuable economic factor because it is the cheapest way of selling goods, particularly if the goods are worthless."

—**Sinclair Lewis**

"I have always believed that writing advertisements is the second most profitable form of writing. The first, of course, is ransom notes."

—**Philip Dusenberry**

"The incessant witless repetition of advertisers' moron-fodder has become so much a part of life that if we are not careful, we forget to be insulted by it."

—**The *London Times* (1886)**

"If advertisers spent the same amount of money on improving their products as they do on advertising, then they wouldn't have to advertise them."

—**Will Rogers**

"Advertising may be described as the science of arresting the human intelligence long enough to get money from it."

—**Stephen Leacock**

"I do not read advertisements—I would spend all my time wanting things."

—**Franz Kafka**

"Advertising nourishes the consuming power of men. It sets up before a man the goal of a better home, better clothing, better food for himself and his family. It spurs individual exertion and greater production."

—**Sir Winston Churchill**

"Man is at his vilest when he erects a billboard. When I retire from Madison Avenue, I am going to start a secret society of masked vigilantes who will travel around the world on silent motor bicycles, chopping down posters at the dark of the moon. How many juries will convict us when we are caught in these acts of beneficent citizenship?"

—**David Ogilvy**

Words and Language

Joseph Stalin banned crossword puzzles in the USSR for being "bourgeois" and "degenerate."

The words *alcohol*, *algebra*, *lute*, and *magazine* all come from Arabic.

The "F-word" was first printed in English in 1475.

In nearly every language, the word for "mother" begins with the "m" sound.

In Japan, the number 4 is considered unlucky because it sounds like the Japanese word for death.

The only English word with three consecutive sets of double letters: bookkeeper.

The longest English surname without hyphens is Featherstonehaugh. (It's pronounced "Fanshaw.")

Illibilli, in Sudan, is the world's longest palindromic place name. Second longest: Nigeria's Uburubu.

The shortest English word to contain the letters A, B, C, D, E, and F is *feedback*.

The only English word that contains the letters X, Y, and Z in order is *hydroxyzine*.

The German language has words to describe 30 different types of kisses.

The only words in English containing the letters "uu" are *vacuum*, *residuum*, and *continuum*.

Assuming you don't leave your touch-typing position, the longest English word you can type with the left hand only is *stewardesses*.

* * *

DID YOU KNOW?

Halloween began in Ireland as a harvest festival named Samhain, which was also a night when the dead came back to earth for a day.

Urine Analysis

When ancient Greek physicians discovered that urine is sterile, they began using it as an antiseptic on wounds. It worked so well that the Romans later used concentrated urine as a toothpaste and dental rinse.

All the human urine produced worldwide in one day would take about 2½ hours to flow over Niagara Falls.

Human urine is 98 percent water and 2 percent sodium, calcium, urea, phosphates, and ammonium.

Frank Lloyd Wright designed a building for Florida Southern University, which he allowed students to help build for a break on tuition. He also let the students help age its copper into a nice green patina by having them pour their urine over it.

The male strawberry poison dart frog keeps its mate hydrated and warm by peeing on them.

The 16th-century insult *pissant* comes from "piss ants," a large wood ant, so called because its anthills smelled like urine.

Researchers in Singapore have created a battery powered by urine. It's about the size of a credit card, and a drop of urine produces 1.5 volts for 90 minutes.

When General George S. Patton reached Germany's Rhine River during World War II, he showed his contempt for the country by peeing in the water.

Tiger pee supposedly smells a lot like buttered popcorn.

Only 20 percent of people admit to having peed in a public swimming pool, but 93 percent of surfers admit to having peed in their wetsuits at least once.

In French, dandelions are called *pissenlit,* which means "pee in bed."

Alkaptonuria is a rare genetic disorder that causes urine to turn black.

The biggest draw at the Harlekin Toilet Museum of Modern Arse (yes, that's the real name) in Wiesbaden, Germany, is a urinal with Adolf Hitler's face painted inside the bowl.

Love to Laugh!

Laughing heartily for 10 to 15 minutes a day will burn about four pounds of fat in a year.

Studies show that up to 80 percent of adult laughter is unconnected to any joke or funny situation. More often, it's an expression of embarrassment, alarm, discomfort, tension, confusion, or anxiety.

The people most likely to laugh at slapstick humor are children, the brain-damaged, and men.

The French equivalent to "lol" in text messages is "mdr," short for *mort de rire*—"died of laughter."

Supposedly, the ancient Greek painter Zeuxis laughed himself to death while looking at his own painting.

The first person to use the phrase "laugh it off" in print was William Shakespeare.

Apes laugh when they're tickled.

The Leaning Tower of Pisa

In the 1980s, the tower was leaning at an angle of 5.5 degrees and the speed of tilt was accelerating. Earlier attempts to fix the tilt had made things worse, but work in the 1990s actually decreased the tilt to a manageable 3.99 degrees. Even better, the tower stopped moving for the first time in its history.

Work began in 1173, but it was another 200 years before the tower was finished...and the last bell wasn't installed until 1655.

The tower leans because one side is built on spongy sand. Part of the foundation began sinking as it was being built, and it only got worse with time.

It's still not clear who designed the tower. (Maybe the architect didn't want to take credit for it?)

The Tower of Pisa is slightly banana-shaped because the builders slanted the upper stories to try to counteract the structure's tilt.

There are 296 steps on the tower's taller side, and 294 on the shorter side.

The tower has no safety rails.

According to Galileo's secretary, the astronomer used the tower to drop objects of different masses to prove they would fall at the same speed, regardless of weight or density.

Buzzzzzz!

The record number of bee stings a person has received in one day and survived is 2,443.

Before 2010, it was illegal to raise bees in New York City because they were classified as a species that was "naturally inclined to do harm."

New beekeepers typically buy honeybees in two- or three-pound boxes. Honeybees don't weigh very much, so a three-pound box contains 6,000 to 9,000 bees.

What was the profession of Edmund Hillary, the first person to climb Mount Everest? Beekeeper.

Largest bee: Wallace's giant bee (*Chalicodoma pluto*). Females can be up to 1.5 inches long. The smallest bee is Australia's *Trigona minima*, sometimes called the dwarf bee. It's stingless and the size of a pinhead.

Bees fly at about 12 mph.

A honeybee can visit up to 2,000 flowers in a day.

Honeybees can be trained to sniff out explosives.

Researchers have monitored bees by attaching tiny bar codes to them.

The Honey Nut Cheerios bee is named BuzzBee.

A honeybee's stinger is finer than the tip of a needle.

Bears don't raid beehives for honey—they're after the larvae. But they'll eat the honey, too.

Honeybees have remained unchanged for 20 million years.

Besides lovers, St. Valentine is the patron saint of beekeepers, epileptics, and plagues.

Elephants are so afraid of honeybees that you can keep the animals out of a field by stringing it with beehives every 32 feet or so.

Most popular official state insect: the honeybee (17 states). The monarch butterfly is #2, with seven states.

Discovered in Dreams

DREAMER: Otto Loewi

DREAM: Two live frogs with their hearts exposed

RESULT: Figured out that chemicals communicate nerve impulses to the body's organs

In the early 20th century, there was a lot of debate about whether nerve impulses were communicated to the organs via electrical or chemical messages. Loewi believed it was chemical but couldn't prove it. Then, one night in 1921, he dreamed of an experiment that would settle the issue. When he woke up, he feverishly scribbled notes but in the morning discovered that his notes were unreadable and he couldn't remember what he had dreamed. Luckily, he had the same dream the next night. It was a gruesome experiment on the still-beating hearts of two frogs. Loewi followed the procedures in the dream: he slowed the heart of one frog using electrical stimuli and collected the chemical secretions that resulted. Then he injected the secretions into the other frog's heart, and it slowed too, proving that chemicals were how the nervous system communicated with a body's organs. Loewi won the Nobel Prize in Medicine in 1936.

DREAMER: Elias Howe

DREAM: Being boiled by cannibals who danced brandishing spears with a hole near the tips

RESULT: The sewing machine

American inventor and former textile-mill worker Elias Howe couldn't quite figure out how to make sewn stitches interlock so that seams didn't pull apart. But in the 1840s, he had a dream about being boiled alive by cannibals who danced while brandishing spears with holes near the tips.

In the dream, the cannibals moved their spears up and down in a rhythmic way. He thought and thought about it, and then one day, inspiration struck: instead of using a standard sewing needle with a hole at the dull end, he needed to use a thread near the sharp *tip*. That kind of needle could pull a loop of thread through the cloth where it could meet on the other side a moving part that would anchor it with a second thread. It was just the breakthrough Howe was looking for and allowed him to make the sewing machine possible.

DREAMER: Mary Shelley

DREAM: A mad scientist creating life in laboratory

RESULT: *Frankenstein*

In 1816, challenged to write a ghost story to amuse fellow guests housebound during a storm, 19-year-old Mary Shelley lay in bed half asleep. She later wrote, "With shut eyes, but acute mental vision, I saw the pale student of unhallowed arts kneeling beside the thing he had put together. I saw the hideous phantasm of a man stretched out, and then, on the working of some powerful engine, show signs of life, and stir with an uneasy, half-vital motion." The next morning, she got up and began writing what became the book *Frankenstein*.

DREAMER: Paul McCartney

DREAM: A lilting melody

RESULT: "Yesterday"

While filming the movie *Help!*, Paul McCartney woke up with a tune in his head and rushed to the piano to play it, singing "scrambled eggs" and other random words in the place of lyrics. He recalled, "I liked the melody a lot, but because I'd dreamed it, I couldn't believe I'd written it." Thinking maybe he had just remembered an old song, he played it for other people, asking if they'd ever heard it before. They hadn't. But they would, repeatedly, for decades. It became the 1965 Beatles hit "Yesterday," one of the most popular tunes ever recorded.

DREAMER: William Watt

DREAM: Being pelted in a hailstorm of perfectly round lead balls

RESULT: Perfectly round musket shot and cannonballs

Eighteenth-century Bristol, England, was known for its industry, especially smelting lead from local mines. Lead balls for muskets and cannons were big business, but were difficult to make round and smooth enough that they wouldn't jam weapons. A plumber by trade, William Watt's dream inspired him to climb to the top of a church steeple and dribble a stream of melted lead into a bucket of cold water far below. Sure enough, like any liquid, the lead formed itself into perfect balls and stayed that way until it solidified in the cool air and cold water. Watt had remarkably figured this out long before high-speed photography proved that raindrops were round and not, as widely believed, teardrop-shaped.

* * *

RIDE 'EM, COWBOY

- The Houston Livestock Show and Rodeo is the world's largest rodeo. It runs for most of March each year, attracting 2 million spectators.
- *Rodeo* is a Spanish word that means "round up."
- The first formal rodeo took place in Cheyenne, Wyoming, in 1872. However, Prescott, Arizona, hosted the first professional rodeo in 1888 with cash prizes and admission charged for spectators.
- Women have competed in rodeos since 1901, but team roping is the only event where men and women compete together.
- Bucking broncos are no longer wild horses being tamed—they're usually bred and trained to buck.
- Rodeo cowboys have their own group—the Professional Rodeo Cowboys Association. But before 1975, it was called the Cowboy Turtle Association because, although the group was slow to organize, the men weren't afraid to "stick their necks out." The group began after a labor dispute with a Boston rodeo promoter.
- The Texas Cowboy Hall of Fame is in the Fort Worth Stockyards west of Dallas. It used to be an actual stockyard, but now is a tourist attraction.

A Lake List

Only one Great Lake has a bottom that's above sea level: Lake Erie.

Isa Lake in Yellowstone Park straddles the Continental Divide and has two creeks leading out of it. One heads east, with its water ultimately reaching the Atlantic Ocean, and the other flows west to the Pacific.

Utah's Great Salt Lake is five times saltier than the ocean. If you evaporated an eight-ounce glass of its water, about an inch of salt would be left on the bottom.

But the saltiest lake in the world is Don Juan Pond in Antarctica. It's so salty that it never freezes, even in winter temperatures below -50°F.

Only one freshwater lake in the world has sharks: Lake Nicaragua.

*   *   *

CLEMSON BLUE CHEESE

Blue cheese requires a long time to age, and its finicky blue mold doesn't survive in warm weather. So it wasn't until 1941 that researchers at Clemson University in South Carolina successfully made blue cheese in the American South for the first time. Using the state's unfinished Stumphouse Mountain Tunnel, which had been idle for about 80 years, researchers drilled into solid blue granite, which maintained a constant temperature of 50°F and humidity of 85 percent. Clemson University has been making blue cheese for sale since the 1950s, but it doesn't use the tunnel anymore.

Court of Last Resort

Most Americans can't name a single Supreme Court justice.

Childhood nickname of Justice Ruth Bader Ginsberg: Kiki.

In the late 19th century, the dairy industry pushed through laws forcing margarine manufacturers to color their product an unappetizing pink. The Supreme Court struck down the laws in the 1880s, and margarine has been yellow ever since.

William Howard Taft (president from 1909 to 1913) also became Chief Justice of the Supreme Court in 1921 and served until his death in 1930, the only person to hold both positions.

In 1895, when Congress tried to pass an income tax on high earners, the Supreme Court ruled that such a tax was unconstitutional. In response, Congress wrote an income tax into the Constitution in 1913 with the 16th Amendment.

Shortest U.S. Supreme Court Chief Justice: Melville W. Fuller (1888–1910). He was about 5'3".

The oldest Supreme Court justice to date was Oliver Wendell Holmes, who was 90 when he retired in 1932.

George Washington appointed the most Supreme Court justices (11), with FDR a close second (9).

Jimmy Carter was the only president who served a full term without appointing a justice.

Roger B. Taney (who served from 1836 to 1864) was the first Supreme Court justice to wear pants under his judicial robes. Before that, justices sported knee breeches.

The first, and last, U.S. Supreme Court justice to wear an English-style powdered wig was William Cushing in 1790. Although still commonly worn in his native Massachusetts, the wig immediately attracted teasing from the other justices and scorn from Thomas Jefferson, who said, "For heaven's sake, discard the monstrous wig which makes the English judges took like rats peeping through bunches of oakum."

Poetry to My Ears

Tryphiodorus was an ancient Greek poet who enjoyed a good *lipogram*—a body of work deliberately written with one letter of the alphabet omitted. Tryphiodorus wrote a poem called *Odyssey* without the letter A. His next poem contained no Bs, and so on.

As far as anyone knows, Anne Bradstreet of the Massachusetts Bay Colony was the first poet to be published in colonial America.

Marguerite Johnson adopted the stage name of Maya Angelou when she became a cabaret dancer at the Purple Onion, a nightclub in San Francisco. Later, when she began writing novels and poetry, she decided to use her stage name as her pen name.

By the time poet John Milton published *Paradise Lost*, he was 45 years old and completely blind.

Don't confuse William S. Burroughs, the Beat poet, with William S. Burroughs, the man who invented the adding machine. The latter was the former's grandfather.

The Mild Bunch

Walmart sells more bananas than any other item.

The high level of potassium in bananas makes them slightly radioactive.

There are no banana trees. The banana plant is classified as an herb because everything aboveground dies as soon as the bananas mature.

"Banana" comes from the Arab word *banan*, which means "finger."

Bananas came from Malaysia, where they've been bred and cultivated for 10,000 years. Wild bananas have large seeds, very little flesh, and are pollinated by bats.

Bananas are the most profitable crop in the world, and the industry employs 400 million people worldwide (most make below-poverty wages).

About 50% of people who are allergic to latex are also allergic to bananas.

Surprisingly, Iceland, located just below the Arctic Circle, is Europe's biggest banana grower. The tropical fruit grows in huge greenhouses heated by geothermal water.

From 1959 to 1994, Osoyoos, BC, located between two banana-shaped lakes, was home to Canada's only banana plantation—just 200 plants located inside a hothouse.

Paper made from banana-plant fiber is stronger than regular paper.

For a museum about the fruit, head to the Musée de la Banane ("Museum of the Banana") on the Caribbean island of Martinique. It's located on a working banana plantation.

According to *Guinness World Records*, the largest bunch of bananas grown naturally came from Spain in 2001: 473 bananas in the bunch.

Bananas grow pointing up, not hanging down.

The Fruit of the Vine

A lover of wine is called an *oenophile*.

One of America's first great wine regions was centered around Cincinnati, Ohio. In the 1850s, the area was known as "the Rhineland of America," making Ohio America's main wine producer at the time. All that ended with Prohibition, and Ohio winemaking never fully recovered.

Today, California produces the most wine in the United States, about 90%. New York and Washington State are second, with about 8% combined.

In the 7th century BC, the Greeks planted the first wine grapes in France in what's now the region around Marseille.

The average French person drinks about 10 times more wine per year than the average American.

Marijuana mixed with a strong wine was the first recorded anesthetic, used by Chinese physician Hua Tuo in the second century AD.

Every book of the standard Bible mentions wine except Jonah. The book of Isaiah even has advice on how to plant a good vineyard.

Ernest and Julio Gallo learned how to make wine from a pamphlet they picked up at the Modesto public library.

Some wine historians believe that wine dates back more than 8,000 years, making it the oldest alcoholic beverage.

That large indentation on the bottom of wine bottles is called the "punt." There are dozens of theories as to why it was put there centuries ago, but now it's just tradition.

All About Beetles

The insect order that outnumbers all the others? Coleoptera—the beetles.

The 350,000 varieties of beetles make up about one-fourth of all known species. Since 1758, species have been identified at an average of four a day.

Tiger beetles run at 5 mph—proportionately, that's equal to a human running at 480 mph.

Bess beetles can make 14 distinct sounds.

One dropping of elephant dung can feed and house up to 7,000 beetles.

Cochineal, a once-popular red dye, was made from crushing scale beetles that live exclusively on the prickly pear cactus.

A male dung beetle creates a ball of poop, pushes it away from the main pile, buries it, and gets a female to nest in it. That dung ball will later provide food for the happy couple's larva.

To make shellac, you have to crush a lot of beetles—about 150,000 per pound.

Potato beetle larvae protect themselves from being eaten by covering their bodies in poisoned poop. Many plants in the potato family—deadly nightshade, for example—have toxic compounds in their leaves. The larvae are able to eat the leaves without harm, but a lot of the poison gets excreted in their dung. They then stay safe from predators by piling that dung on their backs.

Early farmers believed that ladybugs were helpful pest-eaters sent from heaven. The English called them "Our Lady's beetles"; Germans called them *Marienkafer* ("Mary's beetles"); and the French called them *les vaches de la Vierge* ("cows of the Virgin").

Australian ranchers had to import millions of African dung beetles to eat cow droppings because the continent's native beetles preferred marsupial dung.

Weird Beard

Pogonology is the study of beards. *Pogonophobia*, the fear of beards.

Despite legend, shaving hair will not make it thicker or darker.

Russian czar Peter the Great wanted to modernize his country and thought unkempt beards looked "medieval." So he discouraged long beards by taxing them.

Beards grow faster in the summer.

Female goats have beards.

Barbe à papa is what the French call cotton candy. It translates to "daddy's beard."

The band ZZ Top is famous for its beards. The only clean-shaven member is the drummer. His name? Frank Beard.

If an Amish man has a beard, it means he's married.

Treebeard, slow-talking leader of the treelike Ents found in two of the Lord of the Rings books, was based on J. R. R. Tolkien's good friend and fellow author, C. S. Lewis.

80 percent of American presidents with facial hair have been Republicans.

Knock on Wood

In the early 1920s, Henry Ford was disturbed by how much scrap wood was being thrown out from his factories. So he convinced Edward Kingsford, his cousin-in-law, to use it to make charcoal briquettes. The Kingsford Company is still in business.

Lincoln Logs are among the few toys still sold whose wood hasn't been replaced with plastic. Not that they didn't try—from 1970 until 1990, the company sold an all-plastic version, but backed down after getting complaints.

Pound for pound, wood is stronger than steel.

Jenga game pieces are made of alder wood.

The inner layer of pine bark (called the "cambium") is edible.

Many of the trees in Sequoia National Park are more than 2,000 years old.

A wood louse is just another name for a pill bug, doodlebug, or roly-poly.

In 2007 American Kevin Shelley cracked 46 wooden toilet seats over his head in one minute and set a world record.

Every year in the U.S., more trees are planted than are cut down.

More than 96 percent of the old-growth redwoods in California were logged from 1850 to 2000.

Technically, a cord of wood occupies 128 cubic feet. It takes that much wood to make about 1,000 copies of this book.

* * *

CAN YOU HEAR ME NOW?

Harry Houdini died on Halloween in 1926. In the following years, his wife Bess held Halloween séances based on his promise to contact her from "the other side." (He never did.)

You Call That Cabbage?

CORN BY ANY OTHER NAME...

People have been messing with plants since the invention of agriculture, changing them dramatically from their original form. Wild corn, for example, domesticated since prehistory, now has at least nine different subspecies, from sweet corn to flour corn, each with different uses based on their levels of sweetness and starch. But they're still all recognizable as corn.

CULTIVATING CABBAGE

Wild cabbage is a very specialized plant. It grows only on limestone sea cliffs like the chalk cliffs of Dover, England, and is found only on the coasts of the English Channel and the Mediterranean. And even in those places, it was picky and didn't like competition from other plants.

A few millennia ago, though, people noticed how nutritious the plant was and how well it grew in and stored for all seasons, which would help to stave off starvation in winter. So farmers began digging up the cabbages near the edges of the chalk cliffs and moving them to other soils, methodically breeding plants that could grow in different climates and environments. Having noticed that cabbages had several edible parts, each with different textures and flavors, farmers began selecting plants that had bigger and better amounts of their favorite edible part.

After many seasons of artificial selection, the farmers' efforts paid off and produced plants that were so different from each other it was hard to recognize that they had come from the same plant. For example, farmers selecting plants for large bud size produced Brussels sprouts. Selecting for many flower heads produced broccoli. Selecting leafy growth gave us kale; for terminal buds, what we recognize as cabbage; and so on to include cauliflower, collard greens, broccoflower, kohlrabi, savoy, and Chinese kale.

Climb Every Mountain

There's no scientific agreement about how high something has to be before it's called a mountain instead of a hill. In the United States, some researchers say that point is about 1,000 feet. In the UK, the minimum is around 2,000 feet. The UN's definition is more complicated: 2,500 feet normally, but as low as 1,000 if the sides are particularly steep.

17 of the United States' 20 highest mountains are in Alaska.

A coal seam in Burning Mountain, in New South Wales, Australia, has been smoldering for 6,000 years. The flame moves about three feet south every year.

Mount Rainier in Washington State is considered one of the most dangerous mountains in the world because it is mostly hollow inside, and could collapse, which would wipe out Seattle, Tacoma, and the surrounding areas.

Coral, shells, and other sea fossils have been found on the tops of many mountains because the peaks began as flat surfaces underwater and were raised up over millions of years by tectonic pressure.

96 of the world's highest mountains (109 total) are in the Himalayas.

Building Bridges

The world's longest train bridge is China's Wuhu Yangtze River Bridge. It's 6.2 miles long.

The river Thames has seen several London Bridges. The first was a wooden one that was pulled down by rampaging Danes in 1014. A replacement, built in 1087, was destroyed by a tornado in 1091. It was quickly replaced, but burned in 1136. King Henry II built a stone bridge in 1176 that lasted 647 years until 1823. That one, made of granite, was found to be sinking and was sold in 1962 to a developer in Arizona. The final modern structure is still standing.

About 7,000 people cross the Brooklyn Bridge on foot or bicycle daily.

In the 1880s, when the Brooklyn Bridge was being built, its 275-foot towers were seven times taller than Manhattan's four-story skyline.

Con men regularly "sold" the Brooklyn Bridge to unwary tourists and new immigrants.

More than once, the police stopped insistent bridge "owners" from building their own tollbooths on the span.

What was the going rate for the Brooklyn Bridge? Usually about $200, although a pair of bridge-selling brothers once sold it for a mere $2.50 when that was all their "mark" had.

The only place to legally bungee jump from a bridge in California is on "the Bridge to Nowhere"—a never-used concrete bridge in Los Angeles County's rugged San Gabriel Canyon. It was built in 1936 for a highway, but was never used because the river it ran along kept flooding out the road while it was under construction. Today, the bridge is in a remote part of the Sheep Mountain Wilderness, reachable by only a strenuous hike of 10 miles round-trip.

The Boston University Bridge is the only place in the world where a boat can sail under a train running under a car driving under an airplane.

Favorite Haunts

California, Louisiana, and Pennsylvania have the most ghost sightings in the U.S.

In 1993 J. R. Costigan sued a country music bar in Wilder, Kentucky, claiming that a ghost had beaten him up in the men's room. He wanted the bar to give him $1,000 in damages and to post a "Beware of Vicious Ghost" sign on the men's room door. The judge dismissed the case.

The word *poltergeist* means "noisy ghost" in German.

Ghost researcher Dale Kaczmarek says that in 30 years, he's "never met a ghost [he] didn't like."

Motorcyclists riding on Old Creek Road near Ojai, California, have reported seeing a headless "hogman" riding a 1940s motorcycle on dark, foggy nights.

Supposedly, Toronto's Hockey Hall of Fame, located in an old bank building, is haunted by Dorothy, the ghost of a bank teller.

Singer Sting believes in ghosts. He claims one visited him in his bedroom.

Sherlock Holmes's creator, Sir Arthur Conan Doyle, also believed in ghosts…and bought into most psychic tricks he saw.

Noting that the bulk of video game players were male, the designers of Pac-Man went to great effort to make the ghosts "cute," not scary, hoping to attract girls.

World's most haunted city: York, England, with more than 500 reported ghost sightings.

The word "larva" comes from the Latin word for ghost, probably because most larvae are translucent and white.

According to one poll, 34 percent of Americans believe in ghosts, an equal number believe in UFOs, 29 percent believe in astrology, 25 percent in reincarnation, and 24 percent in witches.

Just Deserts

The definition of a desert is an area that gets less than 10 inches of rain per year.

The Sahara, the world's third-largest desert, is nearly as big as the entire United States. About 2.5 million people live there. (It's also the world's hottest desert.)

The only continent that doesn't have a desert is Europe.

North America's largest is the Chihuahuan Desert. It's mostly in Mexico, but crosses the border into Texas, Arizona, and New Mexico.

20 percent of the earth's land surface is considered desert.

The desert tortoise, which lives the Mojave and Sonoran Deserts in the American Southwest, can survive for a year without water.

The longest-lived desert plant is the creosote bush, which can live for thousands of years by splitting and cloning itself into new bushes. One plant has been carbon-dated to 11,700 years ago.

The ancient Egyptians used castor bean oil to protect their skin from the blistering desert sun. Also, the dark kohl they applied around their eyes helped to minimize the glare of the sun.

The driest place in the world is the Atacama Desert in Chile. There are parts that have never recorded rainfall. The only precipitation comes from fog, measuring less than a quarter inch of liquid per year.

Not all deserts are hot. In fact, the world's two largest deserts are very cold: the Arctic and Antarctica.

*   *   *

Some monkeys in Thailand teach their babies to floss their teeth.

Musical Notes

Queen is the only rock group that had at least one hit written by each member of the band.

Most North American car horns are tuned to the key of F.

Street musicians must audition for permission to play in New York City's subway stations.

Which song has the highest sheet music sales? It's "Yes, We Have No Bananas," which sold more than a half million copies over eight months in 1923.

Charles Lindbergh's solo flight across the Atlantic inspired more than 20 pop songs.

Tina Fey's husband, Jeff Richmond, composed all the music for *30 Rock*.

Pianists and woodwind players often get inflamed tendons in their hands and wrists. Brass players can suffer dental problems from pressure on their mouths. Violinists and violists are often pained by neck, back, and shoulder problems.

India's Lata Mangeshkar is the most-recorded musician in history. Over 40 years, she recorded more than 5,200 songs in 20 languages, mostly for Bollywood musicals.

Catgut, a type of strong cord, is not what it sounds like—it's actually made from sheep intestines. Linguists think it got its name from being used as strings on the *kit,* a small violin popular in 17th-century Europe.

Cows give more milk when they listen to music.

Van Morrison and Itzhak Perlman were both born on August 31, 1945.

Michael Jackson got his first gold record at age 10.

Longest-running TV music series of all time? *Soul Train*, which ran for 35 years from 1971 to 2006.

It isn't just rock and roll that damages hearing—many orchestra performers suffer at least some hearing loss, too.

What a Boar

Christopher Columbus brought the first pigs to the Americas (Cuba, actually) on his second voyage in 1493.

Hernando de Soto brought the first pigs to *North* America, landing in Florida with 13 in 1539. The ones that escaped into the swamplands became the first razorbacks.

Pigs get hairballs like cats do, but they can't cough them up. Instead, their stomachs form a rubbery shell around them, and the (harmless) masses remain inside the pig.

The world's largest pig hairball, the size and shape of a football, is on display at the museum of the Mount Angel Abbey in St. Benedict, Oregon.

Pigs don't sweat. They roll in mud to cool off.

We know of three separate historical conflicts called the "Pig War," each of which began with a dispute about a pig.

A pig says "oink oink," right? Well, not everywhere. It's "kryoo kroo" in Russia, "groin groin" in France, "hulu hulu" in China, "rok rok" in Croatia, "hrju hrju" in Vietnam, "grunz grunz" in Germany, and "buu buu" in Japan.

Most flu viruses first infect chickens, then pigs, and then spread to humans.

Humans worldwide eat pork more than any other kind of meat.

If it manages to evade the butcher's knife, a pig's natural life span is 15 to 20 years.

Pigs eat rattlesnakes and appear to be immune to the snakes' poison.

Pigs may look fat and out of shape, but on average, they can run a seven-minute mile.

The largest pig ever was named Big Bill, from Jackson, Tennessee. He tipped the scales at 2,552 pounds in 1933.

You're Getting Sleepy

In a lifetime, the average American will spend about 25 years sleeping.

Carbs make you sleepy. Protein makes you more alert.

Children who don't get enough sleep are 45 percent more likely to be overweight.

Doctors have identified more than a hundred different sleep disorders.

According to a 2002 study, counting sheep doesn't help you get to sleep any faster.

Most people could last for about two months without any food, but only 10 days without any sleep.

Only about 28 percent of American adults get eight hours of sleep a night.

One in four Americans falls asleep with the TV on at least three nights a week.

Some users of prescription sleep medications report a high rate of physical activity during sleep, including making phone calls and driving.

Somnambulism is when you walk in your sleep. *Somniloquence* is when you talk in your sleep.

Lesson learned? 48 percent of new parents say they prefer sleep to sex.

Thomas Edison thought eight hours of sleep was a waste of time. He slept only three or four hours a night.

Albert Einstein, on the other hand, usually slept 10 hours a night.

40 million Americans experience bruxism in their sleep: jaw clenching and teeth grinding.

In the original story, Rip Van Winkle slept for 20 years;

Chromedome

"Cavities" are holes in your teeth, but a "calvity" is a hole in your hair. (Well, sort of. It's another word for baldness.)

To cure baldness, western European doctors prescribed a hair dressing of oil and burned bees or goose poop (ewww!). (It didn't work.)

Cleopatra used a mixture of horse teeth, bear grease, burned mice, and deer marrow to cure Julius Caesar's baldness. (It didn't work, either.)

Baldy was a first-draft name for one of Disney's seven dwarfs.

In ancient Rome, beauticians painted curls directly onto bald scalps.

Don't fixate on the hairs falling out. About a hundred typically fall out every day.

Women don't usually go bald without an accompanying medical condition.

Minoxidil, the chemical used in Rogaine, does slow follicle loss, as long as you don't stop taking it. How does it work? Researchers still haven't quite figured that out. In fact, hair growth was a puzzling side effect when minoxidil pills were originally prescribed...for high blood pressure.

Bottoms Up

Oldest operating tavern in the U.S.: the White Horse Tavern in Newport, Rhode Island, opened in 1673. For about 100 years, the building also operated as Rhode Island's colonial government headquarters.

Along the 750-mile California Melee road rally (an annual parade of old cars), the pit stops are at brewpubs.

President Martin Van Buren was born in a house attached to his father's tavern.

A poll in *Bartender* magazine found that the worst tippers are lawyers and doctors.

Buffalo wings originated at Frank & Teresa's Anchor Bar, which happens to be in Buffalo, New York.

The U.S. Marines' first recruiting station: the Tun Tavern in Philadelphia...in 1775.

Before becoming president, Abraham Lincoln co-owned a bar in Springfield, Illinois, called Berry & Lincoln.

The Green Dragon Tavern in Boston became known as the "Headquarters of the American Revolution": the place where rebels plotted the Boston Tea Party and discussed plans for Paul Revere's famous ride. The original Green Dragon was demolished in 1828.

A company called "Drink Safe Technologies" sells bar coasters that test drinks for date-rape drugs. The coasters turn colors when you spill a contaminated drink on them.

* * *

WHAT'S IN A NAME?

Beginning in the 13th century, Frankfurt, Germany, produced "frankfurters," pork sausages that were a lot like modern hot dogs. Austria's Vienna (German name: Wien), made similar pork and beef sausages called "wieners."

Cowa Dunga!

According to a 2005 Bristol University survey, birds are more likely to poop on white cars.

Wombats have cube-shaped poop—they use it to mark their territory because it can't roll away.

In ancient Egypt, some women used dung as a method of birth control. (It worked like a spermicide.)

The term "butterfly" comes from a Dutch word, *botervlieg* ("butter poop"), referring to greasy yellow residue from the butterfly's pollen-rich diet.

People make paper out of poop from herbivorous animals, including pandas, cows, elephants, moose, donkeys, and horses. One elephant can produce enough dung for 115 sheets of paper a day.

Like dung beetles, burrowing owls line their underground nests with cow dung. The composting dung insulates the nest to maintain a comfortable temperature and attracts insects for the owls to eat.

Bird dung crab spiders in Africa are so named because they look like a dab of bird poop, which camouflages them in the forest.

NASA slang for poop floating in space: "escapees."

Arrrg...Pirates!

Privateers were pirates who were considered legitimate. Wealthy merchants financed their ships for a cut of the loot, and the privateers operated under immunity from their countries' piracy laws, as long as they agreed to ransack only enemy ships.

The term *buccaneer* originally meant "he who cures meat" in French, and France set up ranches in the Cayman Islands so that their ships could get beef to the New World. In the 1600s, though, the meat-curing men with knives and easy access to ships figured out that they could take those ships and make more money as pirates, so "buccaneer" took on a new meaning.

Pirate ships were democratic. All pirates aboard voted on major decisions, and the captain was elected and could be impeached.

In his time, privateer/pirate and tobacco-pusher Sir Walter Raleigh was also a renowned poet. (Historians note that Sir Walter spelled his last name "Ralegh.")

Pirates sometimes tossed people overboard to their deaths, but they didn't really make people walk the plank. That was an invention of Robert Louis Stevenson in *Treasure Island*.

Edward Teach, better known as "Blackbeard," used his fearsome reputation and scary dreadlocked beard to good effect. Most of the ships he attacked surrendered rather than fight his pirate crew. In return, he treated his captives well, not brutalizing or murdering them as some pirates did.

Some crews, like Henry Morgan's, had workman's compensation plans: if a pirate received a career-ending injury on the job, he'd be granted 600 pieces of gold—about $100,000 in today's money.

Not all pirates sailed the open sea. "River pirates" raided vessels on the Mississippi and Ohio Rivers in the 1800s.

Pirates who sailed the Great Lakes plundered whiskey and venison instead of gold.

Pencil Me In

Until rubber erasers were invented, people often used crustless white bread to erase pencil marks.

Pencils are hexagonal because they were originally cut into that shape to keep them from rolling off tables.

A regular wood pencil can write 45,000 words.

Graphite isn't a form of lead, but people once thought it was, so the term "pencil lead" stuck.

Pencil lead is a mixture of graphite and clay. The more clay, the softer the lead.

Mechanical pencils were invented in 1877, but it wasn't until 1976 that somebody figured out how to store lead inside the pencil and feed one after another into the barrel.

Before becoming a writer, Henry David Thoreau worked in his family's pencil factory. Long after, he impressed friends by reaching into barrels of pencils and pulling out a dozen every time.

Hymen L. Lipman was the guy who first thought of putting an eraser on a pencil in 1858.

The world generates more than 14 billion pencils each year, almost two billion in the U.S. alone.

Money!

The Chinese issued the first known paper money. Facing a copper shortage during the early ninth century, Chinese emperor Hien Tsung authorized block-printed paper currency as a replacement for coins.

When Tibetans switched over to paper money in 1913, their rice-paper currency was hand-numbered by Tibetan calligraphers using black ink made from burned yak dung.

While a chemistry professor at Montreal's McGill University in the 1850s, Thomas Sterry Hunt came up with the ink used to make American dollars—it's been used to make greenbacks green since 1862.

It costs 9.6¢ to make a single dollar bill.

Most common name for currencies worldwide: "dollar." Second most common: "franc."

Since the Federal Reserve was created in 1913, the U.S. dollar's value has fallen 98 percent.

Once used as currency: kettle drums (Indonesia), playing cards (Canada), and dogs' teeth (Solomon Islands).

Federal prisoners aren't allowed to carry money, so for many decades cigarettes were used as currency. But when smoking was banned in prisons in 2004, prisoners had to come up with a new gold standard. The solution: "macks," 99¢ plastic-and-foil packs of mackerel from the prison commissary that could be exchanged for shoe shines, stolen food, homemade booze, and other services and contraband.

Pennies rarely stay in active circulation for long. Of all the pennies minted in a year, 70 percent are taken out of circulation within two years: dropped into drawers, grates, piggy banks, car seats, gutters, sofas, etc.

The official exchange rate of Vietnamese dongs is about 20,000 dongs to one American dollar.

Walk Like an (Ancient) Egyptian

Ancient Egyptian doctors used natural anesthesia found in plants, but they also sometimes just knocked patients unconscious with a wooden hammer.

The ancient Egyptians used penicillin before anyone knew what penicillin was. To treat infections, they placed moldy bread over the wound.

Peseshet of ancient Egypt (about 2400 BC) was the world's first known female physician.

King Tut was entombed with 36 ceramic jars of wine…to make his transition to the afterlife easier. He was also buried with plenty of fresh underwear—145 loincloths.

Egypt's most famous queen, Cleopatra, was actually Greek and a member of the Ptolemaic dynasty that ruled Egypt after the empire was conquered by Alexander the Great. She was also the first of the Ptolemaics to learn the Egyptian language and was the empire's last pharaoh.

An earthquake in the fourth century sank Cleopatra's royal palace into the ocean. The ruins were discovered in 1992, in the sewage-filled waters of Alexandria's harbor.

The last known Egyptian hieroglyphic inscription was made in 394.

Egyptian pharaoh Pepi II had his slaves smeared with honey to draw flies away from him.

Some ancient Egyptians shaved their armpits and used citrus-cinnamon deodorant.

Four million embalmed ibis birds were discovered in a single Egyptian cemetery—people sacrificed them to the god Thoth, who supposedly loved the birds.

Ammonia got its name from the Egyptian god Amun.

It took the ancient Egyptians about 2½ months and half a mile of cloth to turn a corpse into a full-fledged mummy.

Sweet Talk

A sweet Persian reed called *kand* gave us the word "candy." Alexander the Great carried the treat back to Macedonia in 340 BC.

The average American will chow down on 24 pounds of candy per year.

Americans collectively buy an estimated 20 million pounds of candy corn for Halloween. Note: One kernel of candy corn provides enough energy for an adult to walk 150 feet.

For at least 3,000 years, licorice has been used to heal peptic ulcers and ease colds and coughs.

Swedish children dress up as witches and walk around neighborhoods collecting candy…on Easter.

During the Berlin Airlift of the late 1940s, after the Soviets sealed the borders of West Germany, the United States and its allies dropped more than 20 tons of candy to German children from airplanes.

Illinois taxes candy at a higher rate than other foods.

The New England Confectionery Company (NECCO) sponsored Admiral Richard Byrd's two-year Antarctic exploration in the 1930s. That explains why he carried with him a daily ration of a pack of Neccos for each crew member—a total of about 2.5 tons of the chalky candy wafers.

October 30 is "National Candy Corn Day."

In 1923 the Curtiss Candy Company held a contest to name its latest candy bar. The winner: a clumsy klutz named Nikola "Butterfingers" Jovanovic, who sent in his nickname.

Eduard Haas III invented Pez in Vienna in 1927. The candy came only in the flavor of *pfefferminz* (peppermint). By taking the letters at the beginning, middle, and end, the company came up with PEZ. The novelty dispensers wouldn't appear until 1955.

Historical Nicknames

Theodore Roosevelt disliked being called "Teddy."

President Steven Grover Cleveland, weighing in at 280 pounds, was called "Big Steve" and "Uncle Jumbo."

Infamous Roman emperor Caligula's real name was Gaius Caesar Augustus Germanicus. He got his nickname "Caligula" as a child. It means "Little Boots."

Richard Nixon's nickname in college: "Gloomy Gus."

During the Mexican-American War, future president Franklin Pierce was struck in the groin by his saddle. He passed out from the pain and got a new nickname: "Fainting Frank."

Ronald Reagan's nickname was "Dutch," short for "fat little Dutchman," which is what his father thought he looked like as an infant.

In 1316 King John I of France was nicknamed and crowned "John the Posthumous" as he emerged from the womb because his father, "Louis X the Quarreler," had died. Alas, the infant lived only five days—murdered, some say, by his ambitious uncle, "Philip the Tall."

Peace, Love, and Litigation

The Beatles were famous ambassadors for peace and love, but they also generated a lot of lawsuits. Here are some of them.

BEATLES VS. EMI: From 1979 through 2006, the Beatles skirmished with the record company EMI five different times. Four times, it was over royalties. The remaining issue was about EMI's plans to release the *Red* (hits from 1962–66) and *Blue* (hits from 1967–70) albums on CD in 1991 without the band's permission. The Beatles won every time, but after winning the last case and establishing their veto rights, they let EMI release the albums anyway.

BEATLES VS. APPLE: Steve Jobs reportedly named his fledgling company Apple in part because he was a Beatles fan and they'd named their own multimedia company Apple Corps, which owned their record company Apple Records. The Beatles threatened to sue, and in 1981, Jobs's Apple settled by paying $80,000 and agreeing to stay out of the music business.

It didn't last long. In 1989 the Beatles' Apple Corps noted that Apple computers were being used to play, record, and mix music. The band sued again. This time, the computer company paid $26 million and won the right to create "goods and services…used to reproduce, run, play, or otherwise deliver" music, but not any actual music.

Then came iTunes, and Apple Corps believed that the music store violated the terms of the agreement. So in 2006, they went back to court, but this time the Beatles lost, with the judge ruling that selling music was not the same as creating it. Faced with the prospect of endless appeals and litigation, the two companies came up with an agreement, reportedly involving Apple Computers spending half a billion dollars to buy the rights to everything called "Apple" and then leasing the music rights back to Apple Corps. Still, Beatles songs didn't appear in the iTunes Store until 2010 because the band's albums were re-released in digitally remastered form in 2009 and Apple Records wanted a year to sell CDs before offering the songs online.

BEATLES PUBLISHER VS. *SESAME STREET*: In 1965, as a way of reducing their income taxes, the Beatles converted their Northern Songs music publishing company into a public company, selling shares of it on the London Stock Exchange. But the tactic backfired, and control of their songs passed out of their hands and to ATV, a large media company that bought controlling interest. ATV was aggressive in protecting its profits and in 1984 sued Sesame Street Records for several million dollars for two parodies that played on *Sesame Street*: "Letter B," sung by puppet beetles in the style of "Let It Be," and "Hey Food," sung by the Cookie Monster in the style of "Hey Jude." The suit ended only when Michael Jackson bought ATV's rights to the Beatles' song collection in 1984. Under Jackson's new management, the lawsuit was settled for $50, which was paid out-of-pocket by composer Christopher Cerf, who wrote the parodies. In return, he got a nice letter from Paul McCartney, who said he liked the songs.

BEATLES PUBLISHER VS. "THE RUTLES": *The Rutles: All You Need Is Cash* was a one-shot TV parody of the Beatles, produced in 1978 by Lorne Michaels of *Saturday Night Live*, and appearing on both British and American TV. *Monty Python*'s Eric Idle wrote the script and starred as the Paul character. The songs were written (in a devastatingly effective imitation of the Beatles' style) by Neil Innes, a member of the surreal Bonzo Dog Band. George Harrison was also in on the joke, and appeared as a TV reporter. As they so often did, ATV sued. In the end, Innes was forced to share half of his songwriting profits with ATV.

BEATLES VS. NIKE: In 1987 Capitol Records and Michael Jackson sold the rights to use the song "Revolution" in a shoe commercial. The Beatles sued, the case ended in a secret settlement out of court, and Nike stopped using the song.

One for the (Ice) Ages

Evidence shows that there have been at least five major ice ages in the earth's history. The earliest happened between 2.4 and 2.1 billion years ago.

The scientific definition of an ice age is any time period during which ice sheets cover "vast areas" of the earth's surface.

So technically, the earth is still in an ice age that began 2.58 million years ago.

The most recent major ice age in North America and Europe ended about 10,000 years ago, but during that time, the ice sheets covering Greenland, northern Europe, Canada, and much of the northern United States were more than two miles deep.

Enormous animals thrived during the last ice age: woolly mammoths, giant sloths, hamster-like creatures that were as big as oxen, armadillos the size of VW Bugs, oversized beavers with six-inch teeth, and a large, scavenging, flightless bird.

The average temperature during the last ice age was between about 46°F and 60°F degrees cooler than our average temperature today.

During the last ice age, elephants roamed every continent but Australia and Antarctica.

A River Runs Through It

The Mississippi River inspired the longest painting in the world. *Panorama of the Mississippi,* by 19th-century American artist John Banvard, measured 1,200 feet long, representing a stretch of the river. (The painting is no longer with us—after Banvard's death it was cut up to make theater backdrops.)

The longest river in the United States is the mighty Missouri, with 2,540 miles. The Mississippi is #2, with 2,340 miles.

Are you safe from sharks if you're in a freshwater river? Not necessarily. Bull sharks frequently swim up rivers from the ocean.

At least 10 of the Amazon River's tributaries are as large as the entire Mississippi River.

At Canada's Bay of Fundy, the Saint John River reverses direction at the bay's high tide. Because of a funneling effect in the bay, the water rises up to 48 feet, and a tidal wave rolls upstream, temporarily drowning rapids and reversing waterfalls.

Before environmental regulations were in effect, many rivers in industrial areas were so polluted that they often caught fire. The Cuyahoga River in Ohio, once among the dirtiest rivers in the U.S., caught fire at least 13 times, between 1868 and 1969.

The Amazon River is home to more species of fish—2,100 and counting—than the Atlantic Ocean.

The United States has 3.5 million miles of rivers.

The word *quebec* literally means "narrow passage," or "strait" in the Algonquin language, referring to the place where the Saint Lawrence River significantly narrows.

The St. Lawrence Seaway opened in 1959. Even now—more than half a century after the St. Lawrence River overflowed ten Canadian villages in 1959—you can see sidewalks, streets, foundations, and factory ruins of the ghost towns from boats and on satellite maps.

The Mettle of Metal

The Mars rovers *Spirit* and *Opportunity* contain pieces of metal from the World Trade Center.

Lead was one of the first metals used by humans, dating back to about 6500 BC.

In 1886 Charles Martin Hall of Ohio and Paul Heroult of Paris each independently discovered a way to make aluminum cheaply. Before that, aluminum was a rare and expensive metal, and aluminum dinnerware, for example, was an extravagance that only the very rich could afford.

Two million pounds of platinum ore may contain just one pound of metal.

Tonka uses 5.1 million pounds of sheet metal every year to manufacture its toy trucks.

The asteroid 3554 Amun, which will cross Earth's orbit around the year 2020, contains an estimated $20 billion worth of metals.

By the 1920s, Henry Ford was already recycling leftover metal from his production line.

The world's largest cast-metal statue is a 56-foot likeness of Vulcan, the Roman god of fire. Made for the 1904 World's Fair in St. Louis, Missouri, it now stands on a hill in Birmingham, Alabama.

Most people have three to four grams of iron in their bodies.

Thin, pointy metal objects like forks generate more sparks in microwaves than thicker, rounded ones like spoons. (But it's recommended that no metal objects be microwaved.)

* * *

DID YOU KNOW?

Felt-tip pens are made of nylon or some other synthetic instead of true felt, which is steamed and flattened wool.

The Straight Poop

Scientific term for insect poop: frass.

Marsupial babies go to the bathroom in their mother's pouches.

Dried dung from grazing animals is a favorite cheap fuel in many parts of the world. It burns well because it's mostly undigested hay, grasses, and other vegetation.

There's a precise and polite word for dog poop: "scumber."

The survival of many plant species depends on the 165 pounds of poop excreted by the average elephant each day. The dung includes thousands of undigested seeds just waiting for a chance to grow in the newly enriched soil.

Armadillos eat a lot of dirt with their diets of small insects and snails, which is why their excrement looks like piles of clay marbles.

Many brands of fertilizer use composted human waste from sewage treatment plants, meaning we pay money to have it taken away and then we buy it back.

In your lifetime, you'll excrete a school bus's weight in poop.

The Longest...

...**Running TV special:** *Rudolph the Red-Nosed Reindeer* has aired annually since 1964. Second-longest: *A Charlie Brown Christmas*, running since 1965.

...**Train journey:** The Trans-Siberian Express from Moscow to Vladivostok takes eight days.

...**Nonstop canoe race:** The annual Missouri 340, in which teams canoe or kayak across the state of Missouri in a whirlwind 88 hours. Total distance: 340 miles.

...**Oscar acceptance speech:** Greer Garson in 1943 spoke for more than seven minutes.

...**Yard sale:** 690 miles along Highway 127 from Addison, Michigan, to Gadsden, Alabama. Founded in 1987, the four-day event begins on the first Thursday in August.

...**Solar-powered plane flight:** 646 miles, by a plane called *Solar Impulse* (2013).

...**Running network TV show of all time:** *Meet the Press* first aired on November 6, 1947, and is still on today.

...**Documented paper airplane flight** (indoors with no wind, starting and ending at ground level): 27.9 seconds, set by Takuo Toda in Hiroshima, Japan, in 2009.

The Shortest...

...**State motto** is "Hope." It comes from the smallest state, Rhode Island.

...**Papal reign in history** ended on September 27, 1590. Pope Urban VII died of malaria just 13 days after his election.

...**Reign of a French king:** 20 minutes. King Louis XIX, appointed king by a faction after the July Revolution of 1830, immediately abdicated in favor of another claimant, Louis Philippe.

...**Known vertebrate:** male stout infant fish. Found around the Great Barrier Reef, the little fish measures about a third of an inch.

...**National anthem:** Japan's national anthem takes about a minute to sing and has only one stanza of four lines. Its 800-year-old lyrics are "May you reign for eight thousand generations, until pebbles grow into moss-covered boulders."

...**River:** the Doe River in Oregon is only 120 feet long—shorter than an Olympic swimming pool.

...**Alphabet:** The Rotokas language, spoken in the Solomon Islands. It consists of only 11 letters: A, E, I, O, U, G, K, P, R, T, and V.

More Baby Talk

On October 28, 1929, a Mrs. T. W. Evans gave birth to the first baby born up in the air—on a passenger plane above Florida.

According to studies, babies who use pacifiers are more prone to earaches.

Approximately 80 percent of babies are born with at least one birthmark.

Worldwide, hospitals give new mothers the wrong babies about 12 times a day.

1 percent of all babies born in the U.S. are conceived through in vitro fertilization.

More babies are born in September than in any other month.

Research shows that women take 2 minutes, 5 seconds to change a diaper, whereas men take 1 minute, 36 seconds.

More babies are born on Tuesday than any other day of the week.

Babies are born with 300 bones, but many fuse together as they get older and the count goes down to 206 in adulthood.

On February 24, 1924, Mrs. J. P. Haskin of Arkansas delivered the heaviest known set of human twins. One was 14 pounds, the other 13.75 pounds, for a combined weight of 27.75 pounds.

Why should you not give cow's milk to infants? It doesn't have enough iron, vitamin C, or vitamin E, and it has too much protein.

Babies double their weight in their first six months, but slow down after that. If they kept doubling their weight every year, a six-pound baby would reach its tenth birthday weighing 6,144 pounds.

*   *   *

"If men had to have babies they would only ever have one each."
—**Diana, Princess of Wales**

Only Skin Deep

In the original story, Sleeping Beauty stayed asleep and beautiful for 100 years.

Cleopatra's beauty secrets: Lead ore on her eyebrows and around her eyes; blue lapis lazuli (a rare semiprecious stone) on her upper lids and green copper ore on her lower, red ocher on her cheeks, and henna on her palms.

Despite all of this, Cleopatra wasn't very attractive (but she's said to have had a beguiling voice and a great personality).

In her time, court artists depicted Queen Elizabeth I as beautiful. But a German visitor in the 1590s described her a little differently: "Her face oblong, fair and wrinkled; her eyes small, yet black and pleasant; her nose, a little hooked, her lips narrow and her teeth black (a defect the English seem subject to, from their too great use of sugar)."

In the 1920s, when Marlboro marketed its cigarettes exclusively to women, the company included "Beauty Tips" around the filters, red bands meant to hide lipstick stains.

In June 2004, a beauty contest was held in western Croatia... for goats.

In Japanese, *bakku-shan* means "beautiful when viewed from behind." (It's not a compliment.)

* * *

BEAUTIFUL WISDOM

"A soap bubble is the most beautiful thing, and the most exquisite in nature. I wonder how much it would take to buy a soap bubble, if there were only one in the world."

—**Mark Twain**

"Real beauty knocks you a little bit off kilter."

—**David Byrne**

Let's Get Hoppy!

Beer wasn't sold in cans until 1935. Before that, it came in bottles. And before that, drinkers had to go to taverns with a pail for them to fill.

In January 1935, the now-defunct Gottfried Krueger Brewing Company became the first to put beer in cans. Pop-tops hadn't been invented yet, so Krueger included a device to punch a hole in the top and printed instructions on the can about how to use it.

According to one estimate, about 10 percent of beer drinkers drink 43 percent of all the beer sold in the United States.

King Henry VIII's ladies at court had a ration of one gallon of beer per day.

Canadian inventor Steve Pasjack came up with the "Scarborough Suitcase" (the 12-pack beer carton with handles) in 1957.

Before a serious hurricane, the top food or beverage item sold at Walmart is beer. (Pop Tarts are #2.)

First high-profile kidnapping in Canada: Beer baron John Sackville Labatt in 1934. (He was eventually released.)

Studies show: Drinkers are likely to rate someone as 25% more attractive after two pints of beer.

Canada is home to Beersville (NB), Keg River (AB), and the Belcher Islands (NU).

According to Guinness, beards and mustaches soak up about 162,719 pints of beer every year.

The average British adult drinks nearly 500 pints of beer a year.

The daily breakfast regimen of Queen Elizabeth I included two pints of "strong beer."

Navy ships carry two cans of beer for each sailor who spends 45 consecutive days at sea.

The first banned substance to disqualify an Olympian? Beer. In 1968 Hans-Gunnar Liljenwall of Sweden had a couple rounds to calm his jitters before competing in pistol shooting.

There's a Name for That

The six most common county names in the United States are Washington, Jefferson, Franklin, Lincoln, Jackson, and Madison.

A 2009 study showed that cows with names produce 3.4 percent more milk than cows without, but the names might not be the reason. Researchers believe that cattle thrive on being talked to and given individual attention instead of being considered just part of a herd.

The "see-no-evil, hear-no-evil, and speak-no-evil" monkeys have names: Mizaru, Kikazaru, and Iwazaru. In Japan, where the three monkeys first appeared in the 1600s carved on a shrine's door, there is sometimes a fourth monkey, Shizaru, with his arms crossed, symbolizing "do no evil."

The study of how bodies of water receive their names is called *hydronymy*.

The NHL's Toronto Maple Leafs were originally called the Toronto St. Patricks.

In 1934 carpenter-turned-toymaker Ole Kirk Christiansen held a contest among friends and employees to name his new company. After getting a number of entries, Christiansen decided he liked his own entry best: "Lego," based on the Danish phrase *Leg godt* ("play well").

The award for the best TV commercials is a Clio, named after the Greek muse of history.

Garci Ordonez de Montalvo's romantic fiction *Las Sergas de Esplandian* (1510) featured an otherworldly island called California. That's where the state got its name.

Rumen, reticulum, omasum, and *abomasum* are the names of the segments of a cow's stomach.

Say Uncle!

Tom Hanks is a direct descendant of Abraham Lincoln's uncle.

Michelangelo wanted to be buried in his home city of Florence, but the pope insisted that he be entombed in Rome. Eventually, Michelangelo's nephew, honoring his uncle's wishes, managed to steal Michelangelo's remains and ship them in an unmarked crate to Florence, where they remain to this day.

"Uncle" Milton Levine got his nickname from his invention, the Ant Farm. Smart alecks kept asking him, "With all of these ants, where are the uncles?" So he added Uncle to his name.

Abe Lincoln's nephew William Todd designed the first California state flag.

Pablo Picasso smoked until he died, swearing that a cigar-smoking uncle had once saved his life. How? At birth, baby Pablo wasn't breathing. The quick-thinking uncle blew cigar smoke into his lungs, causing the infant to choke, cough…and begin breathing on his own.

Paul Terry, who created the *Mighty Mouse* and *Heckle and Jeckle* cartoons, was the uncle of Alex Anderson, who created the characters of Rocky and Bullwinkle and Dudley Do-Right.

Married Folks

When Eleanor Roosevelt married, she didn't have to update her driver's license or stationery. Her birth name had also been Eleanor Roosevelt. She was a distant cousin of Franklin's.

About 20 percent of Roman Catholic priests are married. If a married male minister from another Christian denomination converts, he may be allowed to become a priest.

Patriot Patrick Henry left his estate to his wife, as long as she didn't remarry after his death. (She challenged the will in court and remarried.)

P. T. Barnum's conjoined "Siamese Twins" Chang and Eng married twin sisters in the mid-1800s and had 21 children between them.

Charles Addams, whose cartoons inspired the TV show *The Addams Family*, got married in a pet cemetery.

Stay married for 50 years in the United States and you can get a letter of congratulations from the president. In the United Kingdom, however, a letter from the queen requires 60 years.

* * *

"A good marriage would be between a blind wife and a deaf husband."
—Michel de Montaigne

Prison Yard

In Massachusetts, 1 percent of the construction costs of a prison must be spent on art.

The guy behind bars in Monopoly's jail is called Jake the Jailbird.

Of all the countries in the world, the United States has the highest percentage of adults in prison: 1 in 107. Adding in people on parole and probation, 2 percent of U.S. adults (1 in 50) are under "correctional supervision" at any given time.

Many writers penned classics in prison. Some examples: John Bunyan's *The Pilgrim's Progress* (the first part), Miguel de Cervantes's *Don Quixote*, Oscar Wilde's *De Profundis*, and most of O. Henry's short stories.

52 percent of Americans say they'd rather spend a week in jail than be president of the United States.

In 1904 Rhode Island judge Darius Baker sentenced to jail a man who was speeding through the streets of Newport...at a whopping 15 mph.

Some of the first European inhabitants in the New World were people who chose a sentence of working in labor camps instead of going to debtors' prison.

Nelson Mandela spent 27 years in prison before becoming president of South Africa.

Eye See You

A good custom artificial eye, matching your natural color, will cost at least $3,000. (But don't call them "glass eyes"—they're made from unbreakable plastic.)

Top-selling poster in U.S. history: The Snellen Eye Chart, designed by Dutch ophthalmologist Herman Snellen in 1862.

The spot where your lower and upper eyelids meet is called the "canhus."

Tiny bugs called follicle mites live in your eyebrows and eyelashes. They eat away the dust and dead skin trapped between the hairs.

A bird's eyes cover about 50 percent of its head; a human's, only about 5 percent.

Most apes and monkeys see almost all the same colors we do.

Owls can turn their heads in almost a full circle, but they can't move their eyes.

When a cat looks at you with half-closed eyes, it's a sign of trust. Do it back to them and you'll share a bonding experience.

"Esotropia" means cross-eyed. "Exotropia" means wall-eyed.

Your eyelids are the thinnest area of skin on your body.

The word "pupil" means both student and a part of the eye. Both came from the Latin word *pupilla*, meaning "small child." The eye part was called that because of the tiny reflections of people seen within.

Needles have eyes and potatoes have eyes, but did you know that Swiss cheese has them, too? That's what the holes are called.

Saint Harvey—the patron saint of optometrists—was blind from birth.

Don't panic if your doctor tells you that you have *bilateral periorbital hematoma*. It's just med-speak for a black eye.

He Knows If You've Been Bad or Good

Much of what we believe Santa does on Christmas Eve came from the poem "A Visit from St. Nicholas" (which begins "'Twas the night before Christmas..."). The poem was published anonymously in 1822, but 21 years later, after it became popular, amateur poet Clement Moore took credit for it. The family of another poet, Henry Livingston Jr., however, claims that he was the real author.

Washington Irving's 1809 satirical history book, *A History of New York*, contains the earliest known written reference to Santa Claus.

Canada's postal service offers its own address for Santa letters: Santa Claus, North Pole, Canada H0H 0H0.

Gene Autry wrote the song "Here Comes Santa Claus" in 1946 after hearing kids excitedly shouting the phrase during the Hollywood Christmas parade.

Rudolph, Santa's ninth reindeer, was born in 1939 as a promotion for the Montgomery Ward department stores. The ad copywriter, Robert May, wrote a poem that originally called the reindeer Rollo, and then Reginald, but the store nixed both names, and Rudolph it was. Montgomery Ward passed out 2.4 million illustrated booklets including the poem, which became a song ten years later.

The Business of Balls

The speed at which an item falls depends on its size, shape, and weight. Dropped from a height of a mile, a table-tennis ball would fall at about 20 mph, and a bowling ball, 350 mph.

With the skin of one cow, you can make about 20 footballs or 144 baseballs.

That little ball inside of a whistle has an official name—it's called a "pea."

The Times Square New Year's ball is 12 feet across and weighs 11,875 pounds.

Of the 20 possible answers in a Magic 8-Ball, only five are negative. Ten indicate "yes," and the remaining five tell you to "ask again."

Originally, polo balls were made of willow root, but those were damaged easily. So hard plastic became the norm in the 1970s.

Pinball game designers' rule of thumb: An average player should get about 45 seconds of play per ball. Too much more time and the machine loses money; less, and the players get discouraged and stop playing.

A little ball played a major role in the first successful artificial heart valve in the 1950s. The ball opened and shut the valve with each heartbeat. It worked well, but when patients opened their mouths, anybody nearby could hear the ball clicking.

In the sport of jai alai, the ball is made of goatskin sewed around rubber. That ball travels at up to 188 mph and can be dangerous, occasionally even killing players.

Drop a 100-pound ball of Silly Putty from a height of 100 feet, and the ball—flattened but intact—will bounce back about eight feet into the air.

*   *   *

Every three minutes, five Barbie dolls are sold on eBay.

Musical Matters

Our musical scale is divided into 12 notes, of which we normally sing only seven in any given song (do-re-mi-fa…). Traditional Chinese music uses 5 notes; Indian, 7; and Arabic, 17.

Joni Mitchell didn't play the 1969 Woodstock music festival because her manager urged her to appear on the *Dick Cavett Show* instead. She still wrote a hit song about the festival ("Woodstock") as if she'd been there.

Buddy Miles, Freddie Mercury, and Loudon Wainwright III were all born on September 5, 1946.

Struggling musician John Lennon shoplifted the harmonica he plays on the Beatles hit "Love Me Do."

Louisiana governor Jimmie Davis, elected in 1944 and 1960, is the only governor in the Country Music Hall of Fame. He wrote more than 400 songs, including "You Are My Sunshine."

The Thai Elephant Orchestra is a troupe of up to six elephants that play on large, sturdy versions of traditional Thai instruments—gongs, drums, and a xylophone. Proceeds of their CD sales go to an elephant conservation center in Thailand.

Emperor Nero was a bagpipe virtuoso, playing it regularly at public gatherings. The Romans loved the instrument and carried it all over the world, but most cultures rejected it…except the Scots.

Warner Music still earns up to $30,000 a day in royalties for the song "Happy Birthday to You."

The Beach Boys once recorded a song written by Charles Manson, who had been an acquaintance of drummer Dennis Wilson before he turned murderous. The album now lists the song as "Never Learn Not to Love," but Manson's original title was "Cease to Exist."

Get to Work!

Ratio of pay between CEOs in Japan and their workers: 10 to 1. In America: 380 to 1. In general, your CEO will make more by early afternoon today than you'll make all year.

According to studies, work-related stress can be as bad for a person's health as smoking.

Tuesday is the most productive day of the workweek.

A 2010 study discovered that 33 percent of U.S. workers were chronically overworked.

The word "freelancer" comes from 12th-century knights who lost employment with royal houses and offered themselves as mercenaries to anyone who'd pay.

Odds that you've nearly fallen asleep at work in the last month: 1 out of 3.

The U.S. Congress is one of the few workplaces in the U.S. where it's still legal to smoke indoors.

The average employee switches tasks every three minutes and has a maximum uninterrupted time of about 12 minutes to focus on a task.

A New York City sanitation worker lifts about six tons of garbage every day.

People who love their jobs are called *ergophiles*.

But 25 percent of all Americans polled say their workplace is a "dictatorship." Not coincidentally, 25 percent also say that they're always angry on the job.

If the minimum wage had risen as fast as the salaries of CEOs, the lowest-paid workers would be making $28 per hour.

1.6 million people live in Manhattan, and 1.6 million people commute to work there daily.

Of the people who die at work, 1 percent die by drowning.

Animal Zzzzzs

Which animals sleep the most? First is the brown bat, which sleeps 19.9 hours a day. Right behind are the giant armadillo (18.1 hours per day), python and North American opossum (18 hours), the owl monkey (17 hours), and the human infant (16 hours).

In comparison, your house cat sleeps very little...only about 12.1 hours a day.

Giraffes go into deep sleep for only a few minutes at a time.

Ducks sleep in rows, and the ones on the ends keep one eye open.

Termites never sleep—they work 24 hours a day.

Technically, bears don't hibernate—they just go "dormant" and sleep all winter.

Male gorillas prefer to sleep on the ground, but females nest in trees.

* * *

YUK, YUK

In the early 1800s, nitrous oxide was used solely for entertainment purposes, and "laughing gas" parties became intoxicating pastimes. It wasn't until 1844 that Horace Wells, a dentist in Connecticut, tried some on himself and found that he could extract a tooth painlessly.

A Really Ice Season

According to studies, as much as 85 percent of winter air pollution comes from wood stoves. Particulates get lodged permanently in the lungs, decreasing breathing capacity and increasing the odds of cancer.

The lost settlers who named Death Valley called it that because they passed through in winter and nearly froze to death.

On December 26, 1620, the *Mayflower* landed at Plymouth Rock with 102 people. Unfortunately, they were ill prepared for the rigors of a Massachusetts winter, and 51 died before spring.

In 1873 fifteen-year-old Chester Greenwood came up with the idea of earmuffs while ice-skating near his home in frigid Farmington, Maine. He convinced his grandmother to sew fur ear coverings and attach them to wire, and then he patented the design and started a hometown factory that made his earmuffs for 60 years.

About 90 percent of public transit commuters suffer at least one cold every winter.

Because of its proximity to the North Pole, the town of Barrow, Alaska, sits in the dark for much of the winter and doesn't see the sun rise for 64 days.

In the 1600s, Russians built long, curvy slides out of ice in the winter for thrilling downhill rides. The fun eventually spread across Europe, inspiring the first roller coasters.

In winter, a shrew can lose 50 percent of its body weight, with even its bones, skull, and organs shrinking.

The air in the average American home during the winter is twice as dry as the air in the Sahara Desert.

What would be an inch of rain in warmer months can become 15 inches of dry, fluffy snow or about 5 inches of the soggy stuff in the winter.

Gobbled Up

Nearly 90 percent of American households eat turkey on Thanksgiving—that's about 45 million animals.

Only male turkeys gobble. The hens make a clicking noise.

The red part of a turkey's head is called the "snotter."

The largest turkey on record weighed 86 pounds, about the size of a German shepherd.

More turkeys are raised in California than in any other state. (And Californians eat three pounds more turkey meat than the average American does.)

Unmated turkey hens can lay eggs that hatch into chicks, but the offspring are always sterile males.

* * *

SAVED BY TURKEYS!

The dodo tree, native to the island of Mauritius in the Indian Ocean, had been sliding toward extinction for centuries because its seeds had to pass through a dodo bird's digestive tract before they'd germinate. Because the bird has been extinct since the 1600s, the species had dwindled to just 13 very old trees. Finally, in 1977, a scientist found that a turkey's gullet worked just as well as a dodo's. At least that was the story at the time. It turned out that the seeds' hard outer layer just needed a good scraping. Turkeys are still sometimes used to digest the seeds, but hand-scraping or tumbling the seeds in a gem polisher also works.

Southpaw

More than 2,500 left-handers officially die from accidents caused by "using devices meant for right-handed people."

If you have two left-handed parents, your chance of being left-handed more than doubles. But that still means only a 26 percent chance—leading to the conclusion that most left-handedness is not inherited.

A stressful birth can double the chances of a female baby being born left-handed.

College-educated left-handers earn 10 to 15 percent more than college-educated right-handers.

Left-handers have slightly faster reaction times than right-handers.

You're more likely to bobble a Frisbee thrown by a left-hander because the reverse-spin changes flight patterns and how the disc behaves when it strikes your hand.

Compared to right-handers, a higher percentage of lefties are mentally challenged.

The World's Smallest...

...**Dinosaur** was about the size of a turkey.

...**Bird** is the bee hummingbird, which weighs as much as two dimes.

...**Game of Monopoly** took place on a one-inch-square game board. Players had to look through magnifying glasses to see their pieces during the 30-hour-long game.

...**U.S. president** was James Madison, who stood 5'4" and weighed 98 pounds.

...**Seeds** belong to the orchid. It would take about 1.25 million of them to equal one gram.

...**Country** has 110 acres of land, 826 residents, and a birth rate of 0. It's Vatican City.

...**State park:** Mills End State Park in Portland, Oregon, is 452 square inches.

...**County** in the United States is Kalawao, Hawaii, only 14 square miles.

...**U.S. post office** is a 7 x 8-foot shed in Ochopee, Florida. It serves a town of 11 on the edge of the Everglades, but it has a daily mail route that stretches 132 miles across three sparsely populated counties.

Octopus Danger!

Only about a third of an octopus's intelligence is in its brain. The rest of its neurons reside in its tentacles, each of which can act independently from the brain.

If an octopus loses an arm, it can regenerate a new one. And, because tentacles contain their own neurons, the detached tentacles sometimes continue to crawl along by themselves to distract a predator.

Blue-ringed octopuses live in the ocean between Japan and Australia. They typically have cream-colored skin with dozens of black, blue, and brown spots that look like targets. How do you know you're making them angry enough to bite? If their blue rings pulsate, swim away fast!

An octopus releases a thick, poisonous cloud of black ink in response to predators and then swims away.

If an octopus released its ink inside an aquarium, it would kill everything inside the glass walls...including the octopus.

The mimic octopus can change the shape and color of its body to look like other sea creatures. Their best impersonations are the lionfish, sea snake, or flounder—the octopuses even imitate their movements.

All octopuses use venom to overcome prey and enemies, but only the blue-ringed octopus is poisonous enough to kill humans.

* * *

HANG LIKE AN EGYPTIAN?

In 17th-century England, you could be hanged for "impersonating an Egyptian." How come? The government believed that the nomadic Romani people came from Egypt (they were actually probably from India) and so used the terms "Egyptian" and the shorter "gypsy" interchangeably. Since you could be hanged for impersonating a gypsy, Egyptian impersonators were also out of luck.

Summertime

Children's IQs typically drop a few points over summer vacation.

The "dog days of summer" come between July 3 and August 11. The Romans coined the term, believing that Sirius, the Dog Star, helped the sun warm the earth during that time.

One toad can eat about 10,000 insects in a single summer.

The 1967 "Summer of Love" actually began in January. The kick-off event was a "Human Be-In" free concert in San Francisco's Golden Gate Park, featuring Timothy Leary, the Grateful Dead, Jefferson Airplane, and jazz trumpeter Dizzy Gillespie.

In the summer, lawn mowers account for up to 5 percent of the nation's air pollution.

Because of its proximity to the North Pole, the town of Barrow, Alaska, sees sunshine for 84 straight days in the summer.

Of all the seasons, summer has the lowest mortality rate.

The International Space Station

Sixteen nations collaborated to build the International Space Station (ISS), which combined three separate stations into one: Japan's *Kibo lab*, the partially built Russian *Mir-2*, and the proposed European *Columbus*.

Pieces of the station began arriving in space in 1998 via Russian modules and the space shuttle. By November 2000, the ISS was habitable, and people have been living there ever since.

The ISS circles Earth every 93 minutes and can be seen from the ground on a clear night. Stargazers can sign up with NASA to get e-mail or text alerts when it's going to be whizzing over their location.

Each astronaut is allotted a personal food stash for his or her visit: 1,900 calories (for a small woman) to 3,200 calories (for a large man) each day.

Water on the ISS comes at room temperature or hot, but not chilled. Cooling uses too much energy, so there's no refrigerator. That's also why food comes dehydrated, or in cans or pouches.

They choose their food before they leave, but better not grow tired of it. Astronauts pick eight days' worth of a menu that repeats for their entire stay. (The eight-day menu ensures that they don't have the exact thing every Sunday, for example, giving the illusion of variety.)

The ISS is larger than a five-bedroom house and orbits the Earth at 17,500 mph.

It's the ninth and largest space station so far.

ISS astronauts often change their underwear only twice a week.

Higher Education

When Aristotle opened his school, the Lyceum, people nicknamed it the "Peripatetic School" because "peripatetic" means "walking around" and the teachers taught while leisurely strolling the grounds.

The University of Rochester was once offered $100,000 by a patent medicine company to change its name to Hops Bitters University. The regents declined.

During the Middle Ages, western European university professors taught their lessons orally, so literacy was not a college prerequisite. In fact, many students decided to put off learning to read until after they'd gotten college out of the way.

The Internet started in 1969 as a link among just four schools: Stanford University, the University of California–Santa Barbara, the University of California–Los Angeles, and the University of Utah.

With more than 14 million books, Harvard University has the largest academic library in the world.

In 1960 there were only 16 female students attending Harvard Law School (including future attorney general Janet Reno). Today, women make up about half the student body.

Medieval schools for knights taught jousting and sword fighting, as well as reading, writing, basic math, chess, lute playing, and chivalry.

In 1925 tobacco tycoon James Duke donated $107 million to Trinity College in Durham, NC. Soon after, the administrators changed the school's name…to Duke University.

College with the most U.S. presidents as alumni: Harvard.

The older you are when you graduate from a law school, the more likely you are to take an academic job with a university.

President Millard Fillmore had no formal education. When Oxford University in England offered him an honorary doctorate, he turned it down, saying, "No man should accept a degree he cannot read."

Kid Stuff

During Puritan times, children who cursed at their parents could be put to death.

The United States ranks 84th worldwide in childhood immunizations against measles. It ranks even worse in immunizing children against polio—89th.

The United States passed its first comprehensive law against child labor in 1938. Business owners at the time argued that working in coal mines and textile mills was good for a child's character.

A law in Georgia specifically forbids "selling a minor under age 12…to rope or wire walk, beg, be a gymnast, contortionist, circus rider, acrobat, or clown."

In 2008 South Africa passed a law making it illegal for kids under the age of 16 to kiss.

When Muhammad Ali was a child, he had his brother throw rocks at him to practice his dodging skills. His brother never passed up the opportunity… but never actually hit the future boxer either.

Fluoridated water once decreased tooth decay among kids by 29.1 percent, but now that number is creeping up. One culprit, dentists say, is that many kids now drink bottled water.

Before educator Friedrich Froebel coined the word *kindergarten* ("garden of children"), he called his new classroom *kleinkinderbeschaftigungsanstalt* ("institution where children are occupied").

Known as the "Boy Pope," Benedict IX was only 11 or 12 years old when took the papal seat in 1032.

"La Cucaracha," the Mexican children's song, is about a cockroach that wastes his life away smoking marijuana. As the song ends, the cockroach dies and is carried for burial among buzzards and a church mouse.

The average American kid eats 23 pounds of pizza each year.

Until the 1400s, children of either sex were called "girls."

Paper View

It wasn't until the 1880s that most paper was made of wood pulp. Before that, papermakers generally used recycled rags, making paper expensive and shortages common.

Americans use, toss out, and recycle more than 100 million tons of paper each year. That's enough to build a wall 12 feet high from Los Angeles to New York.

A single mature tree yields about 700 paper grocery bags.

The little paper socks some chefs like to put on the legs of broiled chickens to keep them from drying out are called *papillotes*.

If you keep the string taut, tin-can phones can work pretty well...but paper-cup phones work much better.

What we call "parchment paper" is actually a poor imitation of the real thing. Real parchment is the pressed skin of a goat, sheep, or calf, and it doesn't work well in an ink-jet printer.

It takes 70 percent less energy to produce a ton of paper from recycled paper than from trees.

Setting up a paper-recycling plant is also about 80 percent cheaper than building a new paper mill.

Fears to You

Eisoptrophobia:
Fear of seeing yourself in a mirror.

Venustraphobia:
Fear of beautiful women.

Gephyrophobia:
Fear of crossing bridges.

Porphyrophobia:
Fear of the color purple.

Ephebiphobia:
Fear of young people.

Octophobia:
Fear of the number 8.

Lutraphobia:
Fear of otters.

Cynophobia:
Fear of dogs.

Apeirophobia:
Fear of infinity.

Phobophobia:
Fear of having phobias.

Zemmiphobia:
Fear of the great mole rat.

Taphophobia:
Fear of being buried alive.

Hexakosioihexekontahexaphobia:
Fear of the number 666.

Money Talk

In 1912 a penny was worth about what a quarter is worth now.

In the late 1960s, when Canada experienced a dime shortage, the Royal Canadian Mint contracted with the U.S. Mint to produce half of its 1968 dimes in Philadelphia. Coin collectors can tell which are American-made by the lack of mint marks.

From 1870 to 1923, Canada issued 25-cent banknotes to reduce the circulation of U.S. quarters within the country.

The first U.S. circulating coin to honor a woman appeared in 1979 and featured suffragette Susan B. Anthony. Alas, Susan B. Anthony's dollar got poor circulation and disappeared. Another woman so honored on a dollar coin, Sacagawea, suffered a similar fate.

But despite its disuse in the U.S., the Sacagawea coin is popular in El Salvador and Ecuador, both of which use U.S. money as their official currency instead of issuing their own.

Largest gold coin ever minted: the Canadian $1 million Maple Leaf (diameter: about 20 inches).

A dime used to be 90 percent silver, which is why it's smaller than a penny or a nickel; anything larger would have made the metal worth more than its face value.

The Canadian "Toonie" coin's outer ring is made of nickel—the middle is aluminum, copper, and nickel.

It costs the same to mint a nickel and a quarter, but a dime is a bargain. According to the U.S. Mint, a penny costs about 2.5¢; a nickel, 11¢; a dime, 6¢; a quarter, 11¢; and a dollar coin, 18¢.

The first U.S. coin to feature an African American was the Booker T. Washington Memorial Half Dollar (1946). More than 1.5 million sold, primarily to coin collectors, to fund the Booker T. Washington National Memorial near Hardy, Virginia, the site of the plantation where Washington was born into slavery.

The Undead

Night of the Living Dead (1968), directed by 28-year-old George A. Romero, changed the image of zombies in popular culture from enslaved workers of Caribbean voodoo wizards to hungry all-American flesh-eaters.

The film's budget was tiny: just $114,000. It eventually grossed $30 million worldwide.

The actors who played the zombies were friends and clients of Romero's struggling film production company. They had to provide their own costumes. Their pay? $1 and a T-shirt.

The blood was chocolate syrup, and the gory body parts came from one of the producers who was also a butcher.

The word "zombie" never appears in the movie.

Night of the Living Dead featured an African American as the lead of an otherwise all-white cast. That was almost unheard of in 1968.

The film entered the public domain early because its distributor made a mistake with the copyright. Before copyright laws changed in 1978, creators had to place a specific copyright symbol prominently on their work or it wouldn't be protected. Romero did so in his title sequence, but when the distributor decided at the last minute to change the movie's title (it was originally called *Night of the Flesh Eaters*), he didn't add the copyright symbol and the film lapsed into the public domain.

What's My Lion?

Mountain lions aren't directly related to lions—they're more closely related to house cats.

Mountain lions can weigh between 64 (for a small adult female) and 220 (a large male) pounds.

Mountain lions that live near the equator are the smallest—the animals get progressively larger the closer they live to the North and South Poles.

The mountain lion (*Puma concolor*) has more than 40 other names. Some of the best known include puma, cougar, catamount, mountain screamer, and painter. It's also one of the two separate big cats called a "panther." (Leopards are the other.)

One of the reasons the mountain lion has so many names is that its habitat is so large, ranging across North and South America. Different regions have independently come up with their own names.

Mountain lions can't roar. They're usually silent, but can hiss, growl, purr, snarl, and scream.

Mountain lions usually avoid people, but more reports of encounters arise as people infringe deeper into the cats' isolated habitats. And mountain lions are not to be trifled with: They can leap as high as 18 feet, and 30 feet horizontally. They can run 40 to 50 mph for short intervals, climb trees quickly, and even swim.

The Taj Mahal

The Taj Mahal was built as a domed mausoleum by a grieving emperor, Shah Jahan, to honor his favorite wife, Mumtaz Mahal, who died while giving birth to their 14th child.

More than 1,000 elephants helped haul in building materials, including jewels and huge quantities of white marble.

To complete the Taj Mahal, 20,000 jewelers, sculptors, calligraphers, and masons worked for more than 22 years, finishing in 1653.

Workmen building the Taj Mahal constructed a large brick scaffold to raise the building. When they were done, Shah Jahan decreed that the scaffold's bricks were free to anyone who could haul them away. According to legend, hordes of people dismantled the scaffold overnight.

Several often-reported "facts" about the Taj Mahal that aren't really true: that there was supposed to be an identical building built in black marble and meant to be Jahan's mausoleum; that the workmen were blinded, dismembered, and/or killed to keep them from building anything that would rival the building; and that British colonial authorities had intended to demolish it and sell off the marble and jewels.

Shortly after the Taj Mahal was finished, Shah Jahan fell ill and was deposed by his son, Aurangzeb, who placed him under luxurious house arrest… with his daughter and his jewels.

When Jahan died at age 74, he was interred next to his wife inside the masterpiece he had commissioned.

* * *

58 percent of divorced men say they're happier after the divorce, but 85 percent of divorced women say they are.

Watch Out!

The first spring-powered clocks appeared in the 1400s. But it wasn't until the 1600s that they became small enough to be put into a pocket, and then the watch was born.

Quartz crystal in a wristwatch vibrates at a rate of 32,768 times per second. That vibration keeps the speed of the watch constant.

The minute hand wasn't added to watches until the 1650s.

Say this ten times fast: "Which wristwatches are Swiss wristwatches?"

Bernd Eilts, a German artist, achieved some notoriety in his career by turning dried cow manure into clocks and wristwatches.

A self-winding watch has a tiny pendulum in it that swings back and forth when you move your arm.

How fast does the hour hand travel on a wristwatch? About 0.00000275 mph.

For a hobby, the Dalai Lama likes to repair watches.

Japan's Emperor Hirohito sported a Mickey Mouse watch. He got it at Disneyland in 1975.

River Horses

Hippos go to special aquatic "grooming" spots where fish come to groom them: Labeo carp clean the hippos' hide, garra suckerfish clean wounds, barbus specialize in foot cracks, and cichlids clean hippos' tails.

Hippos dominate Nile crocodiles, pushing them out of choice pools or sunning spots and killing them if they get too close to hippo calves.

An adult hippo eats 55 to 88 pounds of vegetation a day. That's equal to only about 1.5 percent of its total body weight. (Cows eat at least 2.5 percent of their weight per day.)

Only about 10 percent of male hippos get to mate.

All hippos can mate in the water, but only pygmy hippos can also mate on land. Copulation lasts about half an hour, with the female completely submerged. (She raises her nose out the water now and again to breathe.)

The hippo gestation period lasts just eight months. Calfs are born hind legs first, whether on land or in water.

Hippos can live to be 50 years old in the wild.

Hippos graze all night, but don't travel more than a mile from the water to find good grass.

Hippos don't have oil or sweat glands. When they get scared or excited, their skin oozes an acidic, transparent liquid (not blood) that turns orange-red and protects against water loss, sunburn, and infection.

Hippo skin is about 2½ inches thick.

The hippo's closest relatives are whales and dolphins.

Hippos are surprisingly aggressive and are considered one of Africa's most dangerous animals. They often attack humans on land or in boats without warning.

On the Streets

The intersection of Park and North Eighth Streets in Manitowoc, Wisconsin, was the first place in the U.S. to be hit by space junk. In 1962 a 21-pound piece of *Sputnik 4* landed there. (It didn't hurt anybody.)

The name "Tin Pan Alley" was coined in 1908 to describe the area around 28th Street in New York City where many music publishers had offices. In the summer, the sound of pianos wafting through open windows sounded like a metallic cacophony.

There are 6,374.6 miles of streets in New York City.

Wall Street really had a wall running along it in the 1600s, built by the Dutch to keep enemies out. It didn't last long—the British tore down the wall when they moved in.

Warsaw and Budapest both have Winnie-the-Pooh Streets.

Golf carts are street-legal in Palm Desert, California—even on highways.

The oldest street in North America is Water Street, St. John's, Newfoundland and Labrador, Canada. It was built in the early 1500s.

Second Street is the most popular street name in America. Why not First Street? A lot of towns have a Main Street instead of a First Street.

There are 300,000 streetlights in New York City alone.

In 1807 Pall Mall in London became the first street lit by gas lamps...well, half-lit anyway, because the first demonstration lit only one side of the street.

The first American pedestrian killed by a car was Henry H. Bliss, who on September 13, 1899, stepped off a streetcar at West 74th Street and Central Park West in New York City and was run over by an electric taxi.

In Caracas, Venezuela, the streets are blocked off on Christmas Day so people can roller-skate to church.

What Fur?

"Mohair" and "cashmere" are both made from goat hair.

Crabs have small, sensitive hairs on their claws and other parts of their bodies to monitor water currents.

Otters keep warm in cold water thanks to their dense fur, which traps air bubbles and keeps water away from their skin—they have about 650,000 hairs per square inch. (By contrast, a human scalp has only about 1,000 hairs per square inch.)

A "camel-hair brush" never comes from camel hair—most are made from a pony's tail or mane. High-quality ones come from the fur of oxen, goats, ferrets, or squirrels.

The only place a naked mole rat has hair is inside its mouth.

A violin bow contains about 150 hairs from a horse's tail.

Badgers nearly went extinct in the late 1800s because their hair was in high demand for shaving brushes.

The only canine that changes its fur color to suit the seasons is the arctic fox.

Juneau the Capital?

Alaska's state capital is named for Joe Juneau, who discovered gold there in 1880. That discovery helped kick off the great gold rush era and brought more than 30,000 people into the state.

Alaska is the only state whose name can be typed on a single keyboard row.

If you laid Alaska over the lower 48 states, it would extend from coast to coast. The state is bigger than Texas, California, and Montana...combined.

Largest national forest in the U.S.: the Tongass in Alaska. It's larger than West Virginia.

Largest oil field in North America: Alaska's Prudhoe Bay, covering 213,543 acres.

Russia is only two miles away from Alaska over the Bering Strait.

Valdez, Alaska, had the highest one-day snowfall ever recorded in the United States: 47.5 inches over 24 hours in January 1990.

The United States paid Russia $7.2 million, or 2¢ an acre, for Alaska in 1867. At the time, many Americans thought the government overpaid.

The Trans-Alaska Pipeline moves up to 88,000 barrels of oil per hour.

Dogsled mushing was once the primary form of transportation in Alaska. Now it's the state's official sport.

Almost a third of Alaska is within the Arctic Circle.

Alaska's Mount McKinley is the highest point in the U.S. at 20,320 feet above sea level. 17 of the 20 highest peaks in the United States are in Alaska.

Alaska got its name from the Eskimo word *Alakshak*, which means either "great lands" or "not an island."

Of all the states, Alaska has the lowest percentage of senior citizens, but the highest percentage of people who walk to work.

Burgers

The oldest hamburger chain is White Castle, founded in 1921. Cofounder Walter Anderson is also credited with creating the modern hamburger bun in 1916.

A Burger King in Kalamazoo, Michigan, was the site of the first "Elvis sighting" shortly after Presley died. The King was supposedly driving a red Ferrari.

Ray Kroc opened the first McDonald's in 1955 in Des Plaines, Illinois. Original burger price: 15¢.

The Fatburger fast-food chain sells "Hypocrites"—veggie burgers topped with bacon.

Australian McDonald's restaurants used to offer the McOz, a cheeseburger with beets.

The "cheeseburger in a can," made by a European camping-supply company called Trek'n Eat, costs about $6 and comes in a tin a little taller than a tuna can. It's got a one-year shelf life and can be heated by dropping the can into hot water.

In 2012 a McDonald's restaurant in Japan released several Big America Burgers, including a "Broadway Burger" with pastrami and cream cheese sauce, and a "Beverly Hills Burger" topped with avocado sauce and Caesar salad sauce.

The Heart Attack Grill of Las Vegas offers a "Quadruple Bypass Burger": four half-pound patties, tomato, six slices of cheese, 20 slices of bacon, and a bun… offering up 9,982 calories.

* * *

BUTTERFLY HAIR

Around 50 million years ago, butterflies were much hairier than they are now. The fur made them more likely to stick fatally to spider webs, though, so over time, they lost the hair.

Arabic Words

Hundreds of English words come from Arabic. *Al* means "the" in that language, so it's not surprising that English speakers heard a phrase and thought *al* was part of the word. Here are some examples, and what they mean in Arabic.

- **Albacore:** "The young camel" or "the milk cow." Albacore is so called because it's one of the smaller species of tuna.

- **Albatross:** "The diver" or "sea eagle" (a pelican).

- **Alchemy:** "That which is poured out."

- **Alcohol:** "The fine powder." Alchemists in Europe took this definition and transformed it to mean any processed/purified/distilled material. Eventually, the last meaning took over completely.

- **Alcove:** "The vault."

- **Alhambra:** "The red castle." It became the name for a giant fortress in Grenada, Spain.

- **Alkali:** "The saltwort," which was a plant that grew in alkali soil and was used in making glass and soap.

- **Allah:** "The god."

Lady Liberty

The Statue of Liberty's official name is *La Liberté éclairant le Monde* (French for "Liberty Enlightening the World")

The statue represents Libertas, the Roman goddess of freedom often worshipped by Rome's slaves and former slaves.

Sculptor Frédéric-Auguste Bartholdi used his mother as the model for Liberty's face and his girlfriend as the model for her body.

The iron framework inside Lady Liberty was created by Gustave Eiffel, the French engineer who later built the Eiffel Tower.

In 1885 the Statue of Liberty was shipped to New York in 350 pieces packed into 214 crates.

Liberty's torch-holding arm stood on display in Madison Square Park from 1876 to 1882, while the U.S. raised enough money to complete her pedestal.

Each year, maintenance crews at the Statue of Liberty scrape up 39 gallons of chewing gum.

The Statue of Liberty is made of copper but looks blue-green because that's the color of patina, the thin layer of copper rust that protects the metal.

The Statue of Liberty is 111 feet tall, 20 times taller than the average woman. She also weighs 450,000 pounds.

In 50 mph winds, the Statue of Liberty sways as much as three inches in either direction. Her torch sways six inches.

Only 240 people a day are allowed to climb the stairs to the crown, and visitors can make reservations a year in advance.

Fund-raising for the pedestal stalled until publisher Joseph Pulitzer encouraged ordinary Americans to send whatever little they could, promising to publish their names in his newspapers. That opened the floodgates. More than 120,000 Americans responded, most sending less than a dollar (worth about $25 in today's money). Many schoolkids sent pennies (25¢ today).

The Best Policy

Insurance first appeared in ancient Greece around 600 BC, when people paid premiums throughout their lives to provide themselves a proper burial.

Lloyd's of London is famous for insuring goofy things like Betty Grable's legs, but it was also one of the few insurance companies that promptly paid off all claims after the 1906 San Francisco earthquake.

The only U.S. state that doesn't require car insurance is New Hampshire.

Hungarian food critic Egon Ronay took out a $400,000 insurance policy on his taste buds.

The St. Lawrence Insurance Agency offers UFO abduction insurance…with double indemnity if the abduction results in an alien baby.

Travelers Insurance issued the very first car insurance policy on February 1, 1898. It covered liability costs if drivers collided with a horse or horse-drawn vehicle.

Hartford, Connecticut—home to Travelers and many similar companies—bills itself as the Insurance Capital of the World.

The *Mona Lisa* is not insured. Its value is inestimable.

Blue Cross was open only to schoolteachers in 1929. A premium of just $6 per year covered hospital fees for up to three weeks.

How much is hair from Abraham Lincoln, John F. Kennedy, Marilyn Monroe, and Elvis Presley worth? John Reznikoff of Stamford, Connecticut, insured the largest historical hair collection in the world for $1 million.

* * *

Average number of pucks used during a single NHL game: 35.

The First U.S. President...

...born west of the Mississippi River: Herbert Hoover, in Iowa.

...photographed at his inauguration: Abraham Lincoln, 1861. However, the earliest president ever photographed was John Quincy Adams. He went before a camera in 1843, 14 years after he left office.

...to be protected by the Secret Service: Grover Cleveland.

...to ride in an armored car: Franklin Roosevelt. After the Pearl Harbor attack in 1941, he began using a Cadillac that had been seized from Al Capone after his income tax evasion conviction. It had inch-thick bulletproof glass and 3,000 pounds of armor.

...born in the United States: Martin Van Buren, in 1782. The seven before him were born before the Revolution, when the future states were still colonies of England.

...who actually shook hands with people: Thomas Jefferson. His predecessors preferred a slight, dignified bow.

...to coin an advertising slogan: Teddy Roosevelt. When he was visiting the Maxwell House Hotel in New York City, he complimented the coffee as being "good to the last drop." When the hotel began selling the coffee in stores, they used the phrase as their slogan.

...to install an indoor toilet in the White House: John Quincy Adams, in 1825.

...born in a log cabin: Andrew Jackson, in 1767.

The World's Greenest Burgs

GREEN POWER TO THE PEOPLE

Cities put an enormous strain on the environment: They use more than 75 percent of the world's energy and release more than 75 percent of the world's carbon dioxide and other pollutants into the environment. More than half the people on earth (over 3.5 billion) live in cities, and by 2050, that number is expected to reach 70 percent. The future could be bleak: more lung disease from more pollution, increased global warming, mountains of waste, and concrete everywhere. But the people who live in the world's greenest cities are pioneering a future that's very different.

COPENHAGEN, DENMARK

Population: 1.2 million

How green is it? Copenhagen has been addressing environmental issues for decades. The result is that the water in its harbors and canals is so clean that people actually swim in them. There are also more than 186 miles of bike paths in the metro area, and there are places where residents and tourists can borrow bikes for free. (Really.) Some major streets even have a "green wave" system so bike riders can speed through intersections without stopping—they hit timed green lights the entire way. The result is that nearly 55 percent of Copenhageners bike to work or school.

The city is already filled with parks, but plans are in the works to guarantee that by 2015 at least 90 percent of Copenhagen's population will be within walking distance of a park or beach. About 20 percent of the city's electric power comes from wind turbines, hydroelectric power, and biomass (energy from organic matter like wood, straw, and organic waste), but the goal is to stop using coal altogether. The city is encouraging residents to buy electric- and hydrogen-powered cars and is investing more than $900 billion so that, by 2025, Copenhagen will have reduced its coal and oil pollution to zero.

VANCOUVER, CANADA

Population: 603,000

How green is it? Often called the greenest city in Canada, Vancouver has more than 200 parks in a region that's surrounded by spectacular beaches, forests, and mountains. The city leads the world in the production of hydropower, which supplies 90 percent of its electricity. And one of Vancouver's most famous innovations is the use of solar-powered trash-compactor bins on public sidewalks: The bins can hold five times the amount of conventional trash cans, so they need to be emptied only once a week instead of every night, which saves on the need to use the city's gas-powered fleet of garbage trucks.

Vancouver has also been adding new streetcar lines and bike lanes, and it has constructed nearly 250 miles of "greenways," special corridors for pedestrians and cyclists that connect parks, nature reserves, historic sites, neighborhoods, and shopping areas. And 40 percent of commuter and tourist day trips in Vancouver involve walking, biking, or using public transportation.

REYKJAVIK, ICELAND

Population: 120,000

How green is it? In the 1970s Iceland relied on imported coal for 75 percent of its energy. Today all of its electricity is produced from hydroelectric and geothermal power. The hydropower source is flowing water from melting ice that turns turbines to make electricity. The geothermal power uses the heat and steam of Iceland's volcanoes to do the same. The only fossil fuel the city uses is for its cars and fishing fleets.

But Icelanders even consider that to be too much: To get down to zero use of fossil fuels, Reykjavik is working on a changeover to cars and ships fueled mainly by electricity and hydrogen. In 2003 Shell opened its first hydrogen filling station in Reykjavik to service hydrogen-powered public buses. By the mid-21st century, Iceland plans to have most of its fishing fleet running on hydrogen and all of its cars and buses powered by alternative fuels.

SAN FRANCISCO, CALIFORNIA

Population: 805,000

How green is it? San Francisco was the first city in the United States to pass a mandatory recycling law, and the first to ban the use of plastic bags. Meant to lessen the amount of garbage that goes into landfills, those 2009 edicts have worked so well that San Franciscans now recycle 77 percent of their waste. (All that recycled garbage weighs about twice as much as the Golden Gate Bridge!) New laws also mean cleaner air: Public transportation runs on 20 percent biodiesel fuel (made from used cooking oil), and a green taxi law has resulted in 92 percent of the city's cabs running on alternative fuels.

Even though it's famous for its fog, San Francisco has proved that solar can work in overcast locales: The 60,000-square-foot solar system on the city's convention center generates enough electricity to power the entire center during events, and 24,000 solar panels atop a reservoir provide electricity for city buildings, including a hospital, the airport, and police and fire stations.

CURITIBA, BRAZIL

Population: 3.5 million

How green is it? Curitiba is the capital of the Paraná state in Brazil, and despite facing severe poverty and overcrowding, it consistently wins recognition as one of the most beautiful, livable, and green cities in the world. In 1968 the city had less than 10 square feet of greenery per person, but careful urban planning—minimizing urban sprawl, planting trees, and protecting local forests—has turned that into 500 square feet for each inhabitant. Curitiba now boasts 16 parks, 14 forests, and more than 1,000 green public spaces.

Curitiba is also internationally famous for its Bus Rapid Transport (BRT) system. Reliable and cheap, the BRT vehicles run as often as every 90 seconds in dedicated bus lanes. Eighty percent of the residents use the buses—that's more than two million riders a day. Also famous for its garbage disposal system, the city provides an alternative for low-income families who don't have garbage pickup: They can bring in bags of trash or recycling, and exchange them for bus tickets, food, school supplies, or toys. The result: A clean city where the poor live better and more than 70 percent of the waste is recycled.

GREENSBURG, KANSAS

Population: 900

How green is it? It's not a big city, but the small town of Greensburg embodies the spirit of environmentalism. In May 2007 a tornado demolished 95 percent of the town. When the residents rebuilt, they decided that their new buildings would meet internationally recognized standards that would make their town as energy-efficient and environmentally friendly as possible. The winds that once almost destroyed the town now power a wind farm that provides electricity to all of Greensburg's homes and businesses. This incredible comeback has made the town a center for environmental businesses and ecotourism, and young residents who once vowed to go away to college and never come back now say there's no place like home. In 2011 *Budget Travel* magazine put Greensburg on its top 10 list of the "Coolest Small Towns in America." And we think that's pretty cool.

* * *

DID YOU KNOW?

- Roller derby, sometimes known as pro wrestling on wheels, was invented in Chicago in 1935 by sporting promoter Leo Seltzer.

- Jerry Greenfield met his Ben & Jerry's ice cream partner Ben Cohen in gym class while running laps.

- Bald eagles aren't really bald; they have a head of white feathers. They got their name because the word "bald" used to mean "gleaming" or "white."

- In 2009, a group of English scientists built a snowman that was smaller than the width of a human hair.

- Taken literally, "à la mode" has nothing to do with ice cream or pie. It's French for "in the fashion."

Mayhem on Ice

Hockey gets its name from the same root word as croquet and crochet—a Middle French term pronounced regionally as *hoquet* and meaning "shepherd's crook."

In Japan, the movie *Slapshot* was called *Roughhouse Hockey Players Who Curse a Lot and Play Dirty*.

Professional hockey pucks are kept in a freezer before games because warmer pucks bounce too much on the ice.

The world's largest hockey stick and puck reside in Duncan, British Columbia, Canada.

In 1923 hockey announcer Foster Hewitt was the first to shout into a microphone, "He shoots! He scores!"

Despite the game's Canadian roots, the United States had the first pro hockey league.

The first U.S. hockey franchise to win a Stanley Cup was the New York Rangers, in 1928.

In 1987 Philadelphia Flyer Ron Hextall became the first NHL goalie to shoot a puck into the other team's net from the opposite side of the rink. Two years later, he did it again.

Some Like It Hot

India is the world's largest producer, consumer, and exporter of chili peppers.

In 400 BC, Hippocrates recommended black pepper for women's reproductive complaints. A century later, Theophrastus prescribed it as an antidote to hemlock poisoning. (Neither really did much good.)

Since 1868, the hot peppers for Tabasco have been grown and processed on Avery Island, Louisiana.

Christopher Columbus was one of the first Europeans to eat chilis, and he gave them the name "pepper" because their effect resembled that of black pepper. Yet, black pepper is not related to chili peppers.

Portuguese sailors spread hot peppers and seeds around the world.

The blindness and burning of pepper spray, which is made from peppers, can last for 30 minutes.

One red bell pepper contains 148 milligrams of vitamin C.

Jalapeño jellybeans really do have a little of the pepper inside.

The chemical compound that makes peppers so hot is called capsaicin.

Researchers go through multiple pairs of latex gloves when handling Trinidad Moruga Scorpion chili peppers because the capsaicin penetrates the latex.

*   *   *

ANIMAL ANTICS

- Hippos can't float and are lousy swimmers, so they rarely leave shallow water. If they end up in deep water, they leap like chubby porpoises along the bottom.
- African bush babies have "toilet claws" on their hind feet that they use just for grooming.

Hedgehogs

Hedgehogs are spiny and look like porcupines, but the two animals are not closely related.

The average hedgehog has 7,000 spines. (A porcupine, in comparison, has 30,000, but they're longer.)

When a hedgehog is born, its spines stay under a skin-like membrane that dries up and shrinks within 12 hours.

Hedgehogs roll up into a protective, spiked ball when threatened.

Hedgehogs were among the first mammals to appear on earth, and they haven't changed much in 20 million years.

Hedgehogs communicate with squeals, snuffles, and grunts.

In 2006 McDonald's in England changed the shape of their McFlurry containers because hedgehogs, trying to lick out the last remains in discarded cups, were getting their heads stuck in them, sometimes fatally.

Hedgehogs are lactose-intolerant.

Toad Suck, Arkansas

The name for a person from Arkansas can be either Arkansan or Arkansawyer.

Why stop in Dover, Arkansas? Well, there's the Booger Hollow Trading Post, a souvenir shop that serves up "Boogerburgers" and offers seats in its self-proclaimed "World's Only Double-Decker Outhouse."

On August 10, 1936, Ozark, Arkansas, recorded the state's highest temperature of 120°F.

On the Arkansas River northeast of Little Rock lies the Toad Suck Ferry Lock and Dam. Legend has it that back in the 1800s, river men stopping at the local saloon would suck down so much beer they would swell up like toads.

In 1909 University of Arkansas football coach Hugo Bezdek said that his team was like a "wild bunch of razorback hogs." Proud of this lofty praise, they have been the Razorbacks ever since.

Alma, Arkansas, is the self-proclaimed spinach capital of the world. The people of Alma are so proud of their spinach status that the front of their chamber of commerce building sports a giant statue of Popeye.

Crater of Diamonds State Park, near Murfreesboro, is the world's only diamond mine open to the public.

Famous Arkansans include U.S. president Bill Clinton, author and poet Maya Angelou, civil rights activist Eldridge Cleaver, baseball great Dizzy Dean, and five-star general Douglas MacArthur.

The first female U.S. senator was Hattie Ophelia Wyatt Caraway from Arkansas, first elected in 1932 (and again in 1938).

It's against the law in Arkansas to purposely mispronounce the name of the state.

* * *

Gamophobia is the fear of marriage.

Get Your Peanuts

The oldest peanut remains were found in Peru, dated to 7,600 years ago.

Peanut plants self-pollinate and require about five months before the pods are ready to pick.

The United States is one of the world's largest peanut exporters and is #3 in peanut growing. (China and India are #1 and #2.)

Peanut shells can be recycled into plastic, fuel, wallboard, glue, paper, and rayon.

About 1 percent of all Americans have a mild to severe allergy to peanuts, and they account for 50 to 100 deaths in the United States each year.

A NASCAR superstition says that peanuts or their shells in the garage are bad luck.

Peanuts are legumes in the bean family. They grow with their flowers aboveground and their fruit (the peanut shells and seeds) belowground.

Beer Nuts are just sweetened and salted peanuts. They contain no beer.

There are four types of peanuts grown in the United States: Spanish (for their high oil content), runner (good flavor, high yields), Virginia (large peanuts for salting and roasting in shells), and Valencia (best type for boiled peanuts).

* * *

AN EASY, EFFECTIVE FRUIT-FLY TRAP

You can make this in minutes: Place cider vinegar or a slice of a banana in a jar as bait. Roll and tape a sheet of paper into a funnel, and place it in the jar with the small opening at the bottom. Fruit flies will easily fly and crawl in, but won't easily find their way out. The jar can be sealed and the fruit flies released outside.

The Blues

Blue is a hard natural pigment to come by, making it a latecomer in art. That's why you won't find blue in cave paintings. The earliest synthetic blue paint appeared in Egypt around 2500 BC.

Ultramarine was the most expensive color during the Renaissance because it was created by grinding high-grade lapis lazuli stones into powder. The semiprecious stones came from modern-day Afghanistan, and the color is called "ultramarine" because it traveled *ultramarinus*—Latin for "beyond the sea."

Cobalt blue is now a standard color in an artist's palette, but it wasn't available as a paint color until 1802.

It's not just a reflection from the sky—clear water really is (very slightly) blue. You have to look through a lot of it to see the color, though, which is why deep water is such a deep blue and shallow water doesn't seem to show any color.

In Germany, being "blue" means being drunk.

During medieval times, Europeans figured out a cheap way to make blue dye from a plant called woad. The process involved soaking woad leaves in human urine and leaving it out in the sun. As it dried, it slowly turned blue.

Teal blue is named after the color of the blue feathers around the eyes of the teal duck.

* * *

HOW DOC MARTENS WERE BORN

Dr. Klaus Martens, a doctor in the German army during World War II, injured his ankle while skiing during his leave. When he returned to duty, he discovered that army-issued boots didn't provide great support, so he designed his own shoes, creating his first pairs from leather looted from a cobbler's shop and rubber from truck tires.

Cheers & Booze

Pound for pound, women can absorb 30 percent more alcohol into their systems than men.

The Bureau of Alcohol, Tobacco, and Firearms prohibits manufacturers from using the word "refreshing" to describe alcoholic beverages.

During Prohibition, temperance activists proposed rewriting the Bible to remove all references to alcohol, including instances where Jesus drank wine.

The official state distilled spirit of Alabama is Clyde May's Conecuh Ridge Whiskey. From the 1950s to 1980, May, a well-known bootlegger, produced 300 gallons of booze a week in a still he designed and built himself.

The term "booze" comes from the Dutch word *busen* ("to drink heavily").

If you're drinking a tequila *con gusano*, the "worm" is actually the larva of the *Hypopta agavis* moth, which lives on the agave plant that the tequila is made from.

The U.S. city with the highest alcoholism rate: Boston, Massachusetts. The lowest: Provo, Utah.

Change Your Password!

Two computer-jargoned streets in Silicon Valley: Infinite Loop, where Apple is headquartered, and Optical Drive.

Carl Sagan got mad when he discovered that Apple's in-house staff was calling one of its pre-released computers the "Carl Sagan." He complained, so they changed it to BHA. He was placated until he learned that the initials stood for "Butthead Astronomer." He sued and lost.

PCs infected with software that allows hackers to control them remotely are called "zombie computers."

Fox Mulder's computer password on *The X-Files*: TRUSTNO1.

Most-used computer password of all time: password. Second most: 123456.

St. Isidore is the patron saint of computers and the Internet.

In 1946 the University of Pennsylvania built ENIAC, the first fully operational electronic digital computer. It weighed 27 tons and took up 1,800 square feet of floor space.

"Bugs" didn't originate with computers. Thomas Edison used the term in the 1870s when talking about small flaws and difficulties when inventing.

People generally read an item 25 percent more slowly on a computer screen than on paper.

Electronic equipment attracts dust, thanks to electrical fields. It's one reason the first home computers were beige—researchers at Apple determined that it hid dust best.

41 percent of Americans say they've considered attacking their computers—7 percent have done it.

*   *   *

There are 132 countries whose gross domestic product is less than Bill Gates's net worth.

Firefly Facts

Most types of lighting emit a lot of heat—an incandescent bulb, for example, loses 90 percent of its energy to heat. But nearly 100 percent of the energy in a firefly's light goes to illumination, and almost none is heat.

Adult fireflies don't survive over the winter. Their larvae dig into the ground and emerge in the spring.

Each firefly species has its own distinct flash pattern.

Fireflies eat small snails and insects during their one- to two-year larval stage, but many don't eat at all in their adult life.

Special effects in 16th-century theater productions used crushed fireflies as a luminescent powder.

Great Smoky Mountains National Park is home to at least 19 species of fireflies.

A firefly's adulthood lasts only one to two weeks.

It would take more than 40 fireflies to provide enough light to read by.

Technically, fireflies are not flies—they're beetles.

Lightning bugs and fireflies are the same thing, and glowworms are usually their larva. (Sometimes, glowworms are also flightless females.)

Even though fireflies light up, predators generally leave them alone because they taste terrible and are often poisonous.

* * *

DID YOU KNOW?

Solar flares are magnetic enough to disrupt electronics, but they also throw off some animals' navigation. Fish, bees, fruit flies, turtles, birds, and even some mammals use the earth's magnetic field to monitor their movement, location, or altitude.

The Joy of Socks

When Bobby Orr played hockey, he didn't wear socks. Neither did Albert Einstein, who called them an "unnecessary complication." Einstein didn't even wear them on formal occasions, like his citizenship ceremony.

Knitted socks from AD 200 have been discovered in Egyptian tombs.

Women in Texas used to be penalized with prison time if they adjusted their stockings in public. (Fortunately, that law is no longer on the books.)

St. Fiacre is the patron saint of stocking makers.

Cabbies in Halifax, Nova Scotia, are required to wear socks.

In the 1950s, school dances were called "sock hops" because they were usually held in the school gym, and the coaches didn't want the dancers' shoes to ruin the finish on their basketball courts. So the kids danced in their socks.

About half of the socks in the United States are manufactured in Burlington, North Carolina.

The first pantyhose were created for actresses and dancers in the 1940s. To facilitate quick costume changes, their stockings were sewed to their underwear.

Toys for Tots

The doll was probably the first toy in history.

Marbles got their name because, in the 18th century, they were actually made of polished marble.

The powder inside an Etch-A-Sketch is finely ground aluminum.

The largest North American display of toy trains—more than 1,200 train sets in all—is at a theme park called Entertrainment Junction in West Chester, Ohio.

Ruth Handler created Barbie and Ken dolls in the 1950s. She named them after her kids.

When the Hubble Space Telescope's antenna was damaged during its launch in 1990, NASA scientists built a model with Tinker Toys to figure out how to fix it.

What gives crayons their distinctive smell? Beef fat.

Many nonelectronic kids' toys—from Legos to Barbies to soldiers—can be cleaned in the dishwasher. (Small things in a mesh bag, of course.)

A medical student used an Erector Set to design the first artificial heart pump.

Before latex, kids used pig's bladders to make balloons.

Most dollhouses are built at 12:1 scale, which makes things easy—anything that's a foot long in our world becomes an inch long in the dollhouse world.

Full name of toy store magnate FAO Schwarz: Frederick August Otto.

Lego is the world's largest tire manufacturer—they make 306 million toy tires every year.

*   *   *

OLD CHINESE PROVERB
"A child's life is like a piece of paper on which every passerby leaves a mark."

What Americans Do (and Don't) Know

22 percent of Americans can name all five characters in the Simpson cartoon family.

55 percent (wrongly) believe that the Constitution established the United States as a Christian nation.

Only half of Americans know that Judaism is older than Christianity.

40 percent can name all three branches of the government: executive, legislative, and judicial.

1 in 5 Americans believe that a friend or relative was abducted by aliens.

49 percent know that the United States is the only country to have used atomic bombs in war, and 84 percent know the basics of what happened at Pearl Harbor in 1941.

29 percent of Americans between the age of 18 and 24 couldn't point to the Pacific Ocean on a map.

75 percent know that America fought the British for independence.

20 percent believe that the sun revolves around the earth.

41 percent can't name the sitting vice president at any given time.

The Name's the Game

The Rules: We'll give you a collection of words (like goat, club, and hill). You need to figure out a first name that can be added to the beginning or end of each word to create a new word or phrase that makes sense. (If you came up with "billy" as the answer for the example, you're ready to play.)

1. Cat, turkey, thumb, uncle, peeping

2. White, sled, for apples, 's your uncle

3. Swiss, postal, perfectly, furter, 'enstein

4. Cracker, hammer, lumber, car, Monterey

5. Cake, Appleseed, on the spot, here's, come lately

6. Lazy, blackeyed

7. Mafia, Juan

8. Board, fold, duck, of sale, Buffalo

9. Rose, Christmas, 'land, Typhoid

10. Water, trade, hall, German, beauty

11. Runaround, Peggy, for custody

12. Diamond, against, without, chest

Answers
1. Tom, 2. Bob, 3. Frank, 4. Jack, 5. Johnny, 6. Susan, 7. Don, 8. Bill, 9. Mary (or Merry), 10. Mark, 11. Sue, 12. Hope

Thicker Than Water

About 7 percent of a human body's weight is blood.

The length of the arteries, veins, and capillaries in an adult's circulatory system equals about 60,000 miles.

Blood really *is* thicker than water...about five times thicker.

Most phobias cause blood pressure to rise, but *hemophobia*, the fear of blood, causes it to drop, sometimes to the point of fainting.

There are four major blood types: O, A, B, and AB. Type O is a "universal donor" because it can donate red cells to all four. Type A can donate only to A or AB. Type B can donate only to B or AB. Type AB can donate only to AB.

On *Star Trek*, Spock's blood type was "T-negative," presumably an "only in Vulcan" blood type.

Eating too much licorice can cause abnormal heart rhythms—1 to 2 ounces of real licorice per day for two weeks or more can do it.

Just 30 minutes of exposure to secondhand smoke makes platelets in the bloodstream stickier. As a result, blood clots form more easily, which can block arteries and cause heart attacks.

Eel blood is toxic to humans.

Borderline Nations?

NO COUNTRY FOR ANY MEN

The 1783 Treaty of Paris ended the Revolutionary War, but it left in question the exact border between the eastern United States and Canada, which remained under British control. Until 1842, when the Webster-Ashburton Treaty settled most of the questions, there were swatches of land along the New York/Vermont/New Hampshire/Maine borders that didn't technically belong to either country. And in the 60 years between the two treaties, at least three independent "republics" sprang up in the region.

REPUBLIC OF UPPER CANADA

Location: Navy Island in the Niagara River
What happened: In December 1837, after unsuccessfully fighting to win independence from England, a Canadian rebel group led by journalist and former mayor of Toronto William Lyon Mackenzie fled to Navy Island above Niagara Falls, one of the areas that didn't officially belong to either the United States or Canada (today it's Canadian land). They declared the island to be a brand-new country, the Republic of Upper Canada. American sympathizers, still holding a grudge against the British after the War of 1812, supplied the rebels with food, weapons, and money via a steamship called the *Caroline*.

The Republic of Upper Canada didn't last long. In less than a month, British and Canadian loyalists had crossed into New York and captured the ship, setting it ablaze and loose to plummet over Niagara Falls. Mackenzie and his group withdrew from Navy Island in January 1838.

REPUBLIC OF INDIAN STREAM

Location: Between Quebec and New Hampshire
What happened: Indian Stream is a small tributary of the Connecticut River located near the small town of Pittsburg, New Hampshire, but in the early 1800s, it flowed through no-man's-land. In the 1790s, two groups of Canadian settlers got land grants from the Abenaki people, one of the local Native American tribes, to

move in. They didn't take sides in the border disputes initially, but by the 1830s, both the British (who controlled Canada at the time) and American tax collectors came knocking. And so, not wanting to be taxed by either government, the 300 Indian Stream settlers proclaimed themselves the sole inhabitants of an independent country.

That lasted about three years. In 1835, after a sheriff from Canada "invaded" to arrest a man whom the British claimed owed them a tax debt, Indian Stream's citizens fought back, freed the man from debtors' prison, and ultimately joined New Hampshire.

REPUBLIC OF MADAWASKA

Location: Between Maine and New Brunswick

What happened: In the early 1800s, an American settler named John Baker moved from southern Maine into no-man's land along the Maine/Quebec/New Brunswick border. By 1827, Baker was so tired of waiting for the State of Maine to rule that his house was in America (and not Canada) that he decided to start his own country—the Republic of Madawaska, a Maliseet Indian term that meant "where one river runs into another with watergrass." This proclamation was important to Baker because he was fed up with the government, but it was more important to some of his neighbors, Acadians who had been deported as a group from Canada in the mid-1700s because they were the descendants of French Catholics, rather than British Protestants. Although many Acadians immigrated to the American South and become the "Cajuns" of New Orleans, many of Baker's neighbors just wanted a safe place to live that wasn't in Canada, and so they were happy to declare themselves citizens of the new republic.

The British weren't so happy about it, though. On the same day that Baker established his country, British troops from Canada arrested him and put him on trial for conspiracy and sedition. He was ultimately fined £25 and sentenced to prison until he paid it… or two months, whichever came first. This set off an international incident between Canada and the United States that lasted for 15 years. It even triggered a border conflict in 1838 and 1839 called the Aroostook War, which included a lot of diplomatic meetings, threats, shouting, militia-massing on both sides, and incendiary editorials...but no actual combat. Eventually, diplomats from London and Washington negotiated that Webster-Ashburton Treaty of 1842 to settle the northeastern Canada/United States border issue once and for all, and the Republic of Madawaska became part of the Canadian province of New Brunswick.

FUTURE REPUBLICS?

Despite mostly solving the problem by dividing up the border territories, the treaty-makers missed a couple of spots. Even today, North Rock Island and the Machias Seal Island in the Gulf of Maine are *still* in dispute—though if you're thinking of setting up settlements there, be aware that both islands are barren and rocky, with lots of fog and no trees. North Rock is only about the size of a football field and is full of seals. Machias—bigger, but only 20 acres—includes an ancient lighthouse staffed by two members of the Canadian Coast Guard, so expect armed resistance to your plans...or at least polite objections.

* * *

HISTORICAL HODGEPODGE

- Lord Stanley, governor general of Canada, donated the Stanley Cup in 1894, but he never saw a Stanley Cup game. He moved back to England before the first tournament.

- The first American paper currency was a 12-pence note designed by Paul Revere and issued in 1776 by the State of Massachusetts. It's known as the "codfish bill" because of the illustration of a codfish at the top.

- Spokane, Washington, was the first place to celebrate Fathers' Day, on June 19, 1910. It didn't become a permanent national holiday until Richard Nixon signed a bill in 1972.

- In 1829 thousands of high-spirited citizens arrived at the White House to celebrate Andrew Jackson's inauguration. His aides finally lured the mob out of the building with washtubs filled with whiskey and orange juice.

- Ronald Reagan was the first president to nominate a woman to the Supreme Court: Sandra Day O'Connor in 1981.

In Hot Water

For a geyser to occur, it needs a volcano with molten magma bubbling not far from of the surface. Water flows underground until it reaches the hot liquid rock, where steam builds up below it. Eventually the steam explodes, shooting thousands of gallons of water still flowing down from the surface into the air.

Geysers give off a lot of geothermal energy. The world's largest geothermal power plant is the Geysers in Sonoma County, California, which makes enough electricity to power a city the size of San Francisco. And Australia alone has enough untapped geothermal energy to power the country for 2.6 million years.

An accidental, man-made geyser erupts every 40 minutes in Calistoga, California. A man drilling for water in the late 19th century opened a passageway to magma below, allowing groundwater to flow into it.

Hot springs are also heated by water warmed by magma. Some are just warm, but springs heated by molten rock can be scalding.

Mars has geysers, too, except they're dry. During Mars's spring thaw at its south pole, frozen carbon dioxide ("dry ice") melts. The gas it releases shoots jets of sand into the air.

Geyser, by the way, comes from the Icelandic (Old Norse) word *geysa* ("gush.")

Hot springs typically contain sulfur, magnesium, lithium, calcium, and other harmless minerals, but some have radium as well.

Some organisms, viruses, and plants can live in a hot spring's waters. One is the *Naegleria fowleri*, also known as "the brain-eating amoeba."

Half of the world's geysers are in Yellowstone National Park.

GOALLL!

Soccer is the world's most popular sport. It's regularly played by 250 million people in 200 countries and is watched by many more.

In 1863 the newly formed British Football Association met at London's Freemasons' Tavern to codify the uncivil sport of "football" (soccer).

75 percent of the world's soccer balls are made in Pakistan.

In 2007 the Ivory Coast national soccer team helped secure a truce between the government and rebel forces by playing a soccer match that brought both armies together peacefully for the first time.

According to a poll, 1 in 20 British kids thinks Adolf Hitler was a German soccer manager.

Before soccer referees used whistles, they waved handkerchiefs to indicate fouls.

The penalty system of using a yellow card (for a warning) and a red card (for an expulsion from the game) is a pretty new invention The cards were first introduced in the 1970 FIFA World Cup.

The first soccer balls were made of animal stomachs or bladders. They rarely lasted an entire game.

Modern soccer balls aren't round—they're truncated icosahedrons. That means they're made of 12 black panels that are five-sided, and 20 white panels that are six-sided.

The Waves

Q. WHY IS THE SUN ORANGE AND THE SKY BLUE?

A. The sun's light is actually white and the atmosphere around us (made up of gases and dust) is almost clear (which is why we can see the stars at night). "White" light contains every color of the rainbow, as well as many more that are invisible.

When the light from the sun hits the earth's atmosphere, the gases and dust particles scatter it a bit and disrupt all the colors in the light. The red light, traveling in long waves, has to travel through fewer of the particles, so it makes a beeline through the atmosphere. The blue light waves zigzag. (It's like the difference between tossing a rock and a handful of sand.) So when you glance up at the sun, you see its red-yellow waves heading more or less straight toward you, but its blue waves scatter on their way down, lighting up the atmosphere and making the sky look blue.

Q. IS THIS ALSO THE REASON SUNSETS ARE RED AND ORANGE?

A. No. When the sun is near the horizon, its light passes through a lot more of the atmosphere. That atmosphere is often very polluted, and most pollution is orange. The sun's light illuminates that color.

Q. ARE LIGHT WAVES AND RADIO WAVES PRETTY MUCH THE SAME THING?

A. Pretty much. Our eyes can see only a very narrow range of frequencies. The ones we can see are light waves. The ones we can't see are microwaves, X-rays, radio waves, and so on, depending on their length. But they're all electromagnetic waves.

Q. HOW LONG ARE THE OTHER ELECTROMAGNETIC WAVES?

A. That's where it gets a little weird. Light waves are tiny, only about the size of bacteria or even an atom. We see them because there are so many clustered together. Radio waves are longer: they can range from the length of a human to the length of a football field.

Index

animal extinction, 265
animals, 104, 121,
    142–145, 227, 312
Anne, Princess, 211
Anophthalmus hitleri, 53
Ant Farm, 322
ant queens, 196
Antarctica, 158, 297
anthems, 86, 109, 232,
    317
Anthony, Susan B., 342
antiperspirants, 125
Antipode Islands, 158
antipodes, 158
ants, 161, 258, 278, 322
anvil, 75
apes, 279, 325
Apollo 8 spacecraft, 46,
    252
appendix, 241
Apple (company),
    310–311, 367
apple cider, 54
Apple Records, 310–311
apples, 31, 54
Appleseed, Johnny, 55
aquariums, 165
Arabic words, 352
arachibutyrophobia, 23
Aragones, Sergio, 82
archaeologists, 163
archaeology, 163
Archie Comics, 224
Arctic, 297
Arctic Circle, 181, 350
arctic fox, 349
arctic hares, 73
Arctic Pole, 158
arctic tern, 178
arena, 141
Ariadne auf Naxos, 83
Aristotle, 186, 338
Arkansans, famous, 363
Arkansas state song, 86
armadillos, 64, 170, 315,
    330
arteries, 373

artichokes, 78
Aryan race, 167
Asian fruit fly, 251
asphalt, 137
asteroids, 314
astrology, 296
astronauts, 46, 148, 337
Atacama Desert, 297
A-Team, 232
athlete's foot, 186
Atkinson, James Henry,
    273–274
Atlanta International
    Airport, 51
Atlas, 124
atmosphere, 379
atomic bombs, 371
atomic clocks, 76
atomic radiation, 141
ATV lawsuits, 311
Augsburg Cathedral, 189
Australia, 158
Australian dragonfly, 1
authors, 83, 204
autobahns, 69
automobiles. *See* cars
Autry, Gene, 326
autumn, 32
autumnal equinox, 32
averages, 205
Aykroyd, Dan, 16
Azaria, Hank, 147
Aztecs, 53, 101, 108, 187

B
babies, 87, 160, 176,
    318, 330
baby incubators, 160
Babylonians, 124
Bach, Johann Sebastian,
    203
Bacon, Nathaniel,
    111–112
badgers, 131, 349
bagasse, 179
bagpipes, 67–68, 328
Bakelite, 72

Baker, Darius, 324
Baker, John, 375
Baker, Russell, 133
bakku-shan, 319
bald eagles, 359
baldness, 301
Ball, Lucille, 44
balloon animals, 19
balloon incendiary
    bombs, 19
balloons, 19, 370
ballpoint pens, 75
balls, 46, 47, 63, 183,
    327, 378
Bamako, 177
Bambi, 157
Ban Roll-On, 126
banana leaves, 69
bananas, 57, 288
Banvard, John, 313
bar coasters, 302
barbed wire, 13, 78
Barbed Wire Museum, 78
Barbie dolls, 262, 327,
    370
Barking Sands Beach,
    239
Barnum, P. T., 19, 62
Barrow, Alaska, 331, 336
Bartholdi, Frédéric-
    Auguste, 353
baseball, 52, 79, 162,
    269, 327
basketball, 63, 259
Bass Beer symbol, 171
Batman (TV series), 99
bats, 99, 330
Battle of Britain, 105
Battleship, 65
Baum, L. Frank, 104
BB guns, 71
BBC, 167
Beach Boys, 113, 328
beaches, 141
beaks, 178, 223
beards, 123, 291, 320
bears, 13, 157, 281, 330

nose hair, 228
nose jobs, 94
nose picking, 94
nuclear plants, 130
nurses, 166
nuts, 34, 108, 238, 247,
  364

O
Oahu, 239
oak barrels, 184
oak trees, 9
Oakland cemetery, 106
Obama, Barack, 4
obdormition, 186
obesity, 59
O'Brien, Conan, 182
ocean noise, 230
O'Connor, Sandra Day,
  376
octopuses, 176, 223, 335
odontophobia, 35
odors, 94
Odyssey, 287
oenophobia, 23
Offenbach, Jacques, 93
Official Table of Drops, 48
Ogilvy, David, 175, 276
O'Hare Airport, 51
Ohio state flag, 253
Ohio winemaking, 289
oil, 88, 109, 165
oil fields, 350
okapis, 31
Okefenokee Swamp, 106
Oklahoma state song, 86
Old Christians rugby
  team, 194–195
Olympians, 320
Olympic flag, 253
Olympic gold medal, 113
Olympic torch, 134
Olympics, 134, 168–169,
  211, 226, 231
On Civility in Children,
  191
"on the warpath," 275

opossums, 330
optical drive, 367
optometrists, 325
orange peels, 55
orange roughy, 165
orange trees, 55
oranges, 55
orcas, 127
Orchard Place/Douglas
  Field, 51
orchid roots, 216
orchids, 334
Oregon state flag, 253
organs, expendible, 241
organs, pipe, 206
orgasms, 138
Orr, Bobby, 369
Oscars. *See also* Academy
  Awards
osmophobia, 94
Osphresiolagnia, 94
otters, 341, 349
Otto, Frederick August,
  370
owl monkeys, 330
owls, 303, 325
oxygen, 13, 188

P
Pacific Ocean, 371
pacifiers, 318
Pac-Man, 296
page of lists, 212
Paine, Thomas, 30
paint colors, 365
Pall Mall (street), 348
Palm Desert, California,
  348
Pan Am Clippers, 51
Panorama magazine, 113
*Panorama of the
  Mississippi*, 313
panther, 344
pantyhose, 369
Papa Westray, 10
papal reign, shortest, 317
paper, 288, 303, 340

paper airplane flights,
  316
paper clips, 75
paper currency, 251, 376
paper money, 306
papillotes, 340
Paradise Lost, 287
parakeets, 230
Parcel Post, 190
parchment paper, 340
Parker, Isaac "Hanging
  Judge," 240
parks, 356
Pasjack, Steve, 320
passenger pigeon, 150,
  265
passwords, 367
pasta, 132
Pasteur, Louis, 184
pasteurization, 184
Patsayev, Viktor, 254
Patton, General George
  S., 278
pay phones, 22
pea, 327
peanut butter, 108, 238
peanut oil, 109
peanuts, 108, 238, 364
Pearl Harbor, 371
pears, 31
Peary, Robert, 16
pecans, 247
Pelé, 110
Pelletier, Nicolas Jacques,
  48
Penantipodes, 158
pencils, 305
penguins, 196
penicillin, 307
pennies, 55, 306, 342
pens, 75, 314
pepper, black, 361
pepper spray, 361
peppers, 257
Peripatetic school, 338
periscopes, 109
Perlman, Itzhak, 298

punt, 289
pupilla, 325
pupils, 325
Puritans, 66
pygmy shark, 146
pyrethrins, 246
python, 227

Q
Quaker Oats, 141
quarters, 342
quartz crystal, 346
quebec, 313
Quechua language, 250
Queen rock band, 298
Quimby, Harriet, 103
qwylwryghte, 60

R
rabbits, 227
rabies, 136
radiation, 141
radiation sickness, 130
radio, 11–12, 129, 169,
    226
radio, HAM, 11
radio commercials, 129
radio waves, 379
radioactivity, 130
radium, 130
railroad, 102, 210, 229.
    See also trains
railroad stations, 210
rain, 34, 96, 239, 297,
    331
Raleigh, Sir Walter, 304
rams, 154
Ramsey, Alice, 29
Rand, Ayn, 83
Rankin, Jeannette, 103
raspberries, 257
rats, 136, 142, 143, 186
rattlesnakes, 299
Ravenscroft, Thomas, 93
razorbacks, 363
Reagan, Ronald, 4, 173,
    309, 376

recycled garbage, 358
recycled paper, 340
recycling, 314, 340, 358
The Red Balloon, 19
Red Baron, 182, 193
Red Cross, 113
Red Delicious apples, 54
red eye, 73
red wine, 184
Redenbacher, Orville,
    237
redheads, 7
Redwood Highway, 69
redwoods, 292
reference book duos,
    218–220
Reformation, 105
Reich Broadcasting
    Corporation (RRG),
    167–169
reincarnation, 296
religious freedom, 223
Reno, Janet, 338
Republic of Madawaska,
    376
Republic of Upper
    Canada, 374
Republicans, 270, 291
Revere, Paul, 76, 376
The Revlon Revue, 116
"Revolution," 311
Revolutionary War, 374
Reykjavik, Iceland, 357
Reznikoff, John, 44
rhinorrhea, 107
rhinos, 8
Rhode Island, 10
Rice Krispies, 119
Richardson, J. P. "the Big
    Bopper," 97
Richter, Charles, 28
Richter scale, 28
Ride, Sally, 254
Right Guard, 126
Ringling brothers, 62
Rip Van Winkle, 300
Risk board game, 19, 65

Ritter, Frank, 115
river pirates, 304
river routes, 275
rivers, 267, 275, 304,
    313, 317
rivets, 114
Riyadh Airport, 51
roads, 137, 275
robins, 227
Robinson, E. A., 128
Robinson Crusoe, 148
rock candy, 179
rock 'n' roll stars, dead at
    27, 207
Rocket 88 engine, 88
rocket necklace, 198
rockets, 198
Rocky and Bullwinkle, 147
rodents, 143
rodeo cowboys, 284
rodeos, 229, 284
Rodgers, James, 48
Rogaine, 301
Rogers, Fred, 116, 226,
    237
Rogers, Will, 193, 276
roller coasters, 1, 331
roller derby, 359
Rolling Stones, 113
roly-poly, 292
Roman Catholic Church,
    166, 266–268
Roman Catholic priests,
    323
Romani people, 335
Romero, George A.,
    343
Ronay, Egon, 354
Rood, Floyd Satterlee, 47
Roosevelt, Edith, 240
Roosevelt, Eleanor, 20,
    323
Roosevelt, Franklin D.,
    20, 32, 226, 247, 355
Roosevelt, Theodore, 20,
    113, 128, 309, 355
Roper, Silvester H., 135

THE LAST PAGE

FELLOW BATHROOM READERS:
The fight for good bathroom reading should never be taken loosely—we must do our duty and sit firmly for what we believe in, even while the rest of the world is taking potshots at us.

We'll be brief. Now that we've proven we're not simply a flush-in-the-pan, we invite you to take the plunge: Sit Down and Be Counted! Log on to *www.bathroomreader.com* and earn a permanent spot on the BRI honor roll!

If you like reading our books...
VISIT THE BRI'S WEB SITE!

www.bathroomreader.com

- Visit "The Throne Room"—a great place to read!
  - Receive our irregular newsletters via e-mail.
    - Order additional Bathroom Readers.
      - Read our blog.

Go with the Flow...

Well, we're out of space, and when you've gotta go, you've gotta go. Tanks for all your support. Hope to hear from you soon.

Meanwhile remember...

Keep on flushin'!